PRAISE FOR *SPIRITS DISTILLED*

"Spirits Distilled is a new view of booze from the ground up. Beyond illuminating the plants, people, and production of all the major spirits categories, Nat Harry's thoughtful recommendations should empower us to make better choices in the liquor aisle."

— CAMPER ENGLISH, author of *Doctors and Distillers* and *The Ice Book*; publisher of Alcademics.com

"Great for both the casual drinker and the avid spirits connoisseur, *Spirits Distilled* is a valuable resource that goes beyond mere reference guide to show us the intricacies of the agriculture, politics, and culture that go into every bottle of gin, vodka, tequila, and beyond. Nat Harry's genuine curiosity, thorough research, and welcoming approach to sharing their insights makes them the perfect guide for this delicious adventure."

— EMMA JANZEN, award-winning spirits & cocktail journalist; author of *The Bartender's Pantry*

"With clear and concise writing, helpful diagrams, and unbounded enthusiasm, Harry provides drinkers with everything they didn't realize they needed to know about the contents of their glass."

— BETH SQUIRES, Deputy Editor of *The Whiskey Wash*

"Are you a conscientious consumer that wants to drink better, not more? Do you want to understand what actually goes into your drink? Then pick up Nat's book, which is required reading for anyone looking beyond marketing hype to imbibe more thoughtfully and intentionally."

— HEATHER GREENE, author of *Whisk(e)y Distilled*; CEO of Milam & Greene Distillery

"Harry blends hard facts with accessible insights, empowering readers to see beyond marketing hype and misleading labels to better understand the agricultural origins of their favorite drinks. This essential guide for spirits enthusiasts explores the cultural, environmental, and technical factors behind distillation, leading the much-needed push for an industry-wide shift toward greater transparency and informed consumer choices."

— FOREST COLLINS, Academy Chair France, World's 50 Best Bars; author of *Drink Like a Local Paris*

"Harry has succeeded in writing a unique book that needs to exist. Whether you're an avid enthusiast or someone who works in the spirits or hospitality industry, this is a book that needs to be added to your library."

— JACOB KIPER, *Drinkhacker*

"As a chef, I want to know what ingredients I'm putting into my dishes, where they came from, how they were grown or raised. I want to feel and taste that connection to the source. So why not apply that same concept to your evening cocktail? *Spirits Distilled* is a great farm-to-bottle exploration that will make a helluva happy hour to boot."

— GUY FIERI, restaurateur, author, and Emmy Award winning television presenter

"Nat Harry's ambition is to inform with depth the true nature of how our favorite spirits are made—in *Spirits Distilled*, Harry succeeds. With clear prose and unwavering research Harry demands we rethink what's in our glass, delivering *Spirits Distilled* as a trusted, must-have resource for the origins of drink."

— DUGGAN MCDONNELL, author *Drinking the Devil's Acre: A Love Letter From San Francisco & Her Cocktails*

"Spirits judges, master distillers, and cocktail makers all know: the journey to your glass begins long before the distillation process. In *Spirits Distilled*, Nat Harry expertly uncovers the often overlooked but vital foundation of every great drink— the finest raw materials. Blending engaging narrative with in-depth reference, this essential volume is a must-have for any spirits enthusiast's library."

— JEFFREY MORGENTHALER, award-winning bartender and author of *The Bar Book*

"The perfect primer for spirits enthusiasts and beginners alike, Harry expertly guides readers to think beyond the grain, delivering a wonderful world tour on the many ingredients that are transformed into our favorite beverages!"

— TZVI WIESEL, *The Whiskey Wash*

"I've had the pleasure of traveling with Nat and visiting many producers. They advocate for what is good and beautiful in our business. I am certain this book will guide and inspire many readers."

— THAD VOGLER, author of *By the Smoke and the Smell*; founder of the James Beard Award-winning Bar Agricole

"A book that is both as detailed and geeky as it is approachable and digestible to novices and the average spirits drinker. Helpful graphs and breakdowns keep it fun, while categorizing by ingredient is an approach that reminds us all how important it is to know what goes into a bottle, just as we want to know what's in the food we eat. Nat has blessedly written a drink book we didn't yet have—and needed."

— VIRGINIA MILLER, dining, spirits, cocktail, and wine writer and judge; founder of The Perfect Spot

"*Spirits Distilled* is such an engaging read. As an enthusiastic amateur, it gave me a lot to think about and makes me feel more confident in seeking out new (to me) spirits. I started recommending it to people before I even finished it."

— MARY ROBINETTE KOWAL, author of the Hugo and Nebula Award-winning Lady Astronaut series

"Spirits Distilled is a wonderfully educational and insightful resource, whether spirits are your passion or your profession. Harry's 3 P approach—covering plant, place, and production—lays solid groundwork for understanding the pillars of spirits categories, all the while underpinning the importance of transparency for the conscience consumer."

— LEAH VAN DEVENTER, award-winning spirits writer, educator, and judge

SPIRITS
DISTILLED

SPIRITS DISTILLED

A Guide to the Ingredients
Behind a Better Bottle

NAT HARRY

Copyright © 2024, Nat Harry

All rights reserved. No portion of this book may be reproduced or used in any manner whatsoever without the express written permission from the publisher: Westwood Press, PO Box 19326, Portland, Oregon, 97280

Printed in Canada on FSC-certified paper

Library of Congress Control Number: 2024938877

Harry, Nat | Author

Spirits distilled : a guide to the ingredients behind a better bottle / Nat Harry.

Portland, OR: Westwood Press, 2024.
Identifiers: ISBN: 978-1-958510-01-8 (hardcover) | 978-1-958510-02-5 (ebook)
Subjects: LCSH Distillation. | Liquors. | COOKING / Beverages / Alcoholic / General | BISAC COOKING / Beverages / Alcoholic / Spirits | COOKING / Beverages / Alcoholic / Bartending & Cocktails
Classification: LCC TP597 .H37 2024 | DDC 663.5--dc23

10 9 8 7 6 5 4 3 2 1

Cover design by Zoe Norvell and Paul DuVernet
Interior design by Morgane Leoni

www.westwoodpress.com

For Jenn

"When your heart is broken you plant seeds
in the cracks and pray for rain."

—Andrea Gibson

Contents

ABBREVIATIONS

ix

PREFACE

x

INTRODUCTION

xiv

CHERRIES, APPLES, AND PEARS

1

GRAPES

33

BARLEY

69

CORN

101

RYE AND WHEAT
121

RICE
147

AGAVE
169

SUGARCANE
203

ROOT VEGETABLES
243

WOOD
261

STOCKING YOUR HOME BAR . . . WITH BOOKS
280

ABBREVIATIONS

ABV   alcohol by volume

AOC   Appellation d'Origine Contrôlée

AOR   Appellations d'Origine Réglementée

DO   Denomination of Origin

DOC   Denominazione di Origine Controllata

EPA   Environmental Protection Agency

EU   European Union

FDA   Food and Drug Administration

GI   Geographical Indication

GM   genetically modified

GMO   Genetically Modified Organism

TTB   Alcohol and Tobacco Tax and Trade Bureau

UN   United Nations

USDA   United States Department of Agriculture

WTO   World Trade Organization

PREFACE

From my very first visit to Oaxaca, I was hooked. On the food, the people, the culture, and, of course, the Mezcal. While it's hard not to fall in love with this warm and smoky libation, agave—the plant from which Mezcal is made—is the true star of the show. Taking years, if not decades, to grow, the agave is hand-harvested, and its hundred-pound *piñas* (hearts) manually processed and roasted in open, earthen ovens, as they have been for centuries. As I continued to travel to distilleries and farms as a spirits buyer, what started as an agave obsession became so much more. With time, my questions no longer focused solely on a spirit's distillation process but on *what* was being distilled and *how*. How long does it take a spirit-destined plant to grow? Where is it sourced from? How far does it travel to get to the distillery?

When we think of spirits, most of us focus on the final product we drink, not the acres of land on which corn, rye, agave, or sugarcane are grown. Rarely do we consider the hands or machinery that sow and harvest those plants. And if we do, it's usually not with the same care we give to other edible products, like fairtrade coffee, natural wine, organic produce, or pasture-raised meat. But spirits are indeed born of the fruits of the earth. No matter how fancy the label or skilled the distiller, the plant is the foundation.

Just ask yourself: What's the first image that pops into your head when you hear *distilled spirit*? Is it different from those conjured up by the words *liquor* or *booze*? Are you reminded of cocktail soirées with bowtie-wearing mixologists in suspenders? Perhaps a night of overindulgence followed by a wicked hangover? These terms and the images they evoke typically don't lead us back to nature. While browsing for Bourbon in your favorite liquor store, it's more likely you're envisioning the Manhattan you'll be enjoying later rather than the fields where the grains were grown.

So, how did we get to such a narrow understanding of spirits? Well, capitalism, for one. Modern marketing within the spirits industry focuses largely on building a brand. Most ads pitch the imbiber an *experience* rather than share information about the process and quality of the product. (Of course, this isn't unique to the liquor industry—it's the nature of advertising.) But it certainly goes much deeper. Cultural shifts, temperance and tax laws, farming techniques, and globalized industrialization have all influenced how we view and consume liquor today.

Of all the factors affecting spirits, at least in the US, perhaps the most profound was Prohibition (1920–1933). This was a pivotal event that severed farming from the distillation process, taking agriculture out of the discussion altogether. Prior to the banning of alcohol (and its production, importation, and sale), distillation on farms was just another form of preservation, like pickling, canning, or curing. But even after Prohibition's repeal, the increasing systematization of foodways widened the gap. It would take decades (nearly a century, in fact) for Americans to shift their views on beer, wine, and spirits and the distillation process as a whole. This change is due, in part, to the popularity of the farm-to-table movement and the rise of educators focused on the socio-economic impact of food and food systems.

Thankfully, farming is slowly but surely shouldering its way back into the conversation as more distillers realize the importance of highlighting their ingredients and consumers prioritize a more conscientious palate. Meanwhile, farm distilleries are returning to operation (as they did pre-Prohibition), with more small farmers turning to distillation as a secondary source of income. Sure, the biggest players in the liquor industry may still want to sell you an experience, but when we look below the surface, we deepen our understanding of and appreciation for distillation as an intentional agricultural process.

Power and Politics

As we examine individual spirit categories and how they've evolved, one thing is absolutely clear: politics can make or break a distilled or brewed beverage. Alcohol has always been at the government's mercy. Throughout history, the most powerful weapon in any government's arsenal, besides directly stripping away a product's legality, was to tax it. Taxes, prohibitions, and trade embargoes have shaped the trajectory of distilled spirits since their inception. Would Bourbon (a corn-dominant spirit) have reached its current popularity had Prohibition not all but wiped the production of rye (a prominent whiskey grain) off the map? And what would have become of our American rye whiskey and apple brandy if rum and cheap molasses from the French West Indies had continued to flow without British interference?

Governments have even used their power to selectively deem certain alcohols illegal to produce, such as Indigenous beverages like pulque and Mezcal in colonial Mexico. There is a great deal of violence embedded in the history of the spirits industry. Agave, cane, and grape spirits of the Americas were shaped by the blood, sweat, dispossession, and exploitation of Indigenous people, enslaved Africans, and others, who, despite unfathomable odds, left their imprint on the products we enjoy today. What we drink isn't just about what we find palatable. Our access to spirits has been shaped over the centuries by politics, war, religion, and colonialism.

Say, What's in This Drink?

It can be tough to know what's in your drink when its contents aren't legally required to be disclosed. Like many big industries, the spirits sector isn't known for its transparency. Occasionally, the question of what's in a bottle will be met with marketing spin, like a certain whiskey brand that claimed to use "whole apples" in their flavored whiskey when, in fact, they used an extract. (Mind you, it was a lovely extract and made for delicious whiskey.) When pressed, the brand's marketing director confirmed that because the extract itself was made from whole apples, the whiskey could also claim to use "whole apples." Other brands, especially those that produce spirits that can legally contain additives—like Tequila and Cognac—may flat-out lie to their consumers.

So, who decides what has to be disclosed on a bottle's label or a producer's website? In the US, alcoholic beverages are regulated not by the Food and Drug Administration (FDA) but by the Alcohol and Tobacco Tax and Trade Bureau (or just the TTB amongst friends), which sets and enforces rules, definitions, and policies for distilled spirits, beer, and wine. But just how different are the regulations between the two agencies?

Let's take the liquor shop and the candy aisle of the grocery store as an example. The two have quite a bit in common. Products from both face a certain level of social stigma, are unnecessary regarding nutritional value, and can be harmful if not consumed in moderation. And both are dominated by massive, global companies like Diageo and Nestlé. A veritable Russian nesting doll of brands, companies in both sectors rely heavily on marketing, early capitalization on trends, the acquisition of popular brand names, and strategic product placement to reach their consumers. But unlike candy, alcohol lacks the general transparency we've come to expect from the things we ingest. Whereas the FDA has policies regarding the disclosure of product information, the TTB and their liquor laws don't currently require spirit producers to share ingredients, calorie counts, or allergy warnings with their consumers.

So, why do we settle for this opacity when we have such thorough lists of ingredients on just about every other packaged food and drink product? While most imbibers know that wine is made from grapes, cider from apples and pears, and beer from grain and hops, many don't realize additives like caramel, glycerin, food colorings, and heaps of sugar are allowed to silently lurk in many of our spirits. As a conscientious buyer, this overlooked aspect of the industry never ceases to amaze me and is something I wish consumers knew more about.

Buckle Up, Buttercup!

The long of the short of it is that it's up to us as consumers to inform ourselves. When you've finished this book (or at least skimmed it for the juicy bits), I would like for you, dear reader, to be able to do the following:

- Shop for spirits with the same care and values you employ when buying your groceries;

- Hold brands and distilleries to the same ethical standards you would any other company;

- Appreciate the time, work, and labor it takes to create these spirits (especially those that are not mass-produced);

- Know how to spot clever marketing, appreciate it for what it is, and then ignore it; and

- Become a label reader! Notice what's there and, more importantly, what's missing.

Though we'll dig deep at times, this book is not overly technical. You are not meant to walk away an expert in any one category or a master of distillation. Additionally, this book isn't about passing judgment; it's about encouraging transparency, empowering consumers, and, most importantly, closing the gap between (and growing an appreciation for) the raw ingredient and final product. Above all, I hope this book is a seed that reinforces your connection with the earth and with people via the deep history of distilled spirits, starting from the ground up.

INTRODUCTION: PREPARING THE SOIL

As a young bartender in Ithaca, New York, learning the finer points of spirits seemed daunting. On top of committing dozens of cocktail recipes to memory and learning the ropes of bar hospitality, there was also the barrage of industry terminology and a list of seemingly endless categories of liquor, each with—and sometimes distinctly without—its own rules. Eventually, I found myself on the West Coast working as a bar manager at a farm-to-table restaurant in Berkeley, California. Part of my job was creating cocktail menus and understanding how to use ingredients and showcase spirits. But it was when I began working as the spirits buyer for a group of boutique spirits shops based out of San Francisco that I would finally be able to focus on producers and their creative choices, learn to ask different questions, and zero in on the craft of distilling.

Over the years, I've learned to pick up valuable information wherever I can, whether that be from seminars, books, tastings, or, best of all, from the farmers and distillers themselves—something my career has thankfully facilitated. I've had the privilege of chewing on fresh stalks of sugarcane in Martinique, hacking agave from the ground in Oaxaca, drinking freshly pressed cane juice in Michoacán, and tasting *white dog* (unaged whiskey) right off the still in Kentucky. Seeking the most effective way to fuse the vast amounts of information out there for the curious patron has long been one of my goals—making it accessible and digestible for the casual drinker who may not be interested in a long-winded, nerdy treatise on mash bills or pot stills. Meeting folks at their level of interest and understanding takes practice and consideration. (I'm no stranger to the glaze of a customer's eyes when I excitedly describe the phenolic qualities of a peated Islay Scotch.) So, how do I condense almost two decades of knowledge without overwhelming my audience?

I've come to realize that I can demystify just about any category of spirit by approaching it in three parts:

🍾 *Plant* (i.e., the raw ingredients);

🍾 *Place* (i.e., the geography, climate, and elevation); and

🍾 *Production* (i.e., the specialized equipment and processes).

I call this approach the *Three Ps of Spirit-Making*, and with it, you'll be able to easily peel back the many layers of a spirit, including language, culture, and history, to reveal a series of nesting eggs that form the heart of a spirit—the *distiller's cut*, if you will.

xiv　　　　　　　　　　　　　　　　　　　　　　　　SPIRITS DISTILLED

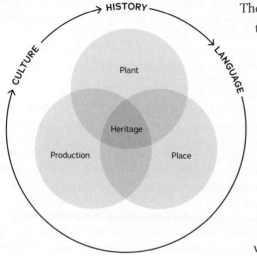

The heart of a spirit.

The Three Ps approach also enables us to pay respect to those spirit categories I consider "vulnerable" or at risk due to the predatory practices of unchecked capitalism. Many spirits found on American shelves are imported—some only recently so, like traditional sugarcane- and agave-based beverages—from countries experiencing deep inequality, economic and political instability, and food insecurity. Additionally, despite mass commercialization, many spirits continue to hold cultural significance for the people who make them (which are not always the same people who own the label). Taken together, widespread consumption of these kinds of spirits merits a conversation about how to best support communities affected by exploitation and the commodification of traditional plants and production methods.

PLANTS: CONSIDERING INGREDIENTS

As the heart and soul of the distillation process, plants—the first of the Three Ps—are the foundation of any spirit. At first glance, we see that corn is the defining ingredient for Bourbon, barley for single malt Scotch, agave for Mezcal, and so on. But when we go deeper, we learn it is more complex than just using the defining ingredient; the quality of said ingredient also matters significantly. Like so many things in life, the output mirrors the input, so if a distiller starts with poor ingredients, they shouldn't expect to turn straw into gold. You can have a beautiful custom-made copper pot still and a knowledgeable distiller, but the key to creating an amazing product will always be, first and foremost, what goes into the chamber.

But there's more to choosing ingredients than determining whether a product is fresh and ripe, just as there's more that goes into grocery shopping than thumping melons or squeezing avocados. So, if you're already a conscientious shopper who prefers products like organic kale or fairtrade coffee, it's time to start considering the ingredients that go into your favorite bottles.

Heirlooms, Hybrids, and GMOs, Oh My!

As we dive deeper into the world of plants as ingredients, it's important to clarify the difference between heirloom, hybrid, and genetically modified (GM) crops. The exact criteria for what makes a plant an *heirloom* is hotly debated, with many in the US relying on an age-based definition (specifically seeds introduced pre-1950). Conversely, Seed Savers Exchange, an organization recognized by the United States Department of Agriculture (USDA), defines an heirloom varietal by "verifying and documenting the generational history of preserving and passing on the seed, emphasizing the seed's tie to a specific group of people." Essentially, heirloom plants are long-standing, stabilized varieties honed through many generations of growth. They must also be open-pollinated, meaning that pollination occurs naturally and that the seedlings are nearly identical in traits to the parent.

Hybrid plants are those that have been cross-bred to feature favored qualities of both parents, like disease resistance, early maturation, or fruit size. For most hybrids, however, pollination must be tightly controlled for each growing season, as seeds produced from natural pollination are not guaranteed to have the favored features of the parent (unlike with heirloom varieties that are the same year-to-year).

Genetically Modified Organisms, or GMOs, are animals, plants, or other organisms whose DNA has been altered via modern genetic engineering. This may include the addition of new genes, the deletion of existing ones, the enhancement of favorable traits, or the muting of others. While in the food world, much of the general discussion around GMOs is focused on safety, in the spirits world, it's about the loss of genetic diversity and, of course, taste—GM crops aren't created to prioritize flavor. To give you an example of the total domination of GM crops, as of 2022, 99.9 percent of all sugar beets, 96 percent of cotton, 94 percent of soybeans, and 92 percent of corn in the US are genetically modified. Just think about how little variety this provides a Bourbon distiller in selecting their raw ingredient!

But it's more than that. These GM crops are often modified to resist certain pesticides or herbicides, which, unfortunately, can kill more than just their plant and animal targets. To make matters worse, GM crops can change the soil and water composition of the surrounding environment and are usually planted as *monocrops* (a single crop grown en masse without rotation), which further contributes to the loss of native plant and animal species.

Perhaps most alarming, however, is the inherent potential of biotechnology companies to control food sources through genetic modification. Created as a response to unwanted cross-pollination between GM and non-GM crops (which heavily favors the GM crop in reproduction), the "terminator gene" entered the scene in the late 1990s and was designed to ensure a plant produced for only one generation. At the time, many feared these seeds could be used to wield power over farmers by controlling the supply. And while the corporation that owns the patent has promised not to use these terminator seeds, it still has the capability to do so.

And it isn't just the threat of terminator genes. Farmers of GM crops must often sign a contract with the biotechnology company selling them seeds. These contracts may (among other terms) prohibit farmers from saving seeds for future use—meaning they must be purchased from the company each growing season—and protect the companies from various liabilities that could arise from using their GM seeds. Of course, these companies claim to have the best of intentions. Still, the truth is they wield an enormous amount of power over all of us, for better or worse, and since we seem to be currently living out our darkest dystopian nightmares, I'm not in the habit of trusting any business to have my best interests in mind.

Generally speaking, in the world of spirits, your interest in GMOs or non-GMOs will largely depend on *why* you care about such things. If you're concerned about the wide-reaching impacts of big agriculture, including biodiversity and farmworker's rights, then you'll likely want to give greater consideration to the ingredients in your favorite spirits. Unfortunately, there's currently no official labeling protocol offered or required by the TTB when it comes to GM ingredients in spirits. While this can be frustrating, it's helpful to know that to be certified as organic by the USDA, the producer must not intentionally use GM crops. Apart from this small reassurance, you'll have to do most of the sleuthing yourself for the time being. The easiest place to begin is by learning which spirits use common GM crops, such as most American whiskeys or vodkas that use corn as their base.

Common	Sometimes/Rarely	Never*
Corn Sugar beets	Sugarcane (Brazil and Indonesia) Wheat (Brazil and Argentina)	Rye Barley Agave

* Not commercially available today.

Genetically modified ingredients used in distillation.

But don't feel like you have to write off your favorite drinks just yet. Some Bourbon distillers, such as Buffalo Trace and Four Roses, don't use any GM corn, and each truck of corn brought to the distillery is thoroughly inspected and graded before it can be accepted and milled, a common practice in quality control. And most, if not all, EU-produced spirits imported into the US will likewise be non-GMO due to EU regulations.

It's Not Perfect, But We Do the Best We Can

Recently, I chatted with some of the most thoughtful distillers I know to get their opinions on sustainability in the industry. Todd Leopold, brewer-turned-distiller, started making organic beer in the 1990s with his brother, Scott. Todd studied brewing in Germany, while Scott, eager to change the world, graduated from Stanford with a master's degree in environmental engineering. At the time, most spirits companies wanted little more than to comply with the Environmental Protection Agency's (EPA) regulations and go about their business. But Scott wanted to prove to manufacturers that creating a sustainable factory blueprint was possible. Together, they started an organic brewery in Denver, Colorado, at a time when organic produce hadn't yet become popular and organic beer had a reputation for being subpar in flavor.

Fast forward thirty years, and Todd and Scott's distillery, Leopold Bros, has something of a cult following in the spirits industry. Today, conscientious distillers juggle many issues, including human labor, quality of ingredients, and environmental impact, and Todd will be the first to admit the concept of sustainability is not black and white. "There's no binary," he told me on my recent visit to their malting floor. "The important thing is that pretty much everybody these days [is] thinking and talking about this to a much greater degree than when we started."

Rob Easter of Workhorse Rye, a former Bay Area denizen I've known for years, has an infectious enthusiasm for heirloom grains and a deep respect for the farmers who supply them for his small, agricultural-focused whiskeys. Like the Leopold brothers, Easter is striving to do better, with the understanding there's no one ideal way to operate. "I'm not trying to be perfect," he confessed when I visited. "I'm just trying to have a good impact." One of the ways he does this is by buying grains from Indigenous growers at a competitive price. Of course, this means his whiskeys aren't cheap, but that's a tradeoff we as consumers make with any of our groceries, whether it be the higher price for organic strawberries or fairtrade cacao. "I'm proud of my distilling, but I didn't create the corn," he said emphatically, acknowledging the growers' contribution. "I've made too much whiskey to not communicate that grains are worth paying for!"

The Importance of Word Choice

While "industry" is an innocuous word, "industrial" is not. Just as with "formula" and "formulaic," these terms take on a different meaning depending on their suffix. In the world of wine and spirits, "industrial" is a bit of a dirty word, as it implies—though does not guarantee—big agriculture, efficiency over nuance, and modern and automated production over traditional processes. In short, industrial spirits can often be basic—that is, consistent, dependable, and crowd-pleasing. But a basic cheeseburger, while perfectly adequate in many ways, eventually leaves you wanting.

Other descriptors, like "craft," while sometimes used to articulate careful or conscientious production, are more often employed as marketing jargon; after all, "craft" has no legal definition, much like other oft-deployed words I love to despise, "premium" or—my personal favorite—"super-premium" (that's "premium" in a cape). "Craft" is a word that distillers often use to signal they aren't like the "big guys" and that they're a small business, work with local farms, and/or use traditional, rather than industrialized, processes. Overall, it comes with no guarantees of quality or expertise.

"Small batch" is another term lacking regulation, whose definition depends solely on context. What is considered a "small batch" is often relative and could mean 100 liters or 1,000+ liters. Furthermore, a spirit distilled in a pot still, by its very nature, is limited by confinements of space and size and can, therefore, also be considered a "small batch." In other words, if no number accompanies the term, you can count on it being entirely subject to the producer's interpretation. That said, mass-produced spirits are not in and of themselves inferior, as long as the product itself is good and the distiller's practices are ethical.

Sustainability

Like the terms "green" or "natural," "sustainable" has become a somewhat diluted buzzword within the spirits industry. In the late 1980s, the United Nations (UN) defined *sustainability* as "meeting the needs of the present without compromising the ability of future generations to meet their own needs." More specifically, many experts define sustainability as having three dimensions, or pillars: *environmental*, *social*, and *economic*. But absent a legal definition, the "sustainable" label doesn't guarantee a commitment to these criteria. Many producers who tout sustainable practices often do so based on a very limited scope of environmental impact alone, skipping over social responsibility practices (e.g., paying a living wage). A spirit producer that strives to be sustainable in the true sense of the word should honor the environment, embrace transparency around the ingredients used, and support the people making the product. Some social scientists argue

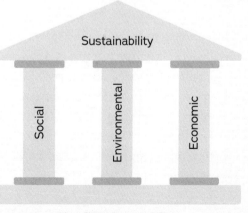

The pillars of sustainability.

that *culture* should be the fourth pillar of sustainability. For the spirits industry, that would mean respecting the intellectual property rights of the people who have historically made the spirit and continue to preserve cultural ties to the plant and its growth, harvest, and/or processing.

For our purposes, truly sustainable spirit producers should demonstrate the following:

- Respect for the natural ecosystem, including practicing responsible farming (e.g., not harvesting a plant before maturity to prevent soil erosion), preserving wildlife and local plant life, engaging in proper wastewater disposal, and committing to biodiversity;

- Respect for cultural ties and traditional production methods (when applicable); and

- Respect for human rights by assuring safe labor conditions both in the field and in production facilities, paying livable wages to workers, and upholding fair pricing and contracts for both raw ingredients and finished products.

PLACE: DENOMINATIONS OF ORIGIN

The second of the Three Ps—place—refers to the geographic location where a product is distilled. It might not surprise you to know that Scotch can only come from Scotland and Irish whiskey from Ireland. However, some industry rules are stricter, with certain spirits required to be produced in specific states, municipalities, or even on a particular parcel of land. Essentially, the product and its place of origin are inseparable.

When it comes to geography and spirits, the primary legal concern is the economic protection of a specific agricultural product that evokes a sense of place, meaning that if the quality, characteristics, or reputation of a product is intrinsically connected to its place of origin, it is under specific protection and regulation. There are many terms used to convey this overall legal concept, including the French Appellation d'Origine Contrôlée (AOC), the Italian Denominazione di Origine Controllata (DOC), and the widely used Geographical Indication (GI). Depending on the country, wine has even more specific terminology protecting and assigning hierarchical value to its various *appellations* (wine-growing regions).

To make matters infinitely more complicated, the US uses Intellectual Property laws already in place for trademarks to enforce these global laws and gives American spirits federal protections and *standards of identity* through the TTB. This accomplishes the same protective goals but with different legal language. Eventually, the alphabet soup thickens to the point of opacity, and while the legal terms aren't always interchangeable (some are more specific than others), we can alleviate confusion by referring to most protected categories simply as a *denomination of origin* (DO). But what exactly does it mean when a product has this acronym-adorned status?

The most digestible explanation I've seen for DOs is in sociologist Sarah Bowen's agave-focused book *Divided Spirits*, in which she explains that DOs are "based on the belief that the environmental and cultural characteristics of particular places—their terroir—are translated into the tastes of the foods and drinks produced there and, moreover, that they deserve to be protected." A lengthy discussion on Comté cheese follows her description, and while this may seem unrelated, some of the most popular cheeses in the world are protected by DOs. Parmigiano Reggiano, Gorgonzola, Asiago, Roquefort, Manchego—each must come from a particular region and follow a specific set of rules to bear the name. Alcohol is no different. Spirits such as Mezcal, Tequila, Scotch, Cachaça, and Pisco are all protected by a DO, as they are considered a reflection of culture, history, and geography.

Why would products like cheese, brandy, or wine need protection? For the same reason a trademark or other piece of intellectual property might require it. Once a food or drink gains popularity, imitations usually follow (the highest form of flattery, I suppose). These homages may cut corners, use different processes that change the expected flavor profile, and ultimately ruin or dilute the reputation of the original product, which was likely painstakingly created. High-value wines and Italian olive oils are examples of products frequently counterfeited. DOs allow for quality maintenance and fraud reduction, especially for products fetching premium prices. At face value, a DO is a form of

---

Champagne's DO

One of the world's most widely known DOs is Champagne. In fact, comedic variations of the internet meme, "It's only Champagne if it comes from the Champagne region of France; otherwise, it's just sparkling wine," have made the rounds in the last few years, giving us gems like: "It's only a coup if it comes from the Coup d'Etat region of France; otherwise, it's just sparkling insurrection." Despite this, in the US, consumers often use the word *champagne* as a catch-all for any sparkling wine in the same way that Band-Aid and Kleenex have become *proprietary eponyms*, or general terms for a product type rather than a brand name.

intellectual property, though it's technically not a trademark, as trademarks are tied to a company rather than a specific geographic location. Instead, in the US, DOs are treated as a "geographic subset of trademarks" and handled by the US patent office.

A geographically protected status is often contingent upon traditional and sometimes historical production methods, an expectation of higher-than-normal quality, and a base of premium raw materials. Additionally, the benefits of a DO are many: regional job creation (especially in smaller, agricultural communities), tourism, and, of course, a higher price per product. At its heart, a DO provides a stamp of authenticity for consumers while protecting the livelihood of those who create the product.

But there's a catch. DOs are complicated and involve political wrangling between nations and complex negotiations that can span years. Countries must agree to recognize and enforce each other's labeling agreements for these rules to have the greatest impact, and protections are typically drafted alongside other trade agreements, further complicating the process. Obtaining internationally-recognized protections can also be more difficult for countries with lower economic standing and less leveraging power. While it may seem like most nations follow the spirit of these designations without much fanfare, that's not always the case. Two current examples are Sotol, protected in Mexico, and Grappa, protected in the EU. Currently, the US doesn't recognize these DOs and allows US distillers to use those terms on their labels as long as they meet the TTB's set standards of identity.

Globalization and National Identity

In the introduction to C.E. Page's book *Armagnac*, published in 1989, he writes, "As trades go, the wine and spirits trade is no worse than most and better than some. Still, in any trade the profit motive rules first and foremost." In the case of spirits, corporations have the unique ability to influence the concept of national identity and what it means for a product to be "local" or "authentic." Furthermore, many "independent" distillers—after demonstrating success—are acquired by major industry players like Diageo, Brown-Forman, and Suntory. And as more and more small brands become part of larger entities, we begin to lose sight of who's pulling the strings.

Take Patrón, for example, one of the most popular brands of Tequila in the world, and at a glance, authentically Mexican. By all accounts, the company is an excellent example of a producer doing things by the book: for instance, using ripe agave and no additives. But Patrón is owned by the transnational company Bacardí, the world's largest, privately-owned spirits company. Originally founded in Cuba, Bacardí, has been producing its eponymous rum in Puerto Rico since the mid-1930s and has since acquired many other non-rum companies, including Patrón. Therefore, while Bacardí owns the Patrón distillery, Patrón can still maintain its identity (and public image) as a Mexican company. Similarly, Bruichladdich, a Scottish, Certified B Corp, farm-focused distillery that grows a portion of its barley on the Scottish island of Islay, is owned by the French-headquartered Rémy Cointreau Group (though, to be fair, for a spirits holding corporation, Rémy Cointreau is on the smaller side and has an intentional and thoughtfully-curated acquisitions portfolio).

Still, not all corporations that acquire smaller companies demonstrate the same level of "hands-off" ownership as Bacardí or Rémy Cointreau. There is always some anxiety and tension from industry professionals and consumers alike when smaller, beloved companies sell to or partner with the "big guys." Concerns abound, including: Will acquisition change the brand's authenticity? Their product's quality? What will the impact on the brand's workforce or social impact be? Will the acquiring company respect the geographical and historical roots of the original business and the products they make?

So, where do we, as consumers, draw the line on what it means to "sell out?" In many cases, the answer isn't straightforward. The reality is that often, an acquisition can boost a brand's visibility, increasing its access to funds and customers that would otherwise be inaccessible. For some brands, such resources can mean the difference between closing their doors or continuing their operation. Take, for instance, Ron Cooper's brand, Del Maguey. Del Maguey specializes in remote, single-village Mezcals known for embodying culture and craftsmanship, and just recently, the brand partnered with industry titan Pernod Ricard after twenty years of independently working and building relationships with various mezcaleros throughout Mexico. Cooper has since retired, leaving the iconic green bottle's fate in the hands of the world's second-largest wine and spirits company. However, the acquisition doesn't appear to have hurt Del Maguey's reputation much, as many still consider it authentically Oaxacan. Still, as consumers, it's hard to know how much profit now returns to the Mexican families who produce the spirit or if the contracts for the agave itself are priced fairly.

PRODUCTION: TOOLS OF THE TRADE

Production—the third "P"—is vital in determining a spirit's category, and there are numerous standards and practices that dictate how specific spirits are to be made (especially if they are protected by a DO). For example, a distiller may use a pot or column still, ferment their product in stainless steel, wood, or concrete, or roast their raw ingredients underground in earthen pits or in above-ground brick ovens. They may distill their spirits to proof or add water to lower the *alcohol by volume* (ABV) after distillation. All of these methods have their own regulations that must be followed, and the distillation practices used are directly related to the type of spirit being produced. In other words, the production of a spirit leaves a fundamental, unavoidable mark on the finished product.

Spirit production includes the technology, labor, and knowledge needed to plant, grow, harvest, and process a raw ingredient, and often has deep cultural and historical roots. Mezcal, for example, is a uniquely Mexican spirit consumed for both small celebrations and momentous occasions. From hand-harvesting and crushing to fermenting with native yeasts and roasting in wide, earthen ovens, the knowledge of Mezcal production has been passed down for generations. Still today, in more rural areas of Mexico, fermentation and distillation of the national spirit is done with cowhide vessels and clay pots—a far cry from the shiny, modern industrial equipment used to mass-produce Mezcal's cousin, Tequila.

It Takes Two (Stills) to Make a Drink Go Right

While many details of early distillation remain hidden in uncharted archaeological territory, we do know that Ancient Mesopotamians were experimenting with conceptions of the *still*, an instrument used to make alcohol by heating a liquid and collecting the vapor, as early as the 4th millennium BCE. The oldest example of a distillation apparatus yet discovered is from the site of Tepe Gawra in Iraq and dates back over 5,000 years. That's a long history for a technology that feels so modern.

While many types of stills exist—some industrial and high-tech, others simplistic and reliant on sensory input—for our purposes, we'll focus on two main designs: the *pot still* and the *column still*. These stills are the foundation of modern distillation and are fundamental to understanding many of the spirit categories and their production processes. Early pot stills, also called *alembics*, provided the blueprint for the modern pot still. The design is often credited to Arab chemist, astronomer, and mathematician Jabir ibn Hayyan and is known to have been used during the Islamic Golden Age (around the 8th century) to distill water, making it safe for consumption.

Today, our modern pot stills retain the moniker *alembic* (from the Arabic *al-inbiq*), though the original shape has since undergone multiple adaptations. A typical pot still is usually forged from copper and has a round, pot-like base (hence the name) with a heat source surrounding it, whether open flame-fired by wood or gas, steam, or electricity. The fermented liquid is heated in the still, causing vapor to rise and travel up through a long neck before cooling and condensing back into liquid that is ready for collection. This process can be repeated at the distiller's discretion (though it is sometimes limited by regulation) to achieve a desired goal, such as a particular ABV or flavor profile. I anticipate a pot-still-made spirit to be rich, oily, textured, and complex. Spirits commonly distilled in this way include whiskey, brandy, rum, and Tequila.

A column still—also known as a *Coffey* or *continuous still*—is a much more recent invention. First developed by Irishman Aeneas Coffey in the 19th century, it was a game changer. Though the end goal is the same, a column still uses a tall, cylindrical (often stainless steel) chamber with horizontal plates spread throughout to facilitate continuous condensation. Think of each plate as being like a little pot still stacked one on top of the other, with the height of the still reflecting the scale of operation (some industrial stills can reach the height of a two- to three-story building). Whereas a pot still must be stopped, cooled, and cleaned between each distillation, or "run," a continuous still makes for a more efficient process as it retains heat during operation. It also strips impurities as the vapor moves along the plates, yielding a final product more neutral than those made with a pot still. I generally expect a continuously distilled spirit to be light, fruity, clean, and simple. Spirits most often made with a column still include vodka, gin, and rum.

Of course, as with everything, distillation methods are often more complicated than they appear. Many spirits, like rum, are made from a mix of distillates produced by both types of stills, similar to how a coffee roaster might blend different types of coffee in an espresso blend to get a balanced output. There are also outliers, such as *traditional stills*, which can be made from a combination of wood, clay, copper, and/or stainless steel, and *hybrid stills*, essentially a pot still and a modestly-sized column still linked together—a more practical option for smaller distilleries who produce a variety of products.

Pot still

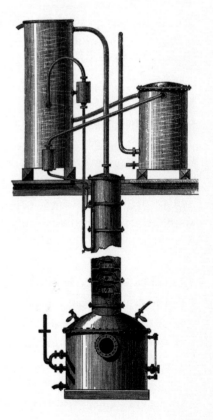

Column still

MANAGING EXPECTATIONS: KNOWLEDGE IS POWER!

Knowing what you like can help ensure you get what you want from your spirit. It's similar to selecting a book; if you are hoping to read science fiction but end up with historical romance, you're likely to wind up dissatisfied no matter the quality of the writing. Your choice of spirit might come down to any number of factors, including your taste preferences, the unique characteristics of your chosen bottle, the season, or even your current mood. The process will likely involve a bit of (fun!) research and trial and error. Here's some advice to get you started:

ASK YOURSELF WHAT YOU WANT FROM THE SPIRIT YOU'RE BUYING. Are you making a cocktail? If so, will the spirit be the star of the show, such as the gin in a gin martini? Or will it be part of the chorus, as is the case with the multi-spirit Negroni? Even the same category of spirits will work differently depending on the goal. You may find a rum that works well in a citrusy and refreshing daiquiri but isn't great for a stirred, spirit-forward drink. Or perhaps you're not mixing the spirit, preferring to sip it neat or with ice. Different spirits are used for different things, so when choosing one, keep in mind the role you want it to play.

FIND YOUR "TYPE." I love red wine, but I don't love *all* red wines. I prefer bold, earthy, tannic wines with structure but shy away from floral wines and those too heavy-handed with oak undertones. As with wine and beer, there are styles within each spirits category. You may prefer a young, sweet, high-corn Bourbon over an older, high-rye mash bill. Or Scotch aged in Sherry casks as opposed to ex-Bourbon barrels. If your first foray into gin is a New American style that tastes like fresh rosemary and you despise it, that doesn't mean you should swear off one of the most versatile and expansive spirit categories; you just may find that you gravitate toward a classic, dry, juniper-forward gin or a floral Spanish style.

TASTE, TASTE, TASTE! Train your palate. This may sound daunting, but anyone can do it—don't be intimidated! You can level up your tastebuds with experience and the learned ability to recognize patterns. Take advantage of spirit and wine flights when bars offer them, or find a bar that specializes in a category you love. Organize a bottle share with friends. Or if you have a favorite watering hole with a well-rounded selection of spirits, ask your bartender to guide you through some of them and make recommendations (assuming it's not Friday night, the bar is four people deep, and tickets are pouring out of the service well; don't be *that* person).

DON'T BUY INTO THE HYPE. As consumers, we're constantly bombarded by ads, articles, and blogs telling us what we should be drinking. For example, American and Japanese whiskey remain the darlings of the spirits world and have been for the better part of a decade. (This is particularly true in the US.) And while their notoriety is fantastic, makers of these spirits can also become victims of their own success. Press and popularity can lead to bottle shortages, real or imagined, causing price inflation—the kind that adds zeroes to the end of the number. So many drinkers, unfamiliar with the categories they're being sold, look for hard-to-find bottles without fully understanding what they're looking for. If you aren't a collector, these bottles are not worth the chase nor the price tag.

DON'T JUDGE BY THE LABEL. Look, we can't be good at everything. Sometimes companies, big and small alike, have UALs (aka ugly ass labels). Think of this as camouflage. *You* know the spirit is good, but plenty of others not in on the secret will overlook the bottle because it looks like it teleported out of the 1980s or was printed by your friend's cousin who's just started design school. Some of my favorite Bourbons, for example, have hideous labels, and that's part of their charm. (There is a simple fix for this; if you're embarrassed to have it on display—buy a decanter! Everyone will wonder what fancy and mysterious spirit is in there.)

DON'T JUDGE BASED ON THE PRICE. Often, a product is more expensive simply because it is in high demand, with its price having nothing to do with quality. On the flip side, you may spot a fantastic bottle of rare, wild agave made by an Indigenous community using labor-intensive, traditional methods in a remote area of Mexico for the low price of $200. (By the time you finish the agave chapter of this book, I hope that price will seem more than reasonable.) Don't let the dent it leaves on your wallet determine whether or not you think a spirit is tasty and/or well-made.

Of course, we all like a good bargain. To that end, if one of your favorite bottles pops up at a warehouse store like Costco or Trader Joe's, fill your cart, my friend. In my experience, these stores have the lowest prices out there, in part because their bottles are likely being sold at wholesale cost or lower, unlike your local bottle shop, which, remember, is selling it for the manufacturer's suggested retail price (MSRP) (or higher depending on demand). And when you do find a spirit priced far above the MSRP, don't get mad at the store selling it! Small shops are just trying to survive, not unlike your local independent bookstore or any other small business. Places like Costco buy in bulk and have hundreds of locations, so they're getting a better deal from distributors, not to mention they can subsidize the cost by selling other products. Your little neighborhood spot likely buys one case at a time, meaning they pay a higher price to stock that item since they don't move the same volume.

BIG ISN'T ALWAYS BAD FOR THE PLANET. Though you might assume that a small, traditionally operated distillery would be more environmentally friendly than a large corporation, some larger companies have taken advantage of their size and wealth to invest in green technology and infrastructure. For example, the American whiskey producer Heaven Hill Distillery rolls out about 400,000 barrels annually at its giant yet highly efficient state-of-the-art facility. When it comes to distillation processes, a continuous still takes less power to operate than a small pot still, while many traditional methods, such as floor malting barley or roasting agave in wood-fired earthen ovens, aren't especially energy- or space-efficient. Don't write off a distillery based solely on its size. Each should be judged on its own merit.

OLDER ISN'T BETTER, AND COLOR DOESN'T SIGNIFY AGE. If you see two 12 Year single malt Scotches, and one is two shades darker, you may wonder how they can be the same age. Is one lying? Surprisingly, a spirit's color and its time spent in barrel don't overlap much on a Venn diagram. A great deal of color actually comes from the kind of char or toast used on the wood of the barrel and the previous liquid it contained. For example, Sherry and wine casks both add a lot of color and hints of sweetness (but so does good old-fashioned caramel additive). In addition, older spirits aged in hot climates take on the qualities of oak barrels faster than those aged in cooler temperatures, making age just a number. In some cases, age may even negatively impact the product, as is the case with peated whiskeys, which tend to lose their savory notes as they get older. So, before you go looking for a 20 Year Bourbon, pinpoint what you like about older American whiskeys rather than focusing on the age statement. You may find those same qualities in a younger spirit without the hefty price tag. Or perhaps you'll find that you got caught up in the romance of an older bottle (understandable). It takes some trial and error, but you'll find what works for you without being overly concerned about age or coloration. Personally, I've found the qualities I like best in Bourbon peak at eight to twelve years. That said, I've also had a knockout single barrel of 7 Year Elijah Craig Bourbon.

Get to Know Importers: The Multitool for Finding Products You Love

Getting to know importers is one of the most overlooked strategies for finding bottles that reflect your tastes and values. An importer is more than just a facilitator of the movement of goods from one country to another. They're the ones who search out quality producers, visit their operations, walk through vineyards and farms, and believe in a product enough to invest in it. A good importer will think about more than just marketability. They'll consider the quality, core values, and practices of potential business partners and create lasting, mutually beneficial relationships with producers (and even their families). At the end of the day, an importer acts as a producer's representative in the country where their bottles will be sold.

I first discovered this hack while entering the world of wine. When I lived on the East Coast, I found that a couple of bottles I enjoyed came from the same importer—Kermit Lynch. At the time, I knew very little about wine other than I liked to drink it and had outgrown my taste for Yellow Tail. After moving to Berkeley, my head (and my wallet) nearly exploded upon finding that Kermit Lynch had an entire storefront just down the road. It was a *eureka* moment. But I didn't come to truly grasp just how helpful importers could be until I became a spirits buyer. Now, it's second nature to turn a bottle around and check for the importer's name.

Finding a few importers whose bottlings you enjoy and who share your tastes and ideals is like scoring an epic cheat sheet of great producers. Go to their websites or storefronts and see what brands they represent. Many tend to have "types" or profiles they favor and often share their mission statement and code of values on their site.

With all this in mind, you're well on your way to choosing your new favorite bottle!

Importers I Love and Trust (and Their Specialties)

- Heavy Métl Premium Imports (Mexican spirits)
- Oliver McCrum (Italian wine and spirits)
- Terranova Spirits (Latin American spirits)
- Craft Distillers (world spirits with a focus on agave)
- Suro International Importers (Mexican agave spirits)
- The Craft Spirits Cooperative (Latin American and world spirits)
- Charles Neal (French wine and spirits)
- Haus Alpenz (central European spirits)
- Back Bar Project (world spirits focused on agave and rum)
- Heavenly Spirits (French spirits)
- Impex Spirits (Scotch and world whiskeys)

CHERRIES, APPLES, AND PEARS

For a food group as familiar as fruit, many of us don't realize how diverse it truly is. So, let's take a moment to nerd out.

According to its botanical definition, fruit is "the mature and ripened ovary of a plant." (Yum!) In addition to looking and smelling great, they are also an essential feature of all flowering plants as they help to protect and scatter the plant's seeds, ensuring future generations of growth. By this definition, some produce we consider vegetables are actually fruits. Tomatoes are a well-known example, as are eggplants, green beans, okra, and avocados. An easy way to remember the difference is that while a vegetable can be any edible part of a plant—root, stem, leaves, and flowers—a fruit must be seed-bearing and derive from the flower.

Grains of wheat and corn are also technically fruits (as are several spices, like the allspice berry, vanilla bean, and black pepper). However, the spirits industry does not group them with other fruits (more on that later). Just know that from here on, we'll use the word "fruit" to mean the sweet and fleshy table fruits we eat every day, like plums, apples, cherries, and grapes.

BRANDY AND EAU DE VIE

Visual guide to fruit spirits.

Almost any fruit can be distilled after being fermented into wine or cider. In the spirits industry, these distillates are commonly lumped under the umbrella term *brandy*, derived from the Dutch word *brandewijn* (meaning burnt or distilled wine). The TTB doesn't add much specificity, defining brandy as a "spirit distilled from the fermented juice, mash or wine of fruit, or from its residue." With such a general description, brandies can vary wildly in style depending on their country of origin and fruit used—though today, most are made from grapes and apples. They can be aged or unaged, but unaged brandies maintain the plant's essence in a purer form (without any influence from a barrel or additives), making them a great place to begin a discussion of the category.

Wasser, schnaps, aguardiente, vinars, aqua vitae; there are many names for the clear spirit the French have dubbed *eau de vie* or "the water of life." Today, it's almost exclusively associated with fruit brandy taken right from the still (i.e., unaged), though historically, the term referred to any distilled spirit and is still occasionally used in France as a catch-all term for liquor. Perhaps not altogether inaccurate since eaux de vie (the plural form of *eau de vie*) are being made today from carrots, basil, and even the buds of the Douglas fir tree! Put simply, eau de vie is a clear, unaged brandy, and while it's often an end-product in and of itself, it may also refer to an unaged grape distillate on its way to becoming Cognac or Armagnac.

Traditionally, eaux de vie were associated with particular regions, and their distillation took place near the farms, orchards, and homesteads where the ingredients were grown. For example, the cherry eau de vie *Schwarzwälder Kirschwasser* is linked to the Black Forest region of Germany and protected through a GI. For the most part, however, there aren't many regional protections for eaux de vie. The flip side to this is that there are amazing examples of the spirit made all over the world, with some using very unexpected ingredients.

Aided by increasingly efficient refrigeration and shipping methods, fresh fruit can now travel long distances, meaning eau de vie can be distilled just about anywhere with a still. Some producers of *Poire Williams* (pear eau de vie), for example, distill their spirits in Eastern Europe but source their pears from Chile. Meanwhile, Chicago-based distillery Rhine Hall meshes traditional Austrian influences with modern sensibilities, making *Bierschnaps* or *Bierbrand* (essentially beer eau de vie), *Kirschwasser* (cherry eau de vie), and *Pommeau* (eau de vie made from apple juice and apple brandy), while introducing tropical fruits like mango and pineapple into the mix. Like I said, eau de vie can be made from *any* fruit!

I grew up knowing this spirit as *schnaps*, the term the Austrian side of my family used for the digestif served straight from the freezer after a heavy meal. But no matter what you call the spirit, expectations for eaux de vie remain the same; they're typically bright, fresh, and lively—aromatic on the nose, yet dry on the palate. At its heart, this spirit should capture and enhance the nature of the raw ingredient.

EAU DE VIE

Plant: Any fruit (though technically and historically, any non-fruit bearing plants as well)

Place: Everywhere fruit is grown

Production: No official regulations, though pot stills are common

Protection: None

Brandy or Eau de Vie?

Inspired by traditional German distilling, Jörg Rupf opened St. George Spirits in Alameda, California, in the early 1980s. Their early bottlings of eau de vie were first labeled as such, though gradually, they replaced the term with the more digestible and generic label of "brandy." "Unfortunately, Americans seem to struggle with asking for spirits when they're unsure of the pronunciation," says Dave Smith, head distiller. "[Our solution] was to inspire palates first [before asking] people to appreciate the specific term."

Bailoni
Austria

Apricot

ORIGINAL GOLD-MARILLENSCHNAPS

This apricot brandy has been made in the Bailoni family's distillery since 1872, using fruit sourced from the Wachau region of the Danube Valley. The distillery also manages roughly 1,500 apricot trees.

Notable European Producer / Regional Typification

R. Jelínek
Czech Republic

Plum

SLIVOVITZ 5 YEAR

R. Jelínek grows a large portion its fruit in orchards across the Bohemia region of the Czech Republic. This 5 Year has top notes of plum jam with a hint of almond and is best served cold or from the freezer.

Notable European Producer / Regional Typification

Rhine Hall Distillery
United States

Mango

MANGO EAU DE VIE

This delightful, fresh, and juicy brandy is made from mangos sourced from central Mexico. While the spirit started as an experiment, it was so well received that it's now a distillery staple.

Modern Yet Artisanal

Clear Creek Distillery
United States

Douglas fir buds

DOUGLAS FIR BRANDY

Using the fresh green buds hand-picked from Oregon Douglas fir trees, this spirit is Christmas in a bottle and will appeal to fans of absinthe. The beverage's green tint comes from a secondary maceration of Douglas fir buds post-distillation.

Funky but Cool

Ventura Spirits
United States

Opuntia

OPUNTIA PRICKLY PEAR BRANDY

Opuntia is the cactus commonly known as "prickly pear" (*nopal* in Spanish). California producer Ventura Spirits makes a unique brandy from its fruit, using over 1 ton per batch! The unique flavor is tropical, with some lingering grassy and herbaceous notes.

Funky but Cool

Guasca
Colombia

Uchuva

UCHUVA

Made with the naturally tart and tangy Andean fruit uchuva/ uvilla (*Physalis peruviana*), also known as "goldenberry" or "Cape gooseberry," this lively spirit is fermented slowly (up to a month!) and is distilled with no extra sugar or additives.

Funky but Cool

CHERRIES

Cherries play a monumental role in the world of spirits, particularly in liqueurs. And, of course, they remain a quintessential and beloved cocktail garnish. How many a wandering hand has been slapped by a bartender for straying too close to the cocktail cherries?

This delicious edible fruit of the cherry tree belongs to the genus *Prunus* (from the Greek word for "plum tree") along with other types of stone fruit, including peaches and nectarines. Botanically speaking, these dangly little orbs are *drupes*, or fruit consisting of skin, flesh, and a single large seed (or "stone"). Today, there are over 120 identified species (and over 1,000 varieties) of cherry, but only 2 species are grown commercially: sweet cherries (*Prunus avium*) and sour cherries (*Prunus cerasus*.) Sweet cherries are generally eaten as table fruit, while sour cherries are more often used for cooking, jams, and distillation.

Despite a wide range of variation, archaeological studies show that all cherries derive from a species native to Western Asia, near the Caspian and Black Seas, and that their domestication predates recorded history. Ancient Greek philosopher Theophrastus provided one of the first known written accounts of the fruit in his *Historia Plantarum* (300 BCE), noting that, at the time of writing, cherries had already been cultivated for centuries. Their later emergence in central and northern Europe has been credited in large part to the Roman Empire and its expansion. The fruit was included in soldiers' rations, and over time, discarded pits grew into a trail of cherry trees (particularly of the Morello variety) along marching routes. These same cherries would later become ubiquitous in Germany and the North Adriatic.

On this side of the pond, there is also a long history of using and enjoying native species of the *Prunus* genus, including black cherries (*P. serotina*), chokecherries (*P. virginiana*), and pin cherries (*P. pensylvanica*). Chokecherries, in particular, were—and still are—culturally vital to many Indigenous people of North America. Besides the medicinal value of their bark and fruit, the local species are consumed fresh, dried, or preserved in traditional foods like pemmican, a dried meat and fruit mixture (essentially a calorie-dense protein bar).

Cherries and Climate Change

Throughout the world, cherry blossoms have traditionally marked the arrival of spring. They are often the first trees to blossom—brilliantly, I would add—and the time between their flowering and fruit harvest is the shortest of any fruit tree species—approximately sixty to seventy-five days total.

However, warmer weather year after year has reduced the *chill hours* available for the fruit to set. To produce fruit, cherries require a certain cumulative amount of time in cold temperatures (around 32°F–45°F). Almost every fruit-bearing tree has a specific number of chill hours it must clock while dormant for the plant to bloom properly. When that requirement is met, the tree is ready to make pretty flowers and invites bees and other pollinators to join the party.

Unfortunately, with unpredictable weather and earlier springs comes premature or uneven blooms at risk of withering during cold snaps. In the US, the Montmorency cultivar accounts for a staggering 98 percent of all commercially grown tart cherries and is grown almost exclusively in Michigan. This overreliance on one type of sour cherry leaves the trees vulnerable to pests, disease, and environmental fluctuations, especially as climate change accelerates. In 2013, Michigan's spring came early, causing all the Montmorency cherry trees to bloom, and because the trees are all genetically related, they all bloomed simultaneously. The early spring was followed by an unexpected cold snap that destroyed the entire year's tart cherry harvest.

Early springs can also be a serious problem for pollinators. A rise of just one-degree Celsius can rouse some wild bee populations from their winter slumber as much as ten days too early. If blooms then fail, the bees awaken to no food and a decreased chance of survival. Meanwhile, the blooms that do survive receive sub-optimal pollination, which threatens the yield and quality of the fruit.

The Sordid Corruption of the Maraschino Cherry

Spirits writer Wayne Curtis once described maraschino cherries as "the cocktail world's essential non-essential." Stoplight bright, these "cherries" exist in many a bar's garnish tray, swimming in their sugar syrup, waiting to be plopped into a '90s-era Manhattan. But these very popular (and very manipulated) cherries are a far cry from anything nature offers.

Cherry Picking

Cherry trees can produce a significant amount of fruit—up to 7,000 cherries per tree once they reach maturity (typically 4–7 years for sweet and 3–5 for tart). Though traditionally picked by hand, since the 1970s, most commercial growers use a mechanical tree shaker to "pick" them. This hydraulic, tractor-like apparatus has an arm that grasps the tree trunk and shakes it vigorously until nearly all the cherries fall into a waiting net. It is very effective, but producers must wait until the trees are mature to harvest this way or risk damaging them. To sidestep this limitation, some tart cherry growers have begun using over-the-row harvester machines that surround a tree and use rotating, rake-like structures to separate the fruit from individual limbs, allowing farmers to harvest earlier in the tree's lifespan.

There are two kinds of maraschino cherries: real and imitation. True maraschinos are made from a type of Morello cherry called Marasca, a small, dark red variety cultivated since the 1800s in Croatia. These cherries were originally preserved by brining them in ocean water (essentially pickling them) and then bottling them with a "liqueur" made from cherry juice, ground-up leaves, and cherry pits (the pit, or stone, imparts a bitter almond flavor). These cherries were so popular that demand soon exceeded supply, leading to their high cost and status as a luxury item. They were also a hit with bartenders—partly because they wouldn't spoil as quickly as fresh fruit—and quickly became a standard garnish for drinks of the era, such as the Sherry Cobbler. Their success also drove competitors and imitators to use shortcuts and substitute different types of cherries unsuited for the task—a perfect example of the kind of issues DOs are meant to solve.

The first maraschino cherries imported to the US were a mix of authentic products and imitations of lesser quality, often loaded with sugar and artificial coloring. Before long, using flavorings and extracts such as almond and vanilla was common practice. At the turn of the 20th century, some manufacturers went so far as to use harmful chemicals to process the fruit, leading to a statement in 1912 by the still relatively young USDA that warned of "imitation cherries" and defined authentic cherries as "Marasca cherries preserved in maraschino." This required producers to print "imitation" on maraschino cherry products that did not meet these requirements.

Even knockoff imports were hard to find (and still expensive), so while European cherry varietals were considered ideal for preservation due to their firmer texture, it didn't take long for the US to join the maraschino-imitation party. In the 1920s, Oregon State University horticulturist Earnest H. Wiegand developed a technique for preserving softer, American-grown cherries like Queen Anne (aka Royal Anne) by adding calcium salts to the preserving liquid. With that, the American imitation maraschino cherry was born.

These days, you may notice the word "imitation" is no longer found on the jars of this classic garnish, a result of the cherry industry successfully lobbying the FDA after Prohibition in 1939. Since then, the cherry industry has further reshaped the definition of maraschino cherries in the US (last revised in 1980). The current policy reads: "the term 'Maraschino Cherries' is regarded as the common or usual name of an article consisting of cherries which have been dyed red, impregnated with sugar, and packed in a sugar syrup flavored with oil of bitter almonds or a similar flavor." What an absolute culinary delight!

CHERRIES, APPLES, AND PEARS

But what happened to the real maraschino cherry? Fear not; the Marasca cherry lives on. Marasca cherries remain a primary crop in Croatia and are also grown widely throughout Eastern Europe, Slovenia, and parts of Italy. However, you may not be able to find them in most mainstream grocers. In the US, real maraschinos are often tucked away with other imported products in specialty shops or high-end liquor stores. Consumers can also order them online, as most don't have an alcoholic component. They'll be more expensive than the imitations but well worth the price. They'll also look nothing like the artificial cherries you may be accustomed to. In fact, they're so dark that many of my bar customers have mistaken them for black olives.

Luxardo

In the late 1800s, the spirits and preserves industry was critically important to the economy of the city of Zadar on the Adriatic coast. This is also where Italian spirits producer Luxardo, the most well-known maker of maraschino cherries, got its start. With over 200 years of expertise, Luxardo's maraschino cherries are the gold standard, with no preservatives, food coloring, or thickeners. The cherries are also pasteurized for food safety purposes and packed in a viscous, non-alcoholic syrup—a delicious cocktail ingredient by itself, so be sure to save it!

Maraska

Croatia

MARASCHINO COCKTAIL CHERRIES

In Zadar on the Adriatic coast, Maraska pulls from history, making authentic maraschino cherries using its own locally-grown fruit.

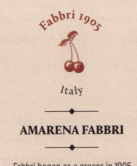

Fabbri 1905

Italy

AMARENA FABBRI

Fabbri began as a grocer in 1905 and later started making syrups and spirits from local fruit. Their Amarena Fabbri uses wild Amarena cherries native to Bologna.

Lazzaroni

Italy

AMARETTO CHERRIES

Lightly flavored with Lazzaroni's Amaretto liqueur (though the syrup and cherries are alcohol-free), these candied cherries are made from wild black cherries harvested from the Apulia region.

KIRSCHWASSER (CHERRY EAU DE VIE)

As we've established, eau de vie is an unadulterated expression of fruit—aromatic yet dry, expressive yet potent. Classic cherry eau de vie, made in Germany, Austria, Switzerland, or Alsace, France, is typically called *Kirsch* or *Kirschwasser* ("cherry water") and can be made from sweet or sour cherries. While Morello cherries are traditionally used in Germany, Kirschwasser can be made from any cherry suitable for distillation, including Brenzer, Dollenseppler, Schwarze Schüttler, and Benjaminler. Some producers, like Swiss distillery Etter, even make their spirits from limited batches of wild cherries. For most people, their first introduction to Kirschwasser comes in a culinary setting, as it is a central ingredient in German Black Forest cake and Swiss fondue. It's an underdog spirit worth using in baking, cocktails, or simply as a digestif.

KIRSCHWASSER

Plant: Cherries

Place: Anywhere (traditionally Germany, Switzerland, and the Alsace region of France)

Production: Pot stills are common, but there are no restrictions on type

Protection: Some regional DOs, such as Schwarzwälder Kirschwasser (Germany) and Zuger Kirsch (Switzerland)

Like many spirits, Kirschwasser's history is a bit fuzzy. It's thought to have originated in the Black Forest region of Germany, known for its abundance of local Morello cherries (perhaps the result of the Roman rations mentioned earlier). It's also believed that Kirschwasser was first made by the medieval monks of Alsace, who distilled eaux de vie in the Vosges Mountains using various wild fruits, including cherries. Either way, both regions have long traditions of distilling fruit. There's even a distillery trail in the Vallée de Villé of Alsace, where you can follow "la route des eaux de vie" to visit a dozen or so producers.

Cherry Crush

Fermentation of the fruit used for Kirschwasser typically takes place in stainless steel containers over ten to fifteen days (a bit on the slow side compared to the fermentation of grain for whiskey), and many distillers

Resting a Spirit

Resting a clear spirit in a neutral vessel like stainless steel is common for many spirits, including Pisco, rum, and Tequila. It allows the spirit to settle, giving the volatile compounds a chance to integrate and the spirit to soften.

choose to keep the pits inside the cherry throughout the fermentation process, as it imparts a noticeable almond flavor to the distillate. The pits are usually removed before crushing the fruit to prevent broken pits from releasing compounds that embitter the spirit. They are then added back to the mash as it continues fermenting. Once fermentation is complete, it's common for producers to double distill and then rest the resulting eau de vie in stainless steel for months or even years.

Cherry crushing, photo courtesy of Rhine Hall Distillery.

The Ambiguity of "Cherry Brandy"

Pick up any vintage cocktail book, flip through the recipes, and you'll undoubtedly find one for cherry brandy. You might assume this means a Kirschwasser, but this isn't necessarily true if the book is from the turn of the 20th century. At that time, cherry "brandy" was made by macerating cherries in brandy or another neutral spirit to make a cherry-*flavored* brandy. To add further confusion, some of those cherry-infused brandies were also sweetened with sugar, technically making them a *liqueur*, a sweet spirit defined by its sugar content (see the chapter on root vegetables).

Cherry Bounce

Black cherry (*Prunus serotina*) is a wild North American tree most widely used by the US furniture industry for its strong and fine-grained wood. Though not widely cultivated for food, the fruit is edible (though it's not the tastiest and is often cooked down into jam or wine). As early as the 18th century, settlers also used the fruit to recreate the English cordial Cherry Bounce, a mixture of fresh sour cherries steeped in a spirit (usually brandy or whiskey), sugar, and sometimes spices. Today, any sour cherry variety will do, though Morellos are preferred.

Cherry liqueurs of this type are typically made using a neutral grain or sugar beet base rather than actual brandy. But if you think all liqueurs are created equal, you've probably been sabotaging your home bar. Mass-produced liqueurs (those typically found on the bottom shelf for under $15) are filled with simple sugars, artificial colors and flavorings, and very little actual fruit. While inexpensive and easy to find, they're liquid candy with little nuance and sometimes heavy on that imitation flavor. In the case of cherries, they have a distinct cough syrup quality. If you're looking for authenticity and to elevate your cocktails, you'll want to spend a little more on your secondary spirits.

Even today, a quick internet search for "cherry brandy" will turn up countless recipes that refer to what are really cherry liqueurs. In most cases, we can assume the creators of these decades-old cocktails intended for the fruitier, sweetened liqueur rather than the dry and expressive eau de vie. However, keep in mind there's room for experimentation and interpretation in these older recipes.

Orchard bloom, photo courtesy of Luxardo.

SPIRITS DISTILLED

Finger Lakes Distilling

Tart

◆

CHERRY LIQUEUR

This New York farm distillery uses no artificial colors, flavors, or additives. They make their cherry liqueur by steeping the fruit in a neutral grape spirit and sweetening it with cane sugar—perfectly tart and ideal in a Blood and Sand.

Artisanal / Farm Distillery

Destillerie Purkhart

A Goldilocks blend of sweet and tart

◆

ROTHMAN & WINTER ORCHARD CHERRY LIQUEUR

This Austrian producer combines a base of eau de vie made from the Austrian sour cherry variety Weichsel with the cherry's fresh, unfermented juices. The result is a fruit-forward distillate that is simultaneously sweet and tart.

A Sense of Place

Heering

Sweet

◆

CHERRY LIQUEUR

Created in Denmark in 1818, this rich, quintessential cherry liqueur somehow made it to the present relatively unchanged. It's made by macerating crushed Steven's cherries (a dark Danish variety) and spices in a neutral grain spirit, then cask-aging for several years.

Tried and True

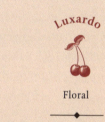

Luxardo

Floral

◆

MARASCHINO ORIGINALE

The clarity of this maraschino liqueur is the first indication it's not your average cherry flavor. Light, floral, and herbaceous, its unique profile comes from macerating the fruit in a neutral beet spirit along with its stems, pits, and leaves, which act as fresh botanicals.

Tried and True

Leopold Bros

Floral

◆

MARASCHINO LIQUEUR

Using Marasca cherries imported from Croatia, Leopold Bros distills the fruit as a base before adding coriander, Montmorency cherry distillate, and honey. It's recommended to refrigerate the bottle and consume it within 3 months.

Artisanal

Merlet

Sweet and tart

◆

SŒURS CERISES

This full bodied liqueur is made using a blend of mostly Morello cherries. The fruit is macerated in a neutral spirit and then blended with small amounts of Cognac and cherry eau de vie. Sweetened with a little sugar, it's rich and aromatic, like liquid cherry pie.

Modern and Artisanal

APPLES

A member of the rose family, apples (*Malus domestica*) have long been a part of our human diet, with domesticated varieties cultivated as early as 10,000 years ago. (The earliest domesticated apples originated in the Tian Shan mountains of Kazakhstan in central Asia, where the small, wild apples of the species *Malus sieversii* still grow today.) Unsurprisingly, throughout millennia, they've become an integral part of mythology and lore in many cultures, symbolic of knowledge, fertility, magic, and even impending death. In Greek mythology, the "Golden Apple of Discord" was said to be the catalyst for the Trojan War, while the Norse considered apples to be a source of immortality, and Snow White just had no idea what she was getting into.

Nature's helping hand has made apples an ideal fruit for "animal dispersal." That trait, combined with trade along the Silk Road, facilitated the apple's journey across Asia and Europe. Sweet apples became particularly popular in ancient Rome (Alexander the Great is said to have even brought apple rootstock from Persia back to Macedonia), and by the 6th century, European monasteries were planting and harvesting apples for food and drink. Fast forward to today, and apples grow worldwide in various climates and soils, including in North America, where they have become an exceptionally successful crop.

Apples are remarkably complex. Their DNA sequence is so large that it humbles our human genome at nearly twice its size. Apples are also highly *heterozygous*, meaning their seeds won't produce fruit identical, or obviously related, to the fruit of the tree they came from. Plant a seed; get a surprise! It's easy to see how nearly 8,000 varieties of apples have been identified, and as many as 20,000 are estimated to exist. Whether or not that estimation is correct, the amount of biodiversity is incredible.

It's worth noting that we, as consumers, enjoy just a drop in the bucket of all the world's apple varieties. Only about 100 varieties are grown commercially in the US, with the top ten (including Red Delicious, Fuji, and Gala) comprising over 90 percent of the crop. Unfortunately, most varieties planted are chosen based on their fruit's appearance and longevity rather than its quality or flavor complexity. A similar situation can be found with tomatoes, though heirloom varieties have started making a comeback thanks in large part to the farm-to-table scene of the last decade. As with most of the fruit industry, this lack of diversity stems not from apple growers' disregard for biodiversity but from their need to keep their businesses financially viable, and most commercial brokers and buyers, like large-scale grocery chains, value shelf life and visual "perfection" over flavor.

CALVADOS

Welcome to Normandy, France, home of over seven million apple trees, three million of which are located in the department of Calvados. Situated west-northwest of Paris, the Calvados landscape is dotted with more orchards than vineyards. Written records from the area date back nearly 2,000 years, and if you're looking for a side quest, there's a 700-page tome on Calvados listed in the "book recommendations" section of the appendix. For now, we'll get right to the juicy bits.

CALVADOS AND CALVADOS PAYS D'AUGE

Plant: Apples (and pears)

Place: Normandy, France

Production: Fixed or mobile column still (Calvados); double-distilled in a pot still (Pays D'Auge)

Protection: AOC

In the 12th century, apple varieties from the Basque Country of the Iberian Peninsula, rich in tannins and ideal for fermentation, arrived in France around the same time as Arab distillation techniques. By 1553, cider was being distilled into *eau de vie de bouche*—later known as *eau de vie de cidre*—and was first described in the writings of Gilles de Gouberville (family name Picot).

A royal forester, farmer, and diarist, as well as cidermaker and recreational distiller, de Gouberville demonstrated great enthusiasm for apples and their cultivation, even encouraging his friends and neighbors to grow specific types. (He was likely the kind of neighbor you avoid getting trapped in conversation with when taking out the trash.) De Gouberville considered himself not just a farmer but an agricultural "artist" and kept detailed records of apple cultivation, documenting the varieties in the Cotentin Peninsula of Normandy, where he lived. He noted at least forty different types and created the four classes of French cider-making apples still used today: bitter, bittersweet, sweet, and acidic.

While de Gouberville is often credited with opening the door to the future of Calvados apple brandy, it would take time for the spirit to be taken seriously in France and beyond. Not until the 1880s (in the novels of Gustav Flaubert, who set many of his stories in Normandy) would the term Calvados appear in print without "eau de vie" preceding it. But just as Calvados brandy began to garner attention, WWI came along. From 1916 to 1939, France instated a state monopoly on alcohol to fuel the supply of industrial-grade ethanol for explosives; apples would have to pull their weight in the war effort. The grape brandies of Cognac and Armagnac were excluded from the mandate due to their economic importance (and preexisting DO protection), but Calvados and other apple-based spirits of Normandy fell subject to the new regulations. As distillers shifted to meet wartime quotas, they

CHERRIES, APPLES, AND PEARS

**Apple Brandy:
It Begins with Cider**

If you've ever bitten into a Granny Smith apple, you know that not all apples are ideal for eating raw. Some are better suited in baked goods, preserves, and juices, while others are best suited for cider and distillation. Apple brandies start with an alcoholic cider, just as Cognac begins with wine.

Cider is the fermented juice of apples and sometimes pears, though pear cider is often referred to by its own name, perry. Like most fermented beverages, cider is relatively low in alcohol and is made using only the tools nature has provided—fruit, yeast, and time.

continued making potable brandy (legally and illicitly), though quality declined. It wasn't long before Calvados gained a reputation for being rough and potent.

The quality of Calvados production didn't bounce back for several decades, especially without a DO in place. However, producers rallied and petitioned the government for the protection of cider spirits, ultimately earning the Appellations d'Origine Réglementée (AOR) status in 1942 for the protection and revival of the category in ten production areas (a separate AOC was also granted at the time for the region of Pays D'Auge).

Apples for Distillation

Around 800 varieties of apples are grown in Normandy, though the DO of Calvados is "restricted" to 230 types of cider apples and 139 cider pears. Essentially, distillers have no shortage of options. When choosing apples for distillation, the key is balance and diversity. Using only sweet or bitter apples in the base cider will create a spirit that is either too high in alcohol or too dry and lacking character. As a result, ciders will typically include a combination of the four classes of apples first identified by de Gouberville. Today, the classes vary slightly by English and French standards, though the differences are subtle.

French cider apple categories	Acidic	Bitter	Bittersweet	Sweet
English cider apple categories	Sharp	Bittersharp	Bittersweet	Sweet
Common Calvados varieties within each category	Petit jaune, Rambault, René Martin	Judor, Avrolles, Mettais	Bisquet, Binet Rouge, Bedan, Frequin Rouge	Rouge Duret, Germaine, Douce Coetligné

French and English cider apple categories.

Apple trees in orchard, photo by Nicholas Klein.

Orchard Life

Normandy's apple (and pear) orchards are well-suited to the region's marine climate, which provides just the right amounts of rain, humidity, and wind (the airflow helps with aeration and keeping the trees dry). The orchards, in turn, provide various benefits, including preventing soil erosion and providing pollinators a home (apples cannot self-pollinate, so they rely on bees and other insects to help them reproduce).

Calvados has specific AOC rules for orchard management, extending down to the percentage of trees that can be planted in one of two styles: *high stem* and *low stem*. High stem planting (or *hautes tige* in French) gives each tree enough space (approximately sixteen feet in width) to comfortably grow and stretch to its full height of twenty-five feet (hence, the name "high stem"). This low-density planting style is the most traditional way to manage orchards in the region, and it has the added benefit of allowing cows and sheep to graze under the trees and graciously deposit their natural fertilizer. High stem plantings are thought to produce fruit that is of higher quality, though the yields per acre are lower than the alternative low stem style. In contrast, low stem plantings (*basse tiges*) are positioned much closer together, with only about three feet between each tree. This high-density planting style benefits newer producers as the trees begin bearing fruit at a younger age since the tree's energy can focus on the fruit rather than the growth of the tree itself.

Producing Calvados is a remarkably low-waste venture when it comes to the farming side of production. The physical appearance of the apples isn't important (unlike in commercial fruit farming), so fewer chemical sprays are needed to prevent blemishes that otherwise do not affect the quality of the apple. As a result, only about 5 percent of a season's harvest goes unused. Additionally, if the trees are properly pruned and maintained, the natural elements—such as wind and sun—are usually sufficient to prevent most diseases in the orchard. (Most disease is the result of excessive moisture/rainfall and harmful bacteria.) To assist their long-term success, the AOC also prohibits orchards from using irrigation beyond the first few years of a tree's life; after that, nature must take care of the rest.

Fallen Apples

Apple harvest in Calvados is unique; rather than picking the fruit from the tree, most apples are collected from the ground after falling. Mature fruit will naturally free itself from the delicate stems and wait on the orchard floor to be collected (either mechanically or by orchard workers who gather them by hand). Different varieties mature and drop at different times, requiring multiple collections in a season, and orchard managers must pay close attention to how long a particular type of apple will keep before beginning to decay.

Adrien Camut

Like many traditionally-produced spirits, Calvados naturally lends itself to a more organic production method. However, the recent popularity of organic farming is a polarizing topic for many producers who view it as little more than a marketing gimmick. Still, some, like grower-producer Adrien Camut, have been farming organically for generations without fanfare. It's just how they've always done things.

The Camut family is now in its 7th generation of grower-producers. Their estate has nearly 4,000 high stem apple trees (in 25 varieties), and their orchards have never been treated with chemicals, though their Calvados are neither certified organic nor publicized that way. The family harvests the fallen apples from the ground using a mechanical sweeper. Following harvest, the fruit ferments in wood for a whopping 10–11 months. (That's a lot of time to develop flavor, and it shows!) A small but conscientious producer, bottles are typically released only once a year and are highly sought after.

VS FINE TROIS ÉTOILES	VIEUX RÉSERVE	VO VSOP VIEILLE RÉSERVE	EXTRA XO TRÈS VIEILLE RÉSERVE NAPOLÉON TRÈS VIEUX HORS D'ÂGES
AGED FOR A MINIMUM 2 YEARS	AGED FOR A MINIMUM 3 YEARS	AGED FOR A MINIMUM 4 YEARS	OAK BARREL-AGED FOR A MINIMUM 6 YEARS

Calvados age statements.

Calvados by AOC

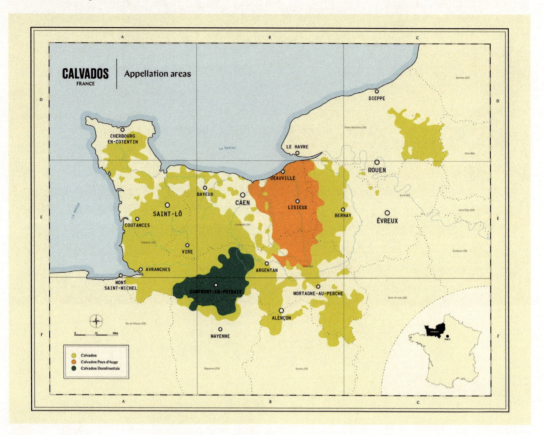

Map of Calvados, courtesy of the Department of Calvados.

Today Calvados has three recognized appellations across lower Normandy and surrounding departments. The Calvados AOC, which was established in 1984 and encompasses the ten protected areas of the previous AOR, provides the general, overarching rules all Calvados producers must follow. But there are two additional appellations in the region—Calvados Pays d'Auge and Calvados Domfrontais—which are subject to both the Calvados AOC as well as their own unique rules and styles. Thirty percent of all Calvados fall under these specialized AOCs.

Part of the rationale for the divided AOC is that climate and soil type varies dramatically across Normandy. Even the subregions have diverse terroirs (natural environments), with soils containing green clay, silt, and/or sand. However, soil composition has a relatively subtle influence on apples (unlike grapes), primarily affecting the growth of trees as well as the acidity of the fruit.

	Calvados	Pays D'Auge	Domfrontais (see the section on pears)
Soil	Variable	Clay and limestone	Granite
Fruit	Minimum 35% high-stem fruit used; covers 230 apple varieties; usually uses apples rather than pears, though there's no requirement	Minimum 45% high-stem fruit used; covers 100 apple varieties; must contain at least 70% apple	Minimum 80% high-stem fruit used; covers 50 apple varieties; must contain at least 30% pear
Distillation	Single distillation in column still is common and traditional but not required	Must be double-distilled using a pot still	Must be distilled using a column still
Age	At least 2 years in oak	At least 2 years in oak	At least 3 years in oak
AOC Established	1984	1942	1997

Calvados regulations by AOC.

Calvados pear harvest, photo courtesy of the Interprofession des Appellations Cidricoles.

Adrien Camut

Calvados Pays d'Auge AOC

♦

6 YEAR

Adrien Camut's 6 Year is their entry-level Calvados and my favorite of their bottlings. It hovers around a hundred bucks and is hard to find, so if you like a good old-fashioned scavenger hunt, you're in for a treat.

Worth the Splurge

Roger Groult

Calvados Pays d'Auge AOC

♦

12 YEAR

This 5th-generation grower-producer family farms about 66 acres of orchards in both high and low stem styles, growing 30 varieties of primarily bitter and bittersweet apples like Frequin Rouge and Bisquet. Their 12 Year retains the fruit while imparting just the right amount of spice.

Typification of the Region

Julien Frémont

Calvados Pays d'Auge

♦

CALVADOS RESERVE

Known for his natural, Basque-style ciders, Frémont's Calvados is no exception, with a lactic hint of blue cheese. Apples are from his certified organic and biodynamic orchard and fermented until the sugar is completely consumed, resulting in a dry cider.

For Cider Lovers

Famille Dupont

Calvados Pays d'Auge AOC

♦

ORIGINAL

Dupont makes both table ciders and Calvados. This expression is made of 80% bittersweet apples, fermented about 2 months, and aged in used oak barrels. Light and fresh, it's a great bottle to experiment with in cocktails or cooking.

For the Cocktail Bar

Calvados Christian Drouin

♦

LE GIN

A gin made from Calvados?! Yes . . . and no. Calvados serves as the base for this gin made from 30 apple varieties, but it also uses 8 botanicals, including cardamom, rose, and lemon. It's an idea so modern that per AOC rules, it can't be labeled a "Calvados."

Expect the Unexpected

On the Lees

The word *lees* (dregs) comes from Old English and refers to the offal (aka waste) produced by raw material: seeds, stems, skins, and dead yeast cells. Resting or aging "on the lees" simply means these byproducts aren't filtered out of the fermenting liquid, creating a unique or complex flavor profile in the final spirit. While the term is most often used in the wine industry, it may also be used to reference Japanese saké production and other facets of distillation (including the production of Calvados).

(AS AMERICAN AS) APPLE BRANDY

Distillation records from North America's early colonial era reveal that much of the distillate made in the colonies was molasses-based. At the time, rum was on track to become the first post-Independence American spirit (cue an eagle's cry here)—and would have if it hadn't been for the British and their pesky taxes and trade blockades, which stopped the flow of molasses from the French West Indies to New England. Instead, apple brandy, historically called "applejack," is considered America's original spirit.

APPLEJACK/ APPLE BRANDY

Plant: Apples

Place: United States

Production: Any still type, though copper pot still is common

Protection: None

The Cider Apples of Johnny Appleseed

In 1792, the Ohio Company of Associates real estate company tried to entice settlers to Ohio by offering 100 free acres to any man (of the adult, white variety) willing to plant 50 apple trees and 20 peach trees on the property within the first three years of their residency. Enter: John Chapman, more commonly called "Johnny Appleseed." In the Disney rendition and grade school folktale, Johnny Appleseed was a barefoot wanderer with a sack of apple seeds, sometimes depicted with a tin pot on his head in place of a hat. Bits of this romanticized narrative are true, but Chapman has largely been fictionalized over the years. He was certainly a nomad and perhaps even a hippie of his time—he became a vegetarian, planted medicinal herbs, and traded apple seeds and trees for his signature rag-tag clothing. But essentially, Chapman was simply a farmer's son with an entrepreneurial spirit. He saw potential in the Ohio Company of Associates' offer and began sowing apple seeds and selling seedlings and trees along the main public routes traveled by settlers. These seeds would go on to randomize the types of apples grown across the states he traversed, though most were considered "spitters"—too bitter to eat. But from the start, Chapman intended for his seeds and their trees to yield cider apples, though most children's tales have scrubbed that particular detail.

Canceled US stamp issued in 1966 featuring Johnny Chapman, aka Johnny Appleseed.

CHERRIES, APPLES, AND PEARS

Laird & Company

In the late 1690s, Alexander (William) Laird emigrated from Scotland to New Jersey. A Scotch distiller back in County Fife, Laird arrived with plans to make malt whiskey but quickly discovered a severe lack of barley (its main ingredient). Undeterred, he took stock of the produce available to him and found apples—a successful crop in the newly-formed colonies—to be plentiful. The Laird family is said to have started distilling as soon they'd settled into their new life in the future town of Scobeyville and crafted applejack at a popular stagecoach stop called Colts Neck Inn. Their reputation grew from there, and in 1780, they were granted the first distillery permit in the US.

Apple Brandy vs. Applejack

There's some confusion surrounding the terms "apple brandy" and "applejack." While often used interchangeably to refer to any American apple brandy, *applejack* involves freezing the apples to reduce their water content, resulting in a higher alcohol content. This process was once called "jacking," but we now know it as *freeze distillation*. Jacking was likely discovered accidentally by colonial distillers who realized the cider that froze over in winter weather was "souped-up" and left terrible hangovers. Nowadays, "applejack" simply refers to an American brandy distilled from apples. However, there is a subtype we should briefly discuss: blended applejack.

Straight applejack (which is most of what's on the market today) is made solely from apples. Until 1972, it was the only kind of applejack that existed. According to Lisa Laird Dunn (a 9th-generation Laird currently at the helm of Laird & Company), in the early 1970s, brandy sales declined as lighter spirits like vodka and gin rose in popularity. To make matters worse, at the time, the distillery could only legally bottle their brandy as straight applejack, leaving them with no easy way to modernize their heavy, traditional spirit. So, they did what many whiskey companies were doing and decided to make a blended brandy (a category that didn't yet exist until the Lairds petitioned the government for a new standard of identity). The resulting product was 35 percent apple brandy, and the rest was a neutral spirit (essentially vodka). Blended applejack, while a good option for cocktails, is light and lacks a pronounced apple character. Luckily, both the straight and blended brandies are available today, so make sure you check the label to know which one you're getting.

As far as rules go, there aren't many for applejack. Aside from being made from apples, the TTB doesn't have a strict definition for the spirit, and there isn't a real industry push to create one, both because of the lack of producers and the generally low consumption of the niche category. The good news is that the lack of regulation allows for many exciting, non-traditional expressions of the spirit.

Jonathan, Winesap, Stayman, Pippin, and various Delicious apples

OLD APPLE BRANDY 7 ½ YEAR

A straight apple brandy aged in hand-selected charred oak barrels, this bottle is wonderful in cocktails and great for the home bar. Best of all, it's ridiculously affordable.

Tried and True

Estate grown apples

BOTTLED-IN-BOND APPLE BRANDY

If you find yourself in Louisville, make time to hop across the bridge to Indiana and visit one of the best-kept secrets in the spirits industry. At Starlight Distillery, you'll encounter beehives, birdhouses, ducks, and, of course, an apple orchard. This limited-run bottle is elegant and sippable, with an Old-World sensibility.

Artisanal

Maryland grown apples

ASIMINA PUMILA

A blend of Maryland apples and Oaxacan traditions, this Pechuga-style (see the chapter on agave), smoked apple brandy uses locally foraged fruits and nuts, including walnuts and pawpaw. A Maryland Country Ham is also hung in the distillation chamber, adding salinity and umami.

Funky But Cool (Though Definitely not Vegan)

Jonagold apples

BOTTLED-IN-BOND APPLEJACK

The fertile land of the Black Dirt Region of New York was once home to several applejack distilleries. Black Dirt Distillery continues this tradition with its Bottled-in-Bond Applejack, made with local Jonagold apples and aged no less than 4 years in new, American charred oak barrels.

A Sense of Place

CHERRIES, APPLES, AND PEARS

PEARS

Like apples, pears are part of the Rosaceae family, and we use them for many of the same ends: snacking, baking, juicing, and, of course, cider- (or perry-) making and distilling. But for a few reasons—namely time, cost, and risk—pears haven't had the same flashy success in the world of cider and spirits as their spotlight-hogging cousin. For one, pear trees are *alternate bearing*, meaning there are some years the trees may not produce fruit (some yield as few as two harvests in five years). And though they are hardier than apples and can tolerate a wide variety of growing conditions, including dense, tough soils like clay, pear trees typically take several years longer to mature and bear fruit. Pear trees are also more susceptible to bacterial infections, such as "fire blight" (a contagious disease that begins in the blooms and spreads throughout the tree), which can easily and quickly devastate an orchard.

Pears are also finicky, especially at harvest time; they ripen from the inside out, so they must be picked when they're mature, but before the ripening is detectable, otherwise the interior flesh can become mushy and unsuitable for distilling. Since their ripening isn't visible, maturity may be detected by weight, ease of picking, slight change of skin color, and/or *brix* values (the measurement of dissolved sugar in a liquid). This risk of over-ripening, combined with their thin skins, make pears more prone to damage and spoilage, and thus, they can't be cellared as easily as apples. As complicated as it might seem, producers have found ways to ease the burden, like using chill storage for a more uniform ripening.

The Orchard of Alcinous

The ancient Greek poet Homer was particularly taken with pears, exalting the ones growing in the garden of Alcinous as "gifts from the gods" in his epic poem *The Odyssey*. And yes, because I'm a nerd, I once had a cocktail on my bar menu called the Orchard of Alcinous.

- 1 ½ oz. white port
- ¾ oz. Pür Spirits pear liqueur
- ½ oz. St. George Spirits Terroir gin
- ½ oz. fresh lemon juice
- 1 oz. Clos Normand apple cider

Shake all ingredients together (including the cider), double strain (using a fine mesh strainer) into a chilled glass, and garnish with a small piece of rosemary.

(original recipe)

DOMFRONTAIS CALVADOS

Were it not for being a defining fruit in the Calvados department, distilled pears, like cherries, would be found primarily in liqueurs and *eau de vie de poire* (pear eau de vie). Thankfully, the spirit has garnered enough admirers to preserve the perry-making tradition along with the more bitter and tannic pear varietals. In fact, the subregion of Calvados Domfrontais requires that at least 25 percent of every orchard be planted with pear trees. As a result, there are roughly 125 varieties of pear grown in this region alone. Furthermore, the Calvados Domfrontais AOC stipulates the spirit must be made from a minimum of 30 percent pear and prohibits pasteurizing, acidifying, or further sweetening the cider or perry before distilling. Only post-distillation additives like caramel coloring and *boisé* (see the chapter on grapes) are allowed.

DOMFRONTAIS CALVADOS

Plant: Pears (minimum 30%) and apples

Place: Domfrontais, Normandy, France

Production: Column still

Protection: AOC

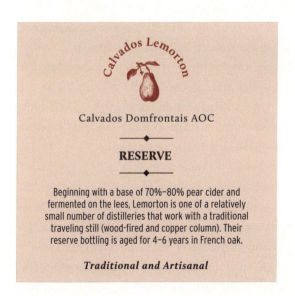

Calvados Lemorton

Calvados Domfrontais AOC

RESERVE

Beginning with a base of 70%–80% pear cider and fermented on the lees, Lemorton is one of a relatively small number of distilleries that work with a traditional traveling still (wood-fired and copper column). Their reserve bottling is aged for 4–6 years in French oak.

Traditional and Artisanal

Harvest Time in Calvados

Rather than grouping pears by their sweet, bittersweet, or acidic nature, pears in the Domfrontais region are categorized according to their ripening time. Early ripening varietals like Bezier Blanc, De Prince, and Mollard are usually ready to harvest by September, while Baignoire, Cartoe De Gilbert, and Gros Blot are harvested in September and October. Late-ripening varietals, like Coq Gris, De Nerf, and Fausset, can be ready to harvest as late as mid-November.

EAU DE VIE DE POIRE

POIRE WILLIAMS

Plant: Williams pear
(aka Bartlett pear)

Place: Historically, the Alsace region
of France and Switzerland (but can
be made anywhere)

Production: Any still type, though copper
pot still is common

Protection: Regional within the EU
(not recognized by the TTB)

Poire Williams is the French name for a pear eau de vie first crafted in and around the German-influenced Alsace region of France and Switzerland. Its early fermentation history mirrors that of Kirschwasser: medicinal application followed by culinary use in the form of preservation through distillation. Because there are no global or North American-specific protections for it, this style of brandy is now widely distilled throughout Europe and North America. Currently, there are only a few DOs in Europe for the spirit, including one for *Eau de vie de Poire du Valais* in southern Switzerland.

While brandies such as Calvados begin with a cider or perry, pear eau de vie is typically made from a whole fruit mash and fermented "on the pulp" (or without first extracting the fruit's juice), though the skins, seeds, and stems are often removed to avoid undesirable flavors. These eaux de vie are juicy and capture the aromatics of the pear as much as the flavor, often mimicking the profile of a fresh piece of fruit. Unlike Kirschwasser, which can be made from a variety of cherries, Poire Williams is made with a specific pear, one you have most likely eaten at some point: the Bartlett pear.

The Williams' Bon Chrétien, or as we know it in the US, the Bartlett pear, is the world's most planted pear variety and a well-known table pear. The Bartlett makes an excellent, fruit-forward spirit, setting it apart from wine and brandy grapes, perry pears, and cider apples, which are typically *not* delicious when consumed fresh. It's also one of the few pears to change colors—the skin gradually turns brighter as it ripens.

Distilling Pears

A member of the genus *Pyrus,* the pear underwent 2 independent domestications, creating 2 distinct genetic populations: Asian pears (including *Pyrus pyrifolia*) and European pears (*Pyrus communis*). Both have been cultivated for thousands of years, but *Pyrus communis* is the species most often used in distilling.

28

SPIRITS DISTILLED

PEAR BRANDY

Often considered the first craft distiller in the US since Prohibition, St. George has been working with pears since 1982. Made with organic, dry-farmed Bartlett pears from the West Coast, each 750 mL bottle contains roughly 30 lbs. of fruit.

Trailblazer

PEAR BRANDY

Made with Bartlett pears from the Finger Lakes region of New York, Finger Lakes Distilling grinds the pears before fermenting the mash of fruit and juice for roughly 10 days, resulting in a bottling that is bright and vegetal with citrusy notes.

Farm Distillery

PEAR WILLIAMS

Using Williams pears from the Alto Adige region (also called Südtirol) on the border of Italy and Austria, this bottling from Purkhart is clean, ripe, and bursting with fresh pear. It's a classic example of a pear eau de vie.

Typification of the Category

POIRE PRISONNIÈRE

For this bottling, whole-crushed Williams pears are fermented for 6 weeks, resulting in a classic profile of juicy, overripe pear. The drunken pear trapped inside can (with some creativity) be extracted.

The Prisoner Pear

PEAR BRANDY

Founded in 1985, Clear Creek sets the bar high for American fruit brandy. They use whole pears grown in the Pacific Northwest for their European-style eau de vie, which packs roughly 20 lbs. of pears into a single bottle.

Modern yet Artisanal

The Prisoner Pear

Whether or not the name *Bartlett* rings a bell, it's likely you have seen the iconic "prisoner" pear in a bottle of pear brandy—a tradition started in Alsace. This is accomplished by carefully slipping the bottle over the newly formed fruit in the springtime and allowing it to mature inside the glass.

PEAR LIQUEUR

Whereas eaux de vie have no sugars added, liqueurs are intentionally sweet, with sugar added post-distillation (see the chapter on root vegetables). Liqueurs can vary in style; some present fresh or overripe fruit profiles, others have a touch of spice that evokes a rich cobbler or pie filling. The difference between using fresh or whole fruit versus artificial flavorings in a liqueur can be an absolute game-changer. When made with care, these lower-proof spirits capture the authenticity of the fruit and make wonderful additions to cocktails, providing depth and sweetness.

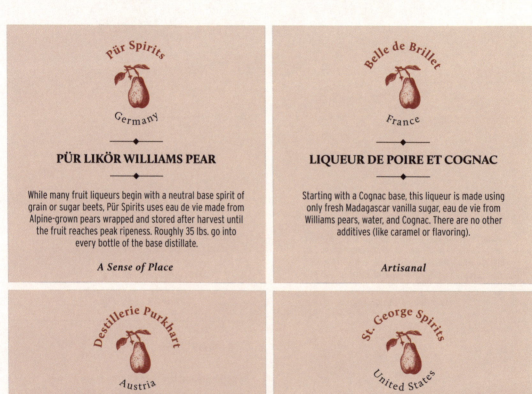

Pür Spirits — Germany

PÜR LIKÖR WILLIAMS PEAR

While many fruit liqueurs begin with a neutral base spirit of grain or sugar beets, Pür Spirits uses eau de vie made from Alpine-grown pears wrapped and stored after harvest until the fruit reaches peak ripeness. Roughly 35 lbs. go into every bottle of the base distillate.

A Sense of Place

Belle de Brillet — France

LIQUEUR DE POIRE ET COGNAC

Starting with a Cognac base, this liqueur is made using only fresh Madagascar vanilla sugar, eau de vie from Williams pears, water, and Cognac. There are no other additives (like caramel or flavoring).

Artisanal

Destillerie Purkhart — Austria

ROTHMAN & WINTER ORCHARD PEAR LIQUEUR

Starting with pear eau die vie as a base and then adding fresh pear juice after distillation, this bottle is fresh and bright, with plenty of juicy pear flavor. As with their flagship pear brandy, the distillery uses Williams pears grown in South Tirol and the Danube Valley.

Orchard-to-Glass

St. George Spirits — United States

SPICED PEAR LIQUEUR

Much more than the sum of its parts, this fall-inspired pear liqueur is made with Bartlett pears, cinnamon, clove, and organic cane sugar (with malic acid for balance.) The base is made of pear brandy, with fresh pear juice added post-distillation to create a rich, immersive profile.

For the Bartender

Ripe pears waiting for harvest, photo by Lya Cattel.

GRAPES

Even if you don't know what Cognac is, you've likely heard of it. Growing up, I associated it with stodgy dens filled with men of a certain age lounging in overstuffed leather chairs. But these days, Cognac has become a global status symbol representing not only success and sophistication but approachability—a testament to ever-evolving consumer tastes and trends.

Cognac was one of the first spirits I purchased as an adult, simply because I liked the idea of it. I didn't know it was made from grapes—it hadn't yet occurred to me to ask those sorts of questions. To younger me, wandering through a North Carolina ABC store, Cognac just seemed interesting and, dare I say, fancy. I decided on a bottle of the ubiquitous yet alluring Hennessy VS—easy on both the palate and a 22-year-old's wallet.

But Cognac is one of many grape brandies made worldwide, which isn't surprising considering grapes are one of the most popular fruits used in distilled spirits. A member of the genus Vitis, there are roughly eighty species of these vining plants, the most recognizable of which is Vitis vinifera, aka the common grape vine. Surprisingly, we interact with relatively few grape varietals in the wine and spirits world nowadays, though they number in the thousands.

Grapes have been with us for quite a while. The earliest evidence of their domestication comes from the country of Georgia, with carbon dating of *pips* (seeds) suggesting domestication as far back as 6000 BCE. As the story goes, the domesticate made its way from the Caucasus region to Central and Western Europe, where it cross-fertilized with native species to create *V. vinifera*, the dominant wine and spirits grape we know today. However, recent research has modified this theory. Genome sequencing (and resequencing) conducted in 2023 shows there were likely two independent domestication centers: one in Caucasia and one in Western Asia. These same genetic studies have also pushed the estimate for domestication as far back as 11,000 years ago, around the advent of agriculture. But that's *V. vinifera*; what about the other dozens of species?

There are a handful of native North American grapes that are influential in their own right. The popular Concord grape, for example, is a cultivar of *Vitis labrusca* (aka the Fox grape). With a skin that slips right off, its easily obtained pulp is often used to make jellies and table wines. And though North American grapes aren't typically used in winemaking and distilling, their rootstocks have played a vital role in the survival and success of their European cousins.

The Grape Destroyer

Phylloxera is a word that strikes fear into the heart of vintners everywhere. While it may sound like a condition you'd need an antibiotic to cure, it's actually the common name of a tiny yet destructive aphid-like insect that devastated the wine and grape industry in the late 19th century. While it's true scientific name is *Daktulosphaira vitifoliae,* it is more commonly known in the spirits world by its original name—*Phylloxera vastatrix,* aka grape phylloxera. Derived from Ancient Greek, the word *phylloxera* essentially means "withered leaf," referring to the effects of the louse's handiwork as it feeds on the root systems of grapevines. However, it's not the feeding itself that kills the plant—it's the wounds left behind on the root systems that allow harmful pathogens and fungi to infect the vines.

Easily spread by trade, grape phylloxera's path across the globe killed vineyards from South Africa to New Zealand to California. It was later discovered that the stealthy pest was unknowingly ferried to Europe from its homeland in eastern North America, possibly on native vines like *V. labrusca*. The irony is that these vines would later become the remedy to what seemed like an incurable problem.

As grape phylloxera ravaged the vineyards of Europe, France—perhaps the most heavily impacted country of all—offered a reward of 20,000 francs for a solution. No option was spared, including the heavy use of chemicals, grape-breeding experiments, and even the flooding of vineyards with white wine. When those tactics failed, vine rows were torn up and burned to the ground in a scorched-earth approach to eradicating the blight. It's believed that by 1878, at least 915,000 acres of French vineyards were irreparably damaged, while more were infected and wasting away, leading many farmers to leave the region for good. Throughout the infestation, France lost an estimated 2.5 million acres of vineyards, and by 1895, grape phylloxera had cut French wine production nearly in half. It took decades to recover from the loss, and the disaster is said to have cost France roughly 10 billion francs (over 50 billion euros today!).

While the French government never got the opportunity to pay that reward, a working solution was eventually found in an unlikely place. Noticing that North American grapevines were relatively unaffected (hello, adaptation), vintners around the world began grafting *V. vinifera* onto phylloxera-resistant North American rootstock in the late 1800s. So effective was the solution that today, it's estimated less than 20 percent of the world's winemaking grapes are grown on their own roots. And since outbreaks continue to rear their ugly head on occasion, especially in warmer areas where the insects tend to thrive, without grafting, the wine grapes we know and love would have been long extinct by now.

The global damage done to *V. vinifera* by one tiny pest is a stark reminder of the inherent risks involved in monoculturalization. Its devastation, both environmentally and economically, should serve as a warning to other spirits industries, like Tequila, which similarly rely on a singular raw ingredient (i.e., Blue Weber agave). And if you ever feel like smuggling a piece of fruit back through customs, consider the story of the grape phylloxera!

COGNAC

Cognac's story begins in France, where it may never have come to the world's attention had it not been for (of all things) the salt trade. Northern European salt traders first encountered the wines of the Charente region in the 11th century CE. Within a couple hundred years, *Vin de Cognac*, an aromatic white wine made from Colombard grapes, had become a popular spirit for export.

COGNAC

Plant: Ugni Blanc (primary), Folle Blanche, Colombard, Montils, Sémillon, Folignan

Place: Cognac, Charente, France

Production: Charentais pot still (double-distilled)

Protection: AOC

Much of the Vin de Cognac, considered unsuitable for table wine, was shipped to the Netherlands (a major importer at the time) to be distilled into *brandewijn*, or "burned wine," (aka brandy). Somewhere along the way, some wise person in France asked themselves: "What if we distill our own brandy at the source?" Setting up a still in Charente proved to be much more lucrative. Along with the increased revenue from selling the finished product, there was a decrease in shipping cost as the spirit took up less space than the base wine. This brandy, distilled at the source, marked the birth of what would later be called Cognac. Transported by ship in oak casks (the primary method of storage at the time), it was soon found that time spent in the wooden barrels vastly improved the product's flavor. Before long, the French brandy began to gain traction throughout Europe, especially in England.

As the spirit's popularity increased, so did its value. To signal the difference in quality between competing products, Charente distillers would add the region's name, Cognac, to their casks to specify that it was the "good stuff." One of the earliest written references comes from a printed advertisement in the 1678 *London Gazette*, though the notice would have called it something like "Cogniak brandy." The spirit would have been a far cry from what we know today, consumed unaged (as eau de vie) or as a relatively youthful spirit rested in the barrel just long enough to transport.

The Grapes of Cognac

Like all grape brandy, Cognac is made from the distillation of what is, essentially, a very unpalatable white wine, typically low in alcohol and very high in acid. Before the grape phylloxera outbreak, Folle Blanche was the favored grape, but after the infestation destroyed the region's vines, Ugni Blanc became the pest-resistant champion. Native to Tuscany, Italy (where it's called Trebbiano), Ugni Blanc is resistant to rot and mold partly because its loose grape clusters allow for airflow. A medium-sized, thin-skinned grape, the varietal produces high-acid, low-alcohol wines that peak at 8–9 percent ABV—ideal for distilling.

Brandy or Cognac?

Distilled from grape wine, Cognac is a type of brandy, but not all brandy is Cognac. This instance isn't the only time you'll see this square vs. rectangle relationship. Nearly every category of protected spirit with a DO has a unique name, differentiated from its parent class. In this case, Cognac takes its name from the region of its production—Cognac, France.

Today, Ugni Blanc accounts for around 98 percent of the grapes used to make Cognac, with modest amounts of Colombard, Folle Blanche, and, less frequently, Montils and Sémillon blended in.

Ugni Blanc, photo courtesy of Cognac Park (Distillerie Tessendier).

DO Rules for Vinification and Distillation

Cognac received its formal DO in 1936, and though technically distilled from wine, it follows a unique set of rules to reach its vinous state. Sulfur dioxide (SO_2) is a common preservative in traditional winemaking, and it even occurs naturally to some degree during fermentation as sulfites are present on the skins of grapes. However, adding SO_2 is prohibited in Cognac production as it risks adding flaws to the distillate. Because the high acidity levels in the grapes act as a preservative (along with natural SO_2 levels), Cognac-destined wine awaits its fate unaltered in pot stills.

Also prohibited in Cognac production is *chaptalization*, or the practice of adding sugar before fermentation to balance out low sugar levels in the grapes, thereby increasing the alcohol content. This is most often done in cooler climates where the brix in grapes is low. Depending on

Harvest and Climate Change

Harvest in the region of Cognac typically begins around mid-September or early October, though this date is inching earlier each year as the planet warms due to climate change (roughly 0.32°F each year since 1981). As hotter weather drives up the sugar content in the grapes and, thus, the alcohol content of the spirit (something distillers don't want in their wines), producers are eager to get the fruit off the vines as soon as possible.

Terroir

If you've ever visited a winery, you're likely to have heard all about *terroir*—the physical elements (i.e., weather, climate, soil, elevation) that combine to create a flavor profile rooted in a sense of place. Terroir bestows grapes with unique characteristics, such as quick aging or a singular aroma. Soil, for instance, doesn't just provide nutrients and minerals; it retains water and heat and challenges roots to dig deeper (or not), among other functions. For example, sandy soil composed of large particles will drain quickly, whereas clay greedily hoards water.

your purist sensibilities, chaptalization can be considered a bit of a cheat, and an interference with the spirit's terroir.

After fermentation, the base wine is distilled twice in Charentais (alembic) pot stills, which must be heated by an open flame. Historically, stills were fueled by wood or coal; today, distilleries can use natural gas (though the "furnace" is usually still encased in a traditional brick façade that once contained the live fire). Continuous distillation is prohibited, and each distillation, or *chauffe*, takes roughly twelve hours to complete. Some producers, especially traditional ones, distill on the lees, that is, without removing the sediment after fermentation, which can provide the final spirit with even more character. As the final step, the *heads* and *tails* (essentially the first and last distillates produced from a distillation run) are discarded, though they may be added back to the fermented wine or first distillate to be distilled again. This process is known as "making cuts."

Vineyard in Borderies, near the town of Jonzac, photo by GAPS photography.

The Six Crus of Cognac: Location, Location, Location

Like French wine, French spirits can be complicated. The region of Cognac is divided into several growing zones (or *crus* if you're feeling proper), each with its own unique soil composition: Grande Champagne, Petite Champagne, Borderies, Fin Bois, Bons Bois, and Bois Ordinaires. Eighty million years ago, the sea covered what is now the prime growing area for Cognac grapes. Over time, calcitic debris shed by plankton and other crustaceans compacted, forming deep bedrocks of chalk now covered in clay-limestone soil. This composition makes the region ideal for viticulture, as the chalky soil helps grapes retain their acidity and allows the roots to penetrate deeper into the ground and absorb valuable minerals.

Grande Champagne

Not to be confused with the sparkling wine of the same name from the Northeastern wine-producing region of France, this is considered the best cru in Cognac and is sometimes referred to as the "Premier Cru de Cognac." Roughly 17 percent of all Cognac grapes are grown in this region. While the name Champagne comes from the word *campagne,* which once meant "countryside" or "field," the term now signals a particular type of soil. According to the distillers at Ferrand Cognac, Grande Champagne essentially translates to "big chalk." These light and floral brandies require a lengthy aging process to reach their peak—up to sixty years in barrel! Notable small producers include Maison Dudognon, François Voyer, Cognac Frapin, Hine, Cognac Grosperrin, and Cognac Paul Giraud.

Petite Champagne

Similar in soil composition to Grande Champagne, this region is larger, and the soil is considered slightly less ideal than its sibling, hence its "little chalk" status. But don't let the name fool you; the region produces just under a quarter of the grapes used in Cognac. And like those from Grand Champagne, these Cognacs are similarly slow to mature in barrel, taking up to thirty to forty years to reach their full potential. Notable

---

What is a Cru?

If you're familiar with French wine, you've probably heard or seen the word cru. Though this term can also mean "growth," when it comes to French wines, it refers to a vineyard or specific growing region, particularly one known to yield high-quality fruit and, thus, high-quality wine. Each region of France has its own ranking system for crus, with Burgundy having hundreds of crus in total and Bordeaux over 60. Cognac has 6.

The "Big Four"

In the entire Cognac region, there are over 4,000 grape growers and roughly 117 distilleries. While that may seem like a lot, many of these growers—and even some of the smaller houses—sell a portion or even all of their grapes (and/or spirit) to one of the "big four" Cognac houses: Hennessy, Martell, Rémy Martin, and Courvoisier—who together, control 90% of the market.

The Industry Today

Founded in 1946 (a decade after the DO for Cognac was formed), the mission of the Bureau National Interprofessionnel du Cognac is to protect the integrity of the Cognac DO. They represent growers, distillers, and merchants within the region and have recently launched a certification program to encourage environmentally friendly viticulture practices, with one of their primary goals being to reduce the carbon footprint of the Cognac-making process from start to finish.

small producers include Cognac Grosperrin, Cognac Lhéraud, and Cognac Park. (You may also see bottles labeled as "Fine Champagne," which means it's a blend of grapes from both the Grand Champagne and Petite Champagne crus.)

Borderies

Small but mighty, this cru yields only a fraction (just 5 percent) of the grapes that become Cognac, and most of it is blended rather than sold as a single cru. The soil here is clay-heavy and mixed with decomposing limestone that becomes flint. Cognacs from this region are quick to age compared to those of the Champagne crus and are typically nutty and floral in flavor. Notable small producers include Camus Cognac and Cognac Park.

Fins Bois

Despite accounting for nearly half of the grapes grown for Cognac, you rarely see a single cru of Fin Bois. Strange, no? That's because this cru does the heavy lifting for the larger Cognac houses, with its grapes often used in their younger spirits, like an entry-level VS (see the section on age designations). Cognacs from Fins Bois tend to reach their peak maturity much earlier than those from other crus, and though they aren't usually showcased on their own, they're great for softening and rounding out blends. A notable small producer of Fins Bois Cognac is Cognac Leyrat.

Bons Bois

The vineyards of this cru form a belt around the Cognac region, and while this is technically the largest cru by area, little of it is actually planted with Cognac grapes (only 12 percent are grown here). The soil is a mix of clay and sand, with some areas of limestone. Cognacs from this region age quickly, yielding exceptionally fruity distillates that lean toward ripe and tropical notes. Similar to those from Fins Bois, these distillates are mostly found in blends. A notable small producer of Bons Bois Cognac is Cognac André Petit.

Bois Ordinaires

Another large tract of land scarcely planted with Cognac grapes, this massive cru stretches along the Atlantic coastal region of France yet only accounts for 1–1.5 percent of Cognac grapes. Often considered one of the least desirable growing regions, some producers believe this cru makes up for its sandy, rocky soil by offering its Cognacs a unique maritime influence and a favorable briny quality. Notable small producers include Cognac Grosperrin and Godet.

Aging and Blending

Cognac age designations can be pesky to learn for two reasons. First, the terms themselves aren't intuitive. And second, age is hard to pinpoint because almost all Cognacs are a blend of vintages, meaning they contain grapes grown in different growing seasons. (Single vintages are rare to find outside of Armagnac country.) On top of that, producers often blend in spirits older than the minimum requirement for the age designation. You may wonder: Why would a producer go above and beyond to add older spirits if it isn't necessary? We often see this with smaller producers and those looking to showcase their craft in competition with more well-known brands.

However, knowing a bottle's exact age is not half as important as knowing whether or not you like it. Some young Cognacs are elegant, fruit-forward, and fresh, while some older ones don't hold up well, taking on too much of the oak during barrel aging or losing their structure over time. Trust your palate!

Say Boisé, Say Boisé

An open secret in the brandy industry—particularly in the world of Cognac, where it's considered a legal and traditional method—boisé is an additive found in most bottles on grocery or liquor store shelves (see the chapter on wood). Made by cooking oak chips in water to create a concentrated tea, boisé can be used creatively to achieve a house style, create a unique flavor profile, or intensify qualities associated with barrel aging (such as notes of vanilla and caramel). However, it can also be added to give the impression of age in younger spirits, leading to its reputation as a controversial additive.

VS (VERY SPECIAL)	**VSOP** (VERY SUPERIOR OLD PALE)	**NAPOLÉON**	**XO**	**HORS D'ÂGE** (BEYOND AGE)
AGED FOR A MINIMUM 2 YEARS	AGED FOR A MINIMUM 4 YEARS	AGED FOR A MINIMUM 6 YEARS	AGED FOR A MINIMUM 10 YEARS	AGED FOR A MINIMUM 30 YEARS

Cognac age statements.

Cognac Park

Borderies

◆

BORDERIES SINGLE VINEYARD

If you've gotten comfortable with Cognac and want to branch out, this single-vineyard bottling from Borderies is the way to go. It's a light, slightly floral expression of 100% Ugni Blanc that first ages in new oak casks for 10 months before moving to older oak casks, where it's aged for 10–15 years.

The Adventurous Palate

François Voyer

Grande Champagne

◆

VS COGNAC GRAND CHAMPAGNE

While this VS Cognac makes a killer Sidecar, I wouldn't be mad at it if I were sitting down with a neat pour. Light, fruity, young, and spritely, this bottle is a wonderful introduction to the category.

Budget and Cocktail Friendly

Léopold Gourmel

Fin Bois

◆

BIO ATTITUDE

Founded in 1972, Léopold Gourmel uses zero chemicals, pesticides, coloring, or additives to produce a very clean and pure expression of Cognac. This bottle showcases both the fruit and the craft. Light and fragrant, it's also suitable for cocktails.

Certified Organic / Sustainable

Distillerie du Peyrat

Fin Bois

◆

ORGANIC SELECTION

It can be difficult to find certified organic spirits that are moderately priced and intended for cocktails. This young brandy is great for Sidecars, and buying a bottle supports organic grape growers and their work to keep pesticides and herbicides out of the soil.

Certified Organic / For the Home Bar

Ferrand Cognac

Grande Champagne

◆

1840

I've always appreciated Ferrand Cognac's dedication to craft cocktail culture and their openness to discussing taboo topics like their use of boisé. This bottle was created in homage to Cognac-based cocktails with the help of cocktail historian David Wondrich.

For the Cocktail Enthusiast

Maison Dudognon

Grande Champagne

◆

10 YEAR RESERVE

This brandy was one of the first "craft" Cognacs to catch my attention. This small, family-owned distillery only distills what they grow, which is impressive considering they have just 24 acres! Their 10 Year is an absolute must.

Artisanal / Grower-Producer

ARMAGNAC

I often describe Armagnac as a distant cousin of Cognac. Though they live in different towns and have different personalities, you can see the genetic relationship. Brandy production in the Armagnac region of France predates that of Cognac by a couple hundred years, making it France's original brandy (though it never saw the same level of success as its cousin). Eau de vie production in the region was first documented by Franciscan Friar Maître Vital Dufour in a medical text published in 1310, where he called the spirit *aygue ardente* ("fire water") and noted its medicinal properties.

ARMAGNAC

Plant: Ugni Blanc, Colombard, Folle Blanche, Baco

Place: Armagnac, Gascony, France

Production: Single distillation in a continuous still (alambic Armagnacais)

Protection: AOC

The region of Armagnac has, for the most part, sandy, heat-retentive soil, which encourages root growth and the early ripening of fruit. It's also what makes the wines of Armagnac ideal for distillation since grapes grown in sandy soils are typically higher in acidity. The other side of this coin is that sand can get very cold during winter, placing the vines at risk during brutal cold snaps, which are not as uncommon in southern France as one might think. In 2020, France declared an "agricultural disaster" after over 80 percent of the country's vines were affected by record-breaking temperature drops. With the increasing speed of climate change, these temperature fluctuations stand to become more and more worrisome.

Typified by its iron-rich "tawny sand" mixed with pockets of soil known as *boulbènes* (a rocky sediment made of clay, silt, and sand), the Bas-Haut Armagnac sub-region accounts for over 67 percent of the grapes grown in Armagnac. But it's not just the sandy soils of this region that make it so special; clay and limestone also feature heavily in the soils of its smaller terroirs: Ténarezè and Haut Armagnac.

Alambic Armagnacais: A Still Well-Traveled

One of the primary differences between Cognac and Armagnac is the distillation method used. Cognac is distilled twice (double-distilled) in specialized pot stills. Conversely, Armagnac is distilled only once using a small-scale, continuous still (which, if you recall, is prohibited in Cognac production). It's important to note that Armagnac continuous stills (called alambic Armagnacais) differ from the enormous continuous stills (often three to four stories tall) that produce light, neutral spirits. Instead, they have an extremely short column for *rectification*, or purification, and are compact enough to be mobile—allowing some distillers to continue the traditional practice of bringing them to the vineyard. Though not legally mandated by French law, around 95 percent of Armagnac producers practice continuous distillation using an Armagnacais still.

So, how does this production method render Armagnac so different from Cognac? Longtime importer of grower-producer wine and spirits Charles Neal believes it creates a thicker, meatier-textured brandy. Single distillation leaves behind more naturally occurring chemical substances that further develop flavors in a wine or spirit, like congeners, esters (see the chapter on sugarcane), and fatty acids, none of which work well in young grape spirits. But these same byproducts of fermentation give Armagnac its unique character, particularly after a decade or more of aging.

In essence, single distillation allows retention of the spirits' imperfections, turning what might be perceived as a flaw into a desired quality during maturation. The congeners and esters need time and even a touch of oxygen to exhibit their true potential. According to Neal, the timeline for this is at least fifteen to twenty years, with the compounds expressing a nutty, even truffle-like quality often referred to in the industry as *rancio*. Alternatively, this also means that Armagnacs will present as more rustic and unpolished than double-distilled Cognacs of the same age.

Folle Blanche

Folle Blanche, also known as Picpoul or Piquepoul, from the French verb *piquer* (to sting), is a white wine grape varietal known for its high acidity and minerality. Once the favored grape for making both Cognac and Armagnac, its career as showrunner was cut short by the grape phylloxera blight in the late 1800s. Today, its role in Armagnac production is minimal, accounting for only 3%–5% of the vines planted. Similar to its role in Cognac production, Ugni Blanc has stepped up to fill the gap and now accounts for over 50% of the grapes used to make Armagnac.

However, young Armagnac is a diamond in the rough, an unpretentious spirit full of texture and rustic charm. (By all accounts, it should be catnip to the average whiskey drinker.) And because Armagnac hasn't seen the popularity and demand of Cognac, it's also an incredible value in the world of spirits. If you like celebrating events with "special bottles," Armagnac is one of the few spirit categories where buying vintage is affordable.

Armagnac still, Distillerie Lafontan Cutxan, photo by Mick Rock.

Sugar and Yeast

As with Cognac, adding additional sugars and sulfites during the fermentation of Armagnac grapes is prohibited by law. Producers who wish to emphasize terroir may choose to use native yeasts (naturally occurring on the skin of the grapes) rather than cultivated yeast to create the wine. As a bonus, this lends a more unique profile to the final spirit.

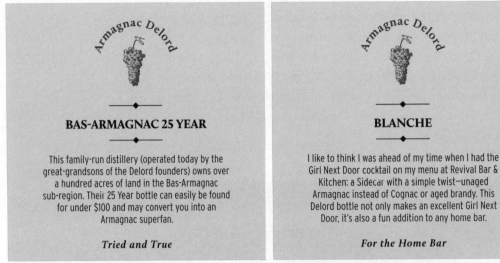

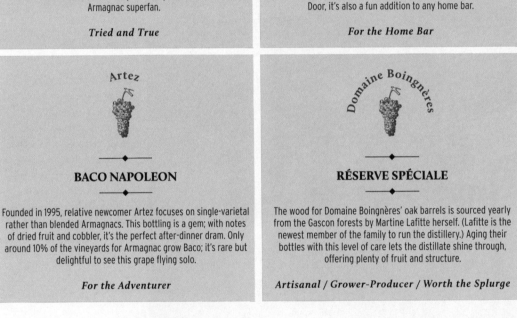

BRANDY DE JEREZ

Brandy de Jerez (or Spanish brandy), which first received its DO in 1987, is an outlier in grape spirits because the plant's terroir is not the most crucial factor. Instead, where (and how) the spirit is aged matters most: specifically, the wine-producing houses (aka *bodegas*) of the Sherry region located in the southwestern tip of Spain. In fact, Airén, the primary grape used to make the base distillate for

Brandy de Jerez, is relatively neutral and is used by distillers as more or less a *tabula rasa* (blank slate) for the flavor imparted by the ex-Sherry (i.e., wine) barrels it's aged within. As such, it's impossible to discuss Brandy de Jerez without discussing Sherry (or Jerez), a fortified wine also produced in the Sherry Triangle. The two drinks are inseparable in both their history and rules of production.

In her book *Sherry: A Modern Guide to the Wine World's Best-Kept Secret,* Talia Baiocchi notes that "applying the word terroir to the location and architecture of a physical structure might seem radical." Nonetheless, the spirit has an assured sense of place. To be labeled a Brandy de Jerez, the spirit must be aged within the limited geographic region of the Sherry Triangle, formed by three cities: Jerez de la Frontera (from which it gets its name), Sanlúcar de Barrameda, and El Puerto de Santa María. And while aging must take place in the Sherry Triangle, the base wines can be distilled anywhere in Spain. This means the geographic protection for this spirit centers solely around its maturation within a particular environment

BRANDY DE JEREZ

Plant: Airén, Palomino (rarely used)

Place: Jerez de la Frontera, El Puerto de Santa María, and Sanlúcar de Barrameda in Cádiz, Spain

Production: Any still

Protection: DO

Vineyard in Andalusia, Spain, photo by Barmalini.

GRAPES 47

The History of Brandy de Jerez

Although wine production was alive and well in Spain as early as 3,100 years ago, distillation wasn't practiced until the 8th century CE when it was introduced to the region by the Moors, also known as the Berbers or North African Muslims. Even then, potable distillates remained relatively uncommon. The earliest official reference to this brandy comes from the recorded minutes of a government meeting held in 1580, which mentioned a "tax on spirits." Although brandy was being distilled at this time, it was primarily used as a fortifying agent for exported Sherry wines, though widespread fortification wouldn't occur until the 18th century.

and microclimate. In other words, Brandy de Jerez is literally absorbing the qualities of Sherry's producing region as it ages.

Foundational to the Sherry Triangle is its Mediterranean climate. The official regulations outlined for the Brandy de Jerez DO state that the unique microclimate of the region—which is surrounded by water and influenced by east-west cross winds that bring in warm humidity from the Mediterranean and cool breezes from the Atlantic—is a key factor that "contributes to [the spirit's] special and unique characteristics."

Barrel Aging and the Solera System

As the wine trade in Europe flourished during the 19th century, Spain began exporting *holandas*—large barrels filled with a grape distillate—to the Dutch, who then sold them via East Indies trade routes. Like most spirits of the time, this brandy wasn't intentionally aged in barrel. The barrel was merely used for storage, not for the flavor it imparted. The Brandy de Jerez we know today was likely discovered as a happy accident, perhaps the result of a shipping delay or a forgotten barrel left in the cellar to mature. The tasty result would soon catch on, and barrel aging would become an intentional stylistic choice, just as with Cognac. According to the DO, Brandy de Jerez must be aged in oak barrels that previously held Sherry wine for at least three years, effectively seasoning the cask. (Interestingly, this is also how Sherry-finished Scotch casks are prepared, but without the minimum age requirement for seasoning.) And, while the type of Sherry doesn't matter for the DO requirements, it will affect the flavor of the brandy and must be accounted for when blending.

Brandy de Jerez is aged using the *solera system*, the same technique used to mature Sherry wines. The method began as a way to ensure that Sherry wines were consistent year to year and to battle the mercurial markets so a single vintage would not be left gathering dust. The system consists of barrels stacked atop each other in rows called *criaderas* (nurseries), with each row containing a particular vintage. Theoretically, the oldest barrels are closest to the ground, and the youngest are on top, though sometimes storing them in this way is not practical. When that's the case, the barrels are often grouped and stored in different areas of the distillery or bodega. In this system, the brandy is first pulled from the oldest barrel, without completely draining it. That barrel is then topped off with the next oldest spirit, and so on and so forth. Over time, as the brandy moves down through the rows, the younger barrels will be topped off as needed. It's a continuous process that is also sometimes called *fractional blending*. This system has also been adopted by a handful of rum and whiskey producers.

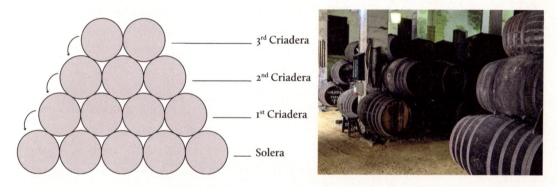

Solera barrels at El Maestro Sierra, photo courtesy of De Maison Selections / El Maestro Sierra.

The Secret Life of Airén

Though you may not have heard of it—it's rarely talked about outside of the production of Brandy de Jerez—Airén is a white wine grape native to Spain and one of the country's most planted varietals. Once widely regarded as the most planted grape varietal in the world, Airén is highly drought-tolerant. The vines can also thrive in less desirable areas, including those with poor soil, and are often planted in a bushier style rather than on trellises. These grapes are primarily grown and fermented in central Spain's La Mancha region and then brought to the Sherry Triangle for aging per the DO requirements. And, while Airén quietly pulls its weight in table wine blends, it's primarily known as the

Palomino Fino

It may be surprising to some that a discussion of grape varietals in the Sherry Triangle would involve any grape other than Palomino, which is historically the foundational grape for Sherry wines. But in truth, very few brandies today are made with Palomino, as it is much too valuable a grape in the world of Sherry wine. The vines of this essential plant prefer Jerez's chalky soils (albariza soil), and like Airén, Palomino is drought-tolerant. The grapes also produce wines prone to oxidization, one of the key qualities of the Sherry style.

backbone of Brandy de Jerez production, producing a neutral wine with relatively low acidity and high alcohol levels—the opposite of what we see in cooler regions such as Cognac and Armagnac.

Production and Distillation

It takes roughly three liters of wine to make one liter of Brandy de Jerez, and though multiple distillations are allowed, the DO only requires one via either a column still or a traditional copper pot still called an *alquitara*. Different still types will produce different distillates. For example, column stills offer a lighter spirit, and pot stills a heavier, fattier one. Based on the wine, still, and methods used, the distillation product falls under one of the following distillate types: *holandas*, *aguardientes*, and *destilados*. These distillates are later blended to create one of three brandy subcategories, each with different aging requirements: *solera*, *reserva*, and *gran reserva*.

Besides differences in the ABV, each class of distillate also has a restriction on "volatile compounds"—essentially a bunch of stuff created during distillation that isn't ethanol (the "good" alcohol). Some are chemical compounds containing desirable flavors, like esters, while others are unwanted byproducts, like methanol—alcohol in its simplest yet most toxic form.

Distillate types	Still	ABV	Amount of volatile compounds permitted (grams per liter)
Holandas	Pot still	< 70%	2-6 g/L
Aguardientes	Column still	70%-86%	1.3-4 g/L
Destilados	Column still	> 90%	<1 g/L

Brandy de Jerez distillate types.

50   SPIRITS DISTILLED

Sherry Flavor Chart: What to Expect

Sherry wine can be simplified into two main categories—dry and sweet—though there is plenty of nuance in between. These flavor profiles also extend to anything aged in an ex-Sherry barrel, including Brandy de Jerez.

DRY ↑

FINO / MANZANILLA: This is a dry, oxidative wine style with notes of aged cheese rind and other savory characteristics referred to as rancio. Additionally, these wines often contain a strong umami quality and can be reminiscent of dry vermouth or oxidized fruit, like brown apples.

AMONTILLADO: These wines begin as Fino/Manzanilla before undergoing a secondary oxidative aging. They have a toasty nuttiness and notes of rancio, dried fruit, herbs, and tobacco.

OLOROSO: Meaning "fragrant" in Spanish, there are both dry and sweet expressions of Oloroso Sherry, though dry is more traditional and carries greater intensity and darker characteristics reminiscent of *nocino* (Italian black walnut liqueur), dried herbs, figs, and balsamic vinegar.

PEDRO XIMÉNEZ: The sweetest of the styles, Pedro Ximénez grapes are sun-dried, yielding residual sugars in the wine and a dark, almost black appearance. These Sherries have a denser texture and notes of dried fruit, dates, figs, raisins, *café de olla* (Mexican spiced coffee), and baking spice.

SWEET ↓

Categories of Brandy de Jerez

- **SOLERA:** Young and fruity, a solera must be no less than 50% holandas and aged at least 6 months in Sherry barrels. It's best suited for cocktails.

- **RESERVA:** To classify as a reserva, a brandy must be at least 75% holandas and aged a minimum of 1 year in Sherry barrels. Reserva brandies are versatile in cocktails but also lovely to sip on their own.

- **GRAN RESERVA:** A gran reserva is 100% holandas and aged at least 3 years in Sherry barrels, though many are aged longer. They're ideal served neat as an after-dinner dram.

Oloroso and Pedro Ximénez Sherry casks

♦

CLÁSICO GRAN RESERVA

With an average age of 15 years, this bottle is an excellent introduction for those who prefer to sip their spirits, as the ex-Pedro Ximénez Sherry casks lend sweetness and approachability. This is one of the first bottles of Brandy de Jerez I tried, and it's still one of my favorites.

Tried and True

Amontillado Sherry casks

♦

SOLERA RESERVA

Similar to the Clásico Gran Reserva, this bottle is aged for roughly 15 years and is the perfect place to begin one's Brandy de Jerez journey. It allows newcomers to familiarize themselves with the oxidized style used in some Sherries and is particularly suited for cocktail experimentation.

Budget and Cocktail Friendly

Oloroso Sherry casks

♦

SOLERA RESERVA

This bottling (which, admittedly, is a bit of a financial investment) has an average age of 20 years, with complex nutty, woodsy, and tobacco-heavy notes provided by the ex-Oloroso Sherry casks. It's also one of the few women-operated bodegas!

For the Adventurous Palate / Funky but Cool

Oloroso Sherry casks

♦

LEPANTO SOLERA GRAN RESERVA

This gem is the only Brandy de Jerez produced with Palomino grapes grown in the Sherry Triangle. Byass uses Charentais pot stills, like those used in Cognac production, before aging the spirit for a minimum of 12 years.

Show Me the Palomino

GRAPPA

Pomace distillate, or Grappa, is a spirit made from the remnants of winemaking, giving the skins, seeds, and stems a second lease on life. Taken from the Latin word *grappapolis,* meaning "a bunch of grapes," Grappa has often been seen as a winemaker's afterthought, with a reputation for being harsh, hot, and astringent. That said, high-quality, elegant Grappa does exist—thanks in part to improved distillation techniques and practices leading to increased consumer demand—and since the 1970s, the overall quality of the category has increased dramatically. So, if you're concerned with the environment and reducing waste, you might consider drinking Grappa.

Grappa has historically been associated with northern Italy and the Friuli-Venezia Giulia and Trentino-Alto Adige regions, though production is now more widespread. In the Middle Ages, pomace "brandies" were cheap, rustic spirits made out of necessity—an attempt to use every bit of the fruit just as one might use every part of the animal. And while there is no exact date for the spirit's official debut, the first written mention of Grappa was in 1451 in Friuli. Today, the region is known for its crisp white wines and prosciutto di San Daniele.

Grappa has a protected DO, but it's only recognized within the EU, meaning the spirit must be made in Italy to be sold in Europe and labeled as such. Furthermore, there are unique geographically-specific regulations for Grappa produced across Italy, including Grappa Piemontese, Grappa di Barolo, and Grappa Friulana. Today, the country has around 130 Grappa distilleries, with most concentrated in the northern regions. (Notably, in the US, the TTB allows distillers who make grape pomace distillates to label it "grappa.")

Recycle, Reuse, Referment

With Grappa, there is no raw ingredient to harvest: it's a salvage mission. The spirit is distilled from grape pomace, also called *vinaccia*, the pulpy mixture of skins, stems, and seeds left over after the grapes have been pressed and relieved of their juice. Nothing goes to waste. Some of the most common pomace used for Grappa comes from Muscat, Chardonnay, Cabernet Sauvignon, and Nebbiolo, and the more aromatic varietals, like Muscat, will yield a more expressive distillate. While most Grappas are traditionally multi-varietal blends, more and

GRAPPA

Plant: Pomace (byproduct of grapes)

Place: Italy

Production: Any still type; steam distillation is common

Protection: DO recognized only in the EU (otherwise none)

Marc

Marc is the French answer to Italian Grappa—a pomace spirit distilled widely throughout the country since at least the 18th century. There are various Marc DOs, including Marc de Champagne, which is made from the pomace of grapes used in French sparkling wine. Additionally, Marc is used to make the washed rind of the notoriously stinky French cheese Époisses.

---

more distillers are beginning to offer single-varietal bottlings following the success of the Nonino family, whose groundbreaking release is often considered the start of the "Grappa revolution." In 1973, the distillery released a Grappa made only of the freshly-pressed pomace of Picolit, a northern Italian white wine grape. In the process, they copyrighted the term Monovitigno, meaning "single varietal."

Vinaccia rossa, photo courtesy of Nonino.

Once the grapes are pressed for wine, the clock starts ticking. To preserve the brightness of the fruit's flavor, the pomace should be as fresh as possible (i.e., unoxidized) when it enters the still. Another reason fresh pomace is so essential is its moisture content, as, by law, no water can be added during the distillation process. Additionally, the longer the pomace sits out, the greater the risk for bacteria and mildew. To combat these natural processes, distillers traditionally traveled to wineries with portable stills to process the pomace fresh after pressing, though now it's more common for producers to bring the pomace back to a distillery, with some using refrigeration to prolong its shelf life.

Artisanal distillers tend to take more care with their raw materials compared to industrial distillers, who may choose to store the pomace in larger, temperature-controlled silos or warehouses for weeks or longer. The Nonino family, for example, streamline the process by sending totes to the winemaker ahead of time so the pomace can be placed into airtight containers immediately after pressing and transported to the distillery as quickly as possible. At the distillery, the material is transferred to stainless steel tanks for anaerobic fermentation (without oxygen) before distillation in one of their sixty-six artisanal pot stills.

There is no restriction on the type of still used for Grappa or how many times the spirit can be distilled. The style and distillation methods are entirely up to the producer's discretion; they can choose a more efficient yet neutral column still or a less efficient but more flavor- and aroma-packing pot still. Distilleria Nardini, Italy's oldest licensed Grappa distillery, uses both methods by operating two distilleries, each with a different focus. Their distilleries in Bassano and Monastier use pot and column stills, respectively, and after distillation, they blend the two spirits for a uniform product. Regardless, to be bottled under the DO, the Grappa must be at least 40 percent alcohol, and the grapes must be grown, vinified, and distilled in Italy.

Aging

Most drinkers are familiar with Grappa in its clear, unaged form; aging is a relatively new phenomenon for the spirit, but it is gaining popularity. Unaged spirits are on the fruit-forward side of the spectrum and have bright aromas, though they're sometimes heady in the same way fresh honeysuckle perfumes the air on a hot day. As wood is introduced, these profiles change to express warmer tones with notes of vanilla, dried fruit, and baking spices. Some regions even infuse the Grappa with citrus or botanicals. As with other spirits, Grappa will take on some of the qualities of the barrel used for aging, often one previously used to age wine. But unlike many other spirits for which the aging container is oak, Grappa can be aged in any type of wood, including cherry, acacia, and chestnut. The longer the Grappa is aged, the more it will take on the characteristics of the barrel, whatever its composition or character, and the grape's essence will fade increasingly into the background.

Fire Power

Unlike most other spirits, Grappa is distilled from solids, specifically grape pomace. Therefore, traditional methods of distillation involving direct fire are tricky, as the flames could easily burn the pomace. In the late 1800s, steam distillation was discovered as the ideal solution, and today, most Grappa (around 90%) is steam distilled.

BIANCA GIOVANE	AFFINATA IN LEGNO	INVECCHIATA	RISERVA OR STRAVECCHIA	AROMATIZZATA
UNAGED/CLEAR BUT RESTED IN STAINLESS STEEL OR GLASS FOR 6 MONTHS	AGED IN WOOD FOR 6–12 MONTHS	AGED IN WOOD FOR AT LEAST 12 MONTHS	AGED IN WOOD FOR AT LEAST 18 MONTHS	CAN BE INFUSED WITH FLAVORINGS AND BOTANICALS (NO AGE REQUIREMENT)

Grappa age designations.

Castello di Verduno

Nebbiolo pomace

GRAPPA DI NEBBIOLO

Produced in the Piedmont region of northern Italy, this single-varietal bottle is an excellent place to start in the world of Grappa. Using artisanal, small batch production, Castello di Verduno ensures their pomace is used within 36 hours after press, giving the spirit lots of grip and a bold, fruit-forward character.

Typification of the Region

Nonino

Moscato pomace

IL MOSCATO

The Nonino family has made Grappa for generations, using only the freshest pomace and small batch distillation. Dedication to the craft and investment in both time and equipment make their distillates a bit pricier, but the result is an elegant, slightly floral, and intensely aromatic spirit.

Artisanal / Worth the Splurge

Distilleria Nardini

Blend of red and white grape pomace

MANDORLA

This bottle from Nardini, infused with almond oils and blended with Marasca cherry eau de vie, tastes like dessert in a glass sans added sugar. Keep a bottle in your freezer and expect it to disappear quickly.

Funky but Cool

Distillerie Bonollo

Amarone pomace

GRAPPA OF AMARONE BARRIQUE

If unaged Grappa still makes you nervous, ease into it with this lovely Amarone Grappa aged in French oak. With notes of tawny port, dried fruit, and sticky toffee, it's a sure bet.

Still Afraid of Grappa?

AGED AMERICAN (GRAPE) BRANDY

Brandy is post-colonial America's first spirit (yes, even pre-dating whiskey). One primary reason for this is that fruit distillates weren't only for casual enjoyment back then. Historically, many types of alcohol were used medicinally, and this was especially true for brandy. (In fact, because of its supposed healing qualities, Cognac was the only imported spirit allowed during Prohibition.) At the time, grape spirits were considered superior to alternatives, and older brandies were considered more effective and potent than younger ones at treating illnesses.

AGED AMERICAN (GRAPE) BRANDY

Plant: Grapes

Place: United States

Production: Any still type

Protection: None

By the late 1800s, "medicinal" brandy was widely used as a sedative, a cardiac stimulant (possibly to resuscitate patients), and to lower fevers. Beyond just drinking it straight, brandy was administered intravenously, and . . . well, other places we won't talk about in polite company. Given its elixir status, it's unsurprising that doctors were sometimes accused of overprescribing brandy to patients, leading to alcohol abuse.

But Prohibition brought all that to a halt. While American brandy limped ahead after Prohibition, it would never bounce back to its previous level of popularity. It was at this moment that whiskey shouldered its way into the spotlight. Fast forward several decades to the 1980s, and American brandy remained unpopular, lacking the reputation of premium French brandies. To compound matters, the US heavy hitters, like E&J Brandy, Paul Masson, and The Christian Brothers, were not particularly known for being of exceptional quality, at least compared to the likes of Cognac.

Some forty years later, the tide is turning—albeit slowly—due in large part to the craft spirits revolution. While Cognac and Armagnac have long-established pedigrees with seemingly unending rules, there are no specialized regions or regulations for brandies made in the US. As with Cognac and Armagnac, caramel and boisé are common additives—though perhaps not as gracefully integrated as they are by French producers—with US distillers sometimes leaning a touch too hard on caramel. But an exciting aspect of American brandy is that this same absence of rules invites a great deal of experimentation into the category, generating some tasty results. For example, up-and-coming distillery Copper & Kings in Louisville, Kentucky (in the heart of whiskey country) makes a variety of brandies aged in ex-Bourbon barrels that heavily embrace more aggressive, spice-forward American whiskey qualities, all while being aged in a hotter climate than most European brandies.

Germain-Robin
CALIFORNIA ALAMBIC BRANDY

Though scooped up by the behemoth E&J Gallo several years ago, Germain-Robin has stayed true to its roots. With the assistance of the original co-founder and distiller Hubert Germain-Robin, this signature brandy, made from Colombard grapes, is distilled in Charentais pot stills and aged in French Limousin oak.

Artisanal / Traditional / European-Inspired

Clear Creek Distillery
AMERICAN POT STILL BRANDY

This French-influenced, youthful spirit is made by aging the eau de vie of grapes grown in Oregon. Though only aged 2 years in French oak, it showcases tons of character, with notes of dried apricot, treacle, currants, and a bit of coffee cake.

Funky but Cool

Copper & Kings
BUTCHERTOWN BRANDY

This overproof brandy (62% ABV) is a flex: meaty, powerful, and ready for cocktails or a holiday punch. Using grapes from California, copper stills, and a combination of charred new American oak and ex-Bourbon barrels, this is a whiskey drinker's brandy and shines in an Old Fashioned.

Modern and Innovative / Funky but Cool

Finger Lakes Distilling
GRAPE BRANDY

For their bottle of grape brandy, Finger Lakes Distilling in upstate New York uses a blend of locally grown *V. vinifera* and native grapes. Made in the Cognac style using alembic pot stills and aged in the distillery's own ex-bourbon barrels, it's the perfect brandy for classic cocktails, like a brandy Old Fashioned.

Grape-to-Glass

PISCO

Despite a wildly popular run during the California Gold Rush, Pisco is often overlooked today. In the mid-19th century, Peruvian Pisco was a staple spirit along the Pacific seaboard, as Peru's capital city, Lima, was a major port of call for aspiring miners, travelers, and fortune-seekers before the construction of the Panama Canal. At this time, San Francisco was considered the "Paris of the West," and the Bank Exchange Saloon was one of its most fashionable drinking establishments. It was here bar manager Duncan Nicol created the Pisco Punch, which many consider to be San Francisco's original craft cocktail. With the drink praised by the likes of Mark Twain and Rudyard Kipling, Pisco's popularity soared.

Despite its historical popularity, few people have written about this potent brandy outside of cocktail blogs and industry-specific producer resources. Ivy Mix, owner of New York cocktail bar Leyenda and author of *Latin American Spirits*, makes an excellent observation when she writes, "grape distillates from Latin America represent a major hole in today's global spirits consciousness." Cane and agave spirits continue to win favor, while this underappreciated grape spirit remains an enigma even to seasoned bartenders.

I asked Kami Kenna, Sales and Marketing Manager of artisanal Pisco producer PiscoLogía, why she thinks the spirit never recovered after the repeal of Prohibition: "Peru has experienced natural, political, and social disasters for much of the latter part of the twentieth century," she replied. "It started making a recovery in the '90s and through the 2010s, and then the pandemic came." Pisco is a relatively vulnerable spirit; not only does it require labor-intensive practices like hand-harvesting grapes in very arid climates, but its production often occurs against a backdrop of deep economic and social struggles. These factors put the spirit and its historical and cultural connections in jeopardy. Similar to what's happening now with Mezcal, some companies are solely profit-motivated, jumping on cocktail trends that don't do justice to the category and often damage it instead. "Pisco [is becoming] a commodity

Pisco Punch

- 2 oz. Pisco
- 1 oz. distilled water
- ¾ oz. pineapple gomme syrup
- ¾ oz. lemon juice

Shake well, strain into a Collins glass, and garnish with a pineapple chunk.

(historical recipe adapted by David Wondrich)

rather than a cultural product; money is driving what's being made and exported. Culture is being lost . . . the industry is becoming a race to the cheapest product," warns Romina Scheufele, president of Capurro Pisco and founder of the Craft Spirits Cooperative.

For those seeking to understand Pisco, a good point of entry is its national origins. The spirit's production occurs in two countries—Peru and Chile—each with its own recognized DO. (Peruvian Pisco is currently more heavily exported and is, therefore, more accessible in the US.) While the raw ingredients of the brandies are similar, the production rules for the two are vastly different and yield very distinct styles. In some ways, these differences are on par with Cognac and Armagnac, which present more as cousins than siblings. In sum, Pisco's two growing regions—long linked by trade, history, language, and culture—reflect its dual identity.

Torontel grapes ready for harvest (left); Quebranta grapes (right); photos courtesy of Capurro Pisco.

Peruvian Pisco

Winemaking and distillation (though not fermentation!) first appeared in Peru and Chile with the arrival of the Spanish, who came rudely knocking in the first half of the 16th century. Eager to set up shop, the Spanish encouraged the cultivation of European staples such as cattle, wheat, figs, and grapes. Sacramental winemaking techniques were also imported, particularly by the Jesuit order of Catholicism. As the population grew, so did the demand for wine. However, importing European wines was expensive and inefficient, so the colonists took it upon themselves to grow their own grapes and make their own wines. By 1539 (just four years after Lima's founding), the colonists had planted enough vineyards to do just that. The vines quickly took to the arid soils of the southwestern region thanks to cooling maritime winds, expansive pre-existing irrigation infrastructure, and the care of Native farmers who had perfected local growing techniques over millennia.

By 1572, the Ica region of Peru (along the country's southern coast) was producing 20,000 barrels of wine per year. The venture was so successful that Spain eventually banned the export of wine from Peru, as it was out-competing Spanish wine. As with most prohibitions, this ban was often skirted, and Peruvian wine was smuggled back to Europe one way or another. The most popular workaround was to distill the wine into a clear brandy, *aguardiente de uva*, before export. (One of the earliest references to this practice comes from a will written in 1613.) Soon, the Spanish relented, deciding instead to tax the spirit. By the dawn of the 18th century, business was booming.

> **PISCO (PERU)**
>
> **Plant (Aromatic):** Italia, Moscatel, Torontel, Albilla
>
> **Plant (Non-Aromatic):** Quebranta, Negra Criolla, Uvina, Mollar
>
> **Place:** The Departments of Lima, Ica, Arequipa, Moquegua, and Tacna
>
> **Production:** Pot still or traditional falca
>
> **Protection:** DO

The Etymology of Pisco

The word *Pisco* comes from the Quechua language (*lingua franca* of the Inca Empire) and means "small bird." It's also the name of the clay vessel the spirit is stored within and the name of a southern port from which it was often shipped. The first written reference to *Pisco* as the distilled spirit we know today would appear in 1825.

The Grapes: Aromatic vs. Non-Aromatic

The DO for Peruvian Pisco allows 8 different grape varietals to be used; these are divided into 2 categories: aromatic and non-aromatic. Aromatic grapes contain higher levels of *terpenes*, the natural compounds responsible for how plants smell. Terpenes can also help attract pollinators to plants. In the glass, this translates to intense floral, heady aromas of honeysuckle and orange blossom water. An example of an aromatic wine grape you may already be familiar with is Gewürztraminer. However, don't let the designation fool you! Non-aromatic varieties aren't devoid of aroma, just less so than their counterparts.

Capurro Pisco

Capurro Pisco entered the US market in 2012—I'm proud to have run one of the first bar programs in the Bay Area to stock their Pisco—but Capurro's biodynamic vineyards have been supplying the grapes for their Piscos for over a hundred years. Founded by Eduardo Capurro, Capurro Pisco has practiced sustainability since its founding, well before it was cool. Today, Capurro's granddaughter, Romina Scheufele, maintains these green values as the company's president, distiller, and importer.

Capurro keeps its vineyards' entire ecosystem in mind during its growing and production process. The distillery grows cover crops throughout, like the Giant Peruvian lima bean, which returns nitrogen to the soil. This method is more time consuming, but produces a better fertilizer. "Biodynamic takes everything into account: the birds, the moon, and the tide," says Scheufele. "It's hard to farm this way on a large scale."

Although labor intensive, the alternative is introducing chemicals or methods that disrupt generations of traditional practices. "In the end, you can taste the intervention. Pesticides kill off indigenous yeasts. One decision starts a chain of events. Your fermentation will be affected," Scheufele stresses. And, of course, one choice eventually trickles down to affect the final distillate. For the Capurro, it's worth the effort.

In addition to biodynamic farming, Capurro doesn't use any machinery in their vineyards, which are planted in a combination of high- and low-trellis systems. High is the more modern approach, and low the more traditional. (The high canopy trellis helps protect the grapes from the sun and prevents the birds from having a little snack.) No machinery means they harvest all the grapes by hand, allowing them to inspect the fruit for insect damage and other issues.

Traditional clay piscos, photo courtesy of Caravedo Pisco.

Production and Distillation

While most grape brandies are destined for the barrel, Peruvian Pisco showcases the fruit and, thus, must remain unaged. At its essence, Peruvian Pisco is grape eau de vie. The distillation of Pisco begins as all grape spirits do: with a wine that's been macerated and sometimes even fermented with must (*mosto*)—a mixture of skins, leaves, and sometimes stems. However, the wine must be filtered and free of all solids before distillation begins.

One of the most unique aspects of Peruvian Pisco is that it must be distilled "to proof" according to the DO regulations, meaning the ABV of the spirit when it comes off the still is its final ABV. No water or other substances can be added at any point in time. Per the DO, the proof must fall between 38 and 48 percent, though in the US, only 40 percent and up can be labeled as Pisco based on the TTB requirements. Essentially, this means distillers have one shot at making their brandy (talk about pressure!). For reference, few spirits are distilled to proof at these ABV levels, except for some Tequilas. However, Tequila producers use double distillation, allowing them to correct any mistakes or make adjustments on the second round of distillation.

Falcas

While a rare sight today, *falcas* are traditional, direct-fire stills very different from those we've seen so far (only about 3 producers still use them). The square base, or "kettle," is positioned underground and insulated with brick, with the flat top of the still flush with the ground. While they have the benefit of using less copper than an alembic pot still, falcas can be tricky to operate at higher elevations as the boiling point of water is lower, and the ability to purify a spirit becomes more difficult, leaving behind more flavor compounds, like congeners.

GRAPES

Pisco below 40 percent ABV can still be imported, but it must be labeled "diluted," which doesn't make sense considering it's straight "off the still" per the rules of Peruvian Pisco, but such is the joy of bureaucracy. To my knowledge, there's no example of "diluted" Pisco currently on the US market.

Singani

South America's much lesser-known grape spirit, *Singani*, shares some commonalities with Pisco. A traditional Bolivian spirit, Singani has been around for about 500 years, yet only received a DO in 1992. The DO is quite restrictive and allows for only a single grape varietal: Muscat of Alexandria. Officially, the grapes can only be grown in the highest elevations of the Andes (such as Potosí, Tarija, Chuquisaca, and La Paz). However, plenty of folks still make "singani" throughout Bolivia, just as distillers make "mezcal" outside the delimited areas. The high elevation gives the grapes a thicker skin and contributes to their intense tropical and musky aroma. Like Pisco, Singani is traditionally distilled in falcas, though pot stills are becoming more common.

Pomace after pressing, photo courtesy of PiscoLogía.

Pisco Styles

- **PURO:** A single-varietal bottling akin to a single-varietal wine.

- **ACHOLADO:** Made from a blend of grape varietals, usually a balance of aromatic and non-aromatic grapes; a favorite for mixing cocktails such as the Pisco Sour.

- **MOSTO VERDE:** A bottling distilled from partially fermented wine, meaning some of the sugars remain, resulting in a sweeter spirit.

Chilean Pisco

The arrival of wine grapes and brandy production in Chile follows a timeline similar to Peru's. Though there is record of the first royal governor of colonial Chile requesting grape vines from the Spanish king in 1545, most sources claim that the first Spanish grapes were planted in Chile in 1549, near the northern city of La Serena.

PISCO (CHILE)

Plant (Aromatic): Moscatel Rosada, Moscatel de Alejandría, Torontel

Plant (Non-Aromatic): Pedro Jiménez, Moscatel de Austria

Place: Atacama and Coquimbo

Production: Batch (aka "discontinuous") distillation (multiple distillations allowed)

Protection: DO

Both Pisco-producing regions in Chile and Peru are arid, sub-desert climates with strong maritime influence. The main difference is that Pisco grapes in Chile are grown further from the ocean and are, therefore, exposed to less humidity. Hot days and cool nights produce grapes with a high brix content. The region's early wines, primarily used for sacramental purposes like their Peruvian counterparts, were sweet, low in acid, and prone to spoilage, meaning shipping them to Europe wasn't practical. To preserve the wine, the alcohol needed to be extracted and concentrated—in other words, distilled. The brandy would then be stored in traditional clay pots, called *botijas*, rather than oak barrels, ensuring no outside flavor was imparted into the spirit.

Chilean Pisco must be distilled in "discontinuous" stills, a less common way of saying it's distilled in batches, and while producers in both Chile and Peru utilize copper pot stills, Chilean production often takes place in a Charentais style still like those used in Cognac. Unlike Peruvian Pisco, which is only distilled once, Chilean Pisco can undergo the process as many times as the producer chooses. However, with each distillation, character is removed from the spirit along with impurities. Every decision a distiller makes comes with a tradeoff.

	Peruvian Pisco	**Chilean Pisco**
Distillation	Single distillation	Multiple distillations
Proof	Distilled to proof, no water added	Dilution allowed, typically proofed down with water
Aging	Unaged	May be aged in wood
ABV	38%-48%	Tradicional: 30%-34.9% Especial: 35%-39.9% Reservado: 40%-42.9% Gran: 43%-50%

Peruvian vs. Chilean Pisco.

Vineyard in the Elqui Valley, Chile, photo by DC Columbia.

PiscoLogía

Peru

Puro of Italia grapes (aromatic)

PISCO ITALIA

This bottle is a lovely example of the category and traditional production methods. Distiller Nati Gordillo double presses the grapes, crushing them by foot, then by hydraulic press.

Artisanal and Traditional

Capurro Pisco

Peru

Puro of Quebranta (non-aromatic)

QUEBRANTA

Capurro's single-varietal expressions were some of the first Piscos I pulled into my bar program. Handpicked grapes are macerated for 12-24 hours and then pressed once. Fermentation occurs in open-air tanks using natural yeasts, which can take 2-4 weeks. The spirit then rests for a minimum of a year.

Sustainable and Biodynamic

Caravedo Pisco

Peru

Acholado of Quebranta (non-aromatic) and Torontel (aromatic)

ACHOLADO

Distilling with a combination of pot stills and traditional falcas, each varietal in this bottle is distilled independently and rested for 4 months before blending and resting for another 5 months. It's a great bottle if you're new to the category.

Nice and Easy

Pisquera Tulahuén

Chile

Acholado of Moscatel de Alejandría and Moscatel Rosada (aromatic)

PISCO WAQAR

Using grapes grown near the distillery (in the foothills of the Andes mountains), this Pisco is distilled once in copper pot stills and proofed down with fresh mountain water. Master distiller Jaime Camposano heats the stills with wood fire and cuts by sensory parameters.

Artisanal

Viñas de Oro

Peru

Puro Albilla (aromatic)

ALBILLA

This family-run distillery is doing exciting things in the world of Pisco by showcasing puros made from single grape varietals not often seen on their own, such as this Albilla, which is delicate and herbal with notes of chamomile.

For the Adventurer

Miguel Torres Chile

Chile

Acholado of Moscatel de Alejandría and Moscatel Rosada (aromatic)

EL GOBERNADOR

Winemakers as well as distillers, Miguel Torres Chile works with sustainable fruit suppliers and is Fair Trade certified. Distilled only once from grapes grown in the Limarí valley, El Gobernador is citrusy, bright, and perfect for classic cocktails.

Fair Trade

BARLEY

I have apparently become the sort of person who travels long distances to stand in fields of grass. Whether it's experimental barley fields in Kentucky, towering corn rows in Indiana, or heirloom rye grasslands in California, watching grass grow is anything but boring when you know that at the end of the season, there's whiskey to be had.

Grains—specifically cereal grains—are the edible seeds of annual grasses in the Poaceae family. Also known as "staple crops," they are used in everything from livestock feed and fuel to cooking oils and alcohol and are native to every continent except Antarctica. Grains have long been a vital part of the human diet, though we don't know exactly when their domestication happened. What we do know is that we were snacking on wild varietals like Einkorn and Emmer at least 75,000 years ago, and the oldest known grain silo—located at the Neolithic village site of Dhra' on the eastern flank of the Dead Sea in Jordan—contains traces of barley and wheat dating back roughly 11,000 years.

In the world of distilled spirits, grains are to whiskey as fruit is to brandy. And while whiskey is the headliner, the show begins with beer—distiller's beer, to be exact—a fermented, typically un-hopped drink made with malted grain. Of course, beer destined for distillation isn't the same type of brew you'd get at your local pub, just as wine destined for brandy isn't meant to be paired with your meal. This initial fermentation is one of the many steps involved in whiskey.

Barley's Origins

While it's believed there were multiple independent domestications, including one in Central Asia, most European and American cultivars used in distilling today descend from *H. spontaneum*, first domesticated in the Fertile Crescent.

Barley (*Hordeum vulgare*) was one of the first—if not the first—grains to be domesticated. While getting a complete picture of barley's deep history is tricky, archaeology and archaeobotany give us a pretty good understanding. Some of the earliest evidence for barley domestication dates to around 10,500 years ago from the site of Abu Hureyra in Syria, which is thought to be one of the earliest farming sites in the world. Only a few millennia later, barley was well on its way to becoming the grain we recognize today. In 2016, a stash of 6,000-year-old seeds was discovered in a cave near the Dead Sea. The seeds were so well preserved—due to the arid environment and protection from the elements afforded by the cave—that archaeobotanists were able to study their DNA and compare them to present-day varieties. Their findings

Experimental barley field at Makers Mark, photo by Nat Harry.

showed that by the time they were stored, significant progress had already been made in breeding for barley's more favorable characteristics. What's more, those ancient grains weren't drastically different from the barley we know today.

For a bigshot grain with a long tenure in brewing and distilling, it's surprising that barley comes in a distant fourth in worldwide grain production behind rice, wheat, and corn. (For perspective, annual barley yield is less than ⅓ that of rice, ¼ of wheat, and roughly ⅛ of corn.) However, though it has a limited range of uses or palatability compared to these more popular grains, barley is the hardiest of the bunch. A generally cool season grass (though there is a summer variety), it can withstand drought, short growing seasons, and extreme cold, including sub-zero temperatures. These features have made it a staple crop, particularly at high elevations and in food-insecure countries.

While it can be made from different types of grains, beer, as we commonly know it, is primarily made from barley, thanks in large part to the fermentable sugars unlocked during the malting process. (Beer made from less common ingredients like corn, sorghum, millet, or buckwheat does, however, offer a gluten-free experience for those willing to break with convention.) In the US, roughly a quarter of American barley production goes straight to breweries after a detour at the malt house. Eventually, the barley from the malt house, brewery, or distillery returns to the farm for one last contribution. *Spent grains* (i.e., the solids left over after fermentation) of all sorts, including barley, are sold or donated to farmers as a feed supplement for cattle and other livestock, a practice going back centuries. Recycle, reuse, ruminate!

The Deep History of Barley Beer

The earliest barley-based beer is often credited to the Sumerians. Residue analysis of a large, 5,000-year-old ceramic jug discovered at the archaeological site of Godin Tepe in Iran showed evidence of "beer stone," a form of calcium buildup and a common byproduct of brewing with barley. The jug was found in what's considered to have been a storeroom supplying travelers and traders along the Great Khorasan Road, a precursor to the Silk Road.

The Magic of Maltsters

While many grains go from the farm to the distillery to be milled and fermented, barley has an extra stop to make. It has a great deal of fermentable sugar to offer, but the catch is that those sugars are not as readily accessible as with other grains. The sugar (aka potential energy) is stored within starch molecules—of which barley has a high concentration—and can only be released by germinating the seed.

Enter: malting, the three-step process of soaking, germinating, and kilning grains (with an optional fourth toasting step). A maltster's first job is to encourage, or "trick," seeds to germinate just long enough to trigger a chemical reaction (causing sugar production), but not so long that the seeds begin developing into a plant. Soaking the seeds in temperature-controlled water triggers them to prepare for sprouting, which requires energy in the form of sugar. In a natural setting, those sugars would go on to feed developing roots and leaves as a built-in source of nutrition. But in malting, germination is halted with heat (via kiln or large oven) to prevent the seed from fully sprouting and to preserve the usable sugar. By the end of the process, a maltster will have successfully duped the barley into handing over its precious food stores, resulting in malted grain, or simply *malt*.

Despite the crucial role maltsters play, we rarely hear about them or the vital functions they perform. Even within the bar and spirits industry, little is known or understood about the malting process or the skilled work of maltsters. And yet, the role of the maltster is essential to so many of our favorite beverages; they're past due for some appreciation.

Barley Varieties

It's hard to know exactly how many types of barley exist around the world, especially when accounting for wild varieties, but a rough estimate puts it at well over 5,000. Despite this range, there are only around 300 recognized heritage barleys worldwide, with scant few in commercial use because, as we've covered, modern farming favors high yields above all else. Modern barley varieties (meaning those bred via selective breeding in the last fifty years or so) used in brewing and distillation typically yield 60–65 percent starch by weight—great for providing the amount of sugar maltsters seek—but they account for only a fraction of barleys out there. In 2023, the American Malting Barley

---

Small But Mighty

Grasses have small but sophisticated structures. Along the plant's central stem are *spikelets* containing specialized leaves and florets that mature into tiny husks with kernels and seeds. But barley is unique in that it has two types of structural arrangements—six- and two-row. With six-row barley, all the spikelets are fertile, whereas in two-row, some are infertile (though the fertile seeds tend to be larger). This means that six-row typically has more protein and enzyme content than two-row barley. Since protein has a negative correlation with starch—and therefore sugar—concentration, six-row barley is usually favored in food production or as livestock feed, and two-row barley in brewing and distillation.

Association, a nonprofit trade organization representing maltsters, brewers, distillers, and other food producers, recommended only about three dozen barley varieties for use, the majority of them two-row varieties coming out of breeding programs rather than heirloom types. Even more limiting, the Maltsters' Association of Great Britain lists only a dozen approved varieties.

European distillers have also been breeding out a problematic compound in barley called glycosidic nitrile (GN), which can occur in high levels in some varieties during and after malting. (Reminder that this process is *not* genetic modification, just selective breeding.) As it turns out, in certain varieties, higher moisture levels during germination and higher temperatures during kilning cause a higher amount of GN when the malt comes into contact with copper, an interaction resulting in the creation of ethyl carbamate, a carcinogenic compound. As copper is the primary material in pot stills used for distilling single malt whiskeys, the UK has been quietly working on a solution for the past ten years and has successfully lowered levels of GN in UK barley varieties. In North America, this is likely to become an issue farm distilleries and barley breeders will need to address sooner rather than later, especially as the American single malt movement continues picking up speed.

Reducing GN in barley is just one of the many success stories of selective breeding. Thanks to breeding programs, today's barley varieties are also more disease resistant (which means less pesticide use) and more likely to produce viable crops every year, even if those crops aren't terribly exciting in terms of flavor, ensuring a reliable supply of malt. However, a side effect of prioritizing yield and performance in these studies is that when fruitful, they often lead to industry overreliance on just a few varieties. The result is a trend toward monoculturalization. If left unchecked, this can lead to damaged or de-nourished land and biodiversity loss, which triggers a cascade of other ecological problems. So, how do we find balance? It might be as simple as asking the right questions and working together.

Rather than focusing on yield, as most programs do, Jamie Sherman, a barley breeder at Montana State University, asked brewers what *they* wanted. The overwhelming answer was flavor. After selecting 300 varieties of barley from seed storage banks across forty-two countries, she began growing all of them, a significant undertaking that continues today. Her team analyzes the metabolites that affect flavor in the various barley strains planted. (We know these classes of flavor metabolites by more familiar names like esters, fatty acids, and aldehydes—the sorts of chemical compounds that arise in fermentation and distillation.) Her lab has also integrated brewing into its research, taking a hands-on approach to better understand what brewers need. "It's important for breeder, grower, maltster, brewer, and distiller to all work together to have a variety that will meet all the needs," Sherman says. "Bridging the gap between growers and producers happens one step at a time."

A Change of Identity: From Barley to Malt

Unlike chefs, who typically have access to a wide range of ingredients, brewers and distillers must often make do with the barley varietal(s)-turned-malt available to them from malting houses. Maltsters tend to categorize their malt based on "type," often labeling it according to the beer it's intended to create. For instance, a distiller might choose between a pilsner or pale ale malt rather than a specific barley variety malt like two-row Copeland.

"In most cases, brewers don't know what variety they have as maltsters create blends. This is a particular issue as we identify flavor profiles related to specific varieties," Sherman says of the current landscape. "Some smaller companies might have a particular variety, [but] the processing chain may not be set up to isolate specific varieties as much as brewers might like." Most malt styles are determined by toasting (or not). The process is a bit like roasting coffee—toasting gives malts their characteristic flavor and deep brown or black color. Pale or pilsner malts tend to be lighter and toasted at a lower heat, akin to a light roast coffee, while brown or chocolate malts will be more like a dark roast, heated to a higher temperature where the sugars begin to caramelize.

Just as brewers don't often know what barley variety is in their malt, the same is true for distillers, though there are some exceptions. For example, smaller distilleries with relationships to craft maltsters or specific farms may have more control over the type of barley/malt they use. On the other end, large producers with deep pockets, such as Macallan, often create proprietary varietals for select projects and limited releases. Leopold Bros makes their own whiskey malt, appropriately named "Whiskey Floor Malt," designed especially for distilling. The malt is kilned at higher temperatures and is meant to "[shine] a light on those crucial differences between beer and whiskey fermentations."

Scotch distillers or producers of single malts are the most likely to use a specific barley variety. Popular ones include Optic, Belgravia (often used in Springbank malts), and Concerto. In comparison, mid-sized Westland Distillery in Seattle blends five different malt types, both local and imported, in their flagship American Single Malt Whiskey—Washington Select Pale Malt, Munich Malt, Extra Special Malt, Pale Chocolate Malt, Brown Malt, and Bairds Heavily Peated Malt—none of which emphasize a particular barley variety or carry its name. This use of blends and lack of varietal control is one of the reasons whiskey is rarely associated with terroir.

An Exception to Every Rule: Green Malt

Green malt is the rebel of the single malt family. Green malt is not a malt at all; it's simply sprouted (germinated) barley, with the grain technically having undergone three-quarters of the typical malting process—sans the final step of kilning. This means the *mash* (the base for whiskey, see the chapter on corn) is made while the seed is still attempting to become a plant. The grain is very wet, fussy to distill, and prone to spoilage, and therefore, not commonly used by distillers today. So, why would anyone take the risk?

Barley before malting, Leopold Bros distillery, photo by Nat Harry.

In Scotland and Ireland, *peat* is a traditional fuel source made of decayed organic material. Harvested in the summer and burned in the winter, it has been used to heat malting kilns for centuries. However, peat smokes quite a bit when burned, meaning that centuries ago, it would have attracted the unwanted attention of English authorities. So, as a workaround for paying those pesky malt taxes to the crown in the 18th century, the Irish began using green malt instead. Today, green malt is the defining ingredient for single pot still Irish whiskey, such as Redbreast's.

Green malt whiskeys are a look back in time, and perhaps not every malt drinker's cup of ale, as they add herbaceous and vegetal notes that may come across as sharp or spicy. Only a couple of distilleries in the US make whiskey with green malt, notably Coppersea Distilling in New York's Hudson Valley, which doubles down with a 100 percent green malt expression based on an old Scottish distillation handbook.

The Few, the Proud, the Floor Maltsters

Just as most bakeries don't mill their own flour, most whiskey distilleries, regardless of size, don't malt their own barley. Malted barley is typically sourced from maltsters, who primarily use modern methods like rotary drums and state-of-the-art pneumatic kilning vessels—a far cry from the traditional and laborious process of *floor malting*. As the name implies, the process needs a lot of flat space (around the size of a tennis court, depending on the malting house), a temperature-controlled environment, manual labor for turning the grain, and a kiln for drying it.

Today, floor malting is rare, though it's been making something of a comeback in the last decade. Not terribly efficient or cost-effective, floor malting is a true labor of love. If you're already producing the whiskey, floor malting makes the process more self-contained, gives greater control over the results, and, some argue, provides more complex flavors to the finished product.

What is Peat?

Peat is often mentioned when talking about single malt whiskey and whiskey in general. But what is it exactly? Peat is a compressed and partially decayed organic material found in wet, oxygen-deprived freshwater wetlands called bogs. Over time, plant matter accumulates in these bogs (at a glacial pace of 1 mm per year), forming an ancient layer cake of trees, grasses, and native vegetation. Because it's readily available throughout Scotland and Ireland, peat has traditionally served as fuel for kilning malted barley, a decision based more on practicality than flavor (though these days, it's largely the other way around).

Admiral Maltings

Opened in 2017, Admiral Maltings is California's first floor malting facility and the US's largest to date. They source all their grains from California farms and work directly with growers and brewers, sometimes playing the role of matchmaker for unique ingredients. "It's a good way to connect people to the soil and to the source of what we're selling," says co-founder Ron Silberstein. Building his reputation in the Bay Area with the certified organic brewery Thirsty Bear, Silberstein believes in bridging the dissonance between drink and plant. "Whiskey and beer are agricultural products, and we should never forget to tell people that."

In a former US Navy air hanger in Alameda, the facility malts both organic and conventional grains. It works with barley, wheat, rye, and sometimes oats, as well as forgotten grains like Atlas barley, a six-row heirloom named after Morocco's Atlas Mountains, where it was first cultivated. Brought to the Americas by the Spanish, it took hold in the Sacramento Valley and became a popular export to England from the mid-1800s until World War II, when its sluggish malting time led to its fall from favor.

Floor malting of barley at Admiral Maltings, photos by Nat Harry.

Sprouted barley at Leopold Bros, photo by Nat Harry.

Floor malting, like farming, involves humans managing nature. First, floor maltsters steep the grain in cool water, which can take several days. As the grain absorbs the moisture and expands, enzymes in the seed's proteins begin breaking down the starch and releasing sugar. Then, once the grains have reached about 43 percent moisture, they are spread out in thick layers, around 6–8 inches, on the malting floor. The wet grain is turned, or raked, at regular intervals to ensure the temperature remains consistent, as the sprouting seeds create an exothermic reaction that builds up a surprising amount of heat. Raking helps lower the temperature so the process won't end prematurely. Germination can take an average of five days, depending on the grain, and requires regular tending.

So, how do the maltsters know when it's time to begin drying and toasting the grain in a kiln? A mix of intuition and science. For Todd Leopold and other floor maltsters, it's both a craft and an art. On a visit to Leopold Bros's floor malting facility, Leopold demonstrated the intuition of the "maltster's thumb" by crushing a grain of barley in his fingers, which left behind a coarse paste. To Leopold, that consistency signals that the malt has one more day to go if the embryo's growth is to be stopped before it consumes the starch.

Kilning is a delicate process; low and slow is the way to go. Too high a temperature can render enzymes ineffective and negate all the hard work. Leopold uses an old-fashioned-style kiln—one rarely seen these days—called a Doig kiln. With its pagoda-style roof, it looks as distinctive as it does out of place, just as it might have when Scottish architect Charles Doig first plopped one down in the Dailuaine distillery in 1889. Its unique chimney design draws airflow through the kiln from all sides, effectively removing smoke. Walking inside is like stepping into a giant oven. The barley is stacked three feet high and enters with about 45 percent moisture content that needs to be reduced to 15 percent. The key is to start low, around 100°F, and slowly raise it in stages. Lighter malts, like Pilsner, tend to stay under 200°F, while darker malts may hit temperatures around 400°F.

Todd Leopold showing the maltsters thumb, photo by Nat Harry.

Doig kiln and grain silos at Leopold Bros, photo by Nat Harry.

BARLEY

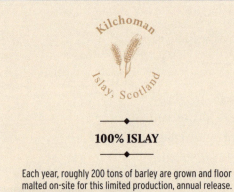

100% ISLAY

Each year, roughly 200 tons of barley are grown and floor malted on-site for this limited production, annual release. Expect umami (a phenolic smoky quality) and salinity from the maritime influence. Typically bottled without an age statement, this peated whisky shines in its youth.

Floor Malted

HAZELBURN 10 YEAR

Commanding a steeper price than most 10 Year Scottish single malts, the craftsmanship of Springbank Distillers speaks for itself. They've been floor malting since before it was cool again, and they're the only Scottish distillery to floor malt 100% of their barley!

Floor Malted

ESTATE SINGLE MALT

This whiskey may not be for everyone, as it has a unique profile and lacks a true comparison to familiar whiskeys. The grain is front and center with oily notes of peanut and almond butter and whole grain bread. It's a bit savory, extremely aromatic, and not very subtle.

Floor Malted

AMERICAN SMALL BATCH WHISKEY

While barley gets the most attention in single malts, Leopold Bros uses their floor malt to make this off-the-radar sour mash whiskey with a respectable 21% barley in the mash bill—a great example of how a "supporting" grain can make a big difference.

Floor Malted

SINGLE MALT SCOTCH WHISKY

Of all the whiskey categories, single malt is the easiest to keep track of in terms of ingredients, as it's only ever made from a single type of malted grain—barley. And while it's technically true that you can malt any grain, seeing the word "single malt" on a bottle of whiskey is *always* an indicator of barley.

Scotch whisky, like Cognac, has a long and tumultuous history. The oldest surviving evidence of the spirit comes from a 1494 tax record detailing a request by King James IV for "aqua vitae" to be made from "eight bolls of malt" (about 1,900 pounds) and distilled by Friar John Cor. By today's measurements, this would have produced somewhere around 1,250 bottles of liquor. However, it's unknown whether the commissioned spirit was intended as a beverage, for the manufacture of gunpowder, or for medicinal use as either an elixir or preservative (the same king would later extend the exclusive right to make and sell aqua vitae to the Guild of Surgeon Barbers in Edinburgh).

Uisge Beatha, the Scottish Gaelic aqua vitae, or "water of life," would continue to develop and evolve in style, although not without a few hurdles. In 1560, the Catholic Church and Catholicism itself were outlawed across Scotland. The officially Protestant country then dissolved its monasteries and sent monks—with expertise in distillation—to live amongst the general population. It wasn't long before this monastic knowledge became integrated into the farming cycle, and distillation caught on as a preservation method for excess crops. At first, farmers used whatever cereal grains they had on hand: barley, of course, but also wheat and oats and sometimes spices, botanicals, and sugar to improve flavor—a far cry from what we consider Scotch whisky today.

SCOTTISH SINGLE MALT

Plant: Barley (malted)

Place: Scotland

Production: Pot stills; double distillation is common, though triple is allowed

Protection: DO

Tensions with England over the next 200 years, coupled with issues of food insecurity, would heavily affect the path of Scotch whisky as it evolved. The British Malt Tax of 1725, imposed across Great Britain, was passed to fund wars abroad. However, the regulation simultaneously struck at Scottish autonomy by taxing an ingredient essential to brewing, baking, and distillation (i.e., malted barley). The Scottish, who had previously been exempt from these sorts of levies, erupted in protest in Glasgow and across the country in what would come to be known as the Malt Tax Riots. Though home distillers weren't subject to the levy so long as they used grains grown on their property and kept the spirit for non-commercial use, the tax heavily impacted brewers, raising the price of beer, which was more than just a working-class drink enjoyed for leisure. At this time, "small" or session beers—those with low alcohol levels—were considered a safe alternative to clean drinking water (which was difficult to come by).

Decades later, amid massive crop failures across Great Britain in 1957, the government intervened again to enact a total ban on commercial distillation, arguing that all food and agriculture must go to humans and livestock (i.e., not be used for nonessential items like alcohol). Registered distilleries went out of business en masse over the three-year enforcement period. As in 1725, home distillation wasn't subject to this ban, a loophole leading to illicit distillation and significant smuggling.

Whisky eventually bounced back, thanks partly to an unexpected sales boost during the grape phylloxera plague. At the time, brandy and soda, a drink we know today as a highball, was the favored boozy libation of the English middle class. When the brandy dried up, blended whisky (a cheaper, lighter grain whisky) was there to save the day. Its popularity as a substitute quickly eclipsed brandy, and before you know it, less reputable peddlers emerged, especially those catering to the lower classes.

Centuries of lax laws governing whisky production meant corners were cut, quality declined over time, and an unholy list of additives rushed in. Glycerin, green tea, caramel, and prune wine were just a few of the deceptive, though relatively innocuous, additives used. But ether, turpentine, and sulfuric acid became justifiable causes for concern and remained legal additives until the 1870s. Stringent rules shaping Scotch weren't created until 1909 as part of the Royal Commission on Whisky and Other Potable Spirits, and there have been many additions since.

Modern Malts and Blends

There are several categories of Scotch whisky, the two most familiar being blended Scotch and single malt Scotch. (The lesser-known

---

Golden Promise Barley

Golden Promise barley, a classic British spring malt variety, was once the favored barley of Scotch producers from the 1970s to the 1990s. Bred by English seed company Miln Marsters, Golden Promise was a result of "mutation breeding" using gamma rays to alter the characteristics of a barley called Maythorpe. Golden Promise was the first barley variety protected by the UK's Plant Varieties and Seeds Act (1964) and was recommended for planting in Scotland 4 years later. Its arrival significantly altered the farming landscape of Scotland, which had previously relied on native barley varieties and their ability to thrive in local microclimates. However, because of these geographic limitations, the amount actually grown for malt was limited, and most was imported from the UK. Today, Macallan is one of two Scotch producers who continue to use a percentage of Golden Promise in production.

SPIRITS DISTILLED

categories—vatted malts and single grain—are primarily appreciated by enthusiasts, which is a shame, as each offers something unique.) Blended Scotch, though often unfairly considered a "cheaper" or "lesser" substitute, was once the most common way to enjoy Scotch and Irish whiskies before single malts gained favor.

- **SINGLE MALT**: 100% malted barley grown in a single season and distilled by a single producer in a copper pot still; the resulting distillate is usually heavy, rich, and oily.

- **VATTED MALT**: A blend of malt distillates from different distilleries.

- **SINGLE GRAIN**: Any grain or mix of grains (corn, wheat, rye, or barley) grown in a single season and distilled by a single producer in a column still; the resulting distillate is usually light, fruity, and clean.

- **BLENDED WHISKY**: A blend of malt whisky and grain whisky (i.e., whisky made, at least partly, from a grain other than malted barley; typically comes from multiple distilleries.

The Gift Basket

- 1 ¾ oz. blended Scotch (such as Compass Box's Glasgow Blend)
- ¾ oz. Broadbent's 5 Year Madeira
- ½ oz. Amaro Nonino
- 1 dash each Angostura and orange bitters

Stir until chilled and diluted, about 20-30 seconds. Strain into a chilled cocktail glass and garnish with an orange twist.

(original recipe)

When Scotch whisky first gained international traction, malt and grain whiskies were typically sold and consumed as a blend, meaning grocers and public houses would often purchase barrels in bulk from distilleries and practice "independent bottling," aging the spirit further or blending it with other whiskies. Back then, the rules of whisky were loose compared to today. A legal definition for Scotch whisky wasn't even created until 1933, followed by the Scotch Whisky Act of 1988. Neither of these laws mentioned the term "single malt." However, by the late 1970s, Scotch whisky sales had declined overall, so distilleries began discussing new approaches to promotion and marketing. The collective goal was to champion "single malts" as superior to blends—with Glenfiddich leading the charge—and by the 1980s, the industry had successfully boosted sales and increased exports, solidifying the perception of single malt Scotch as a "premium" spirit. Despite this, independent bottling

BARLEY 83

and blending continues to this day and has even rebounded in popularity recently thanks to whisky enthusiasts. The rules and definitions surrounding Scottish whisky continue to be revisited and were most recently updated in 2009 to reflect current trends and categories—a testament to history, politics, consumer attitudes, and the power of marketing.

To be classified as a single malt whisky made in Scotland (aka Scotch), a distiller must follow a strict set of rules, primarily: it must be made from 100 percent malted barley, come from a single distillery during a single season, be twice distilled using copper pot stills, and be aged a minimum of three years. Compared with whiskey from other parts of the world, Scotch leans conservative in creativity, with most experimentation occurring during maturation (barrel aging), which accounts for about 70 percent of the spirit's flavor. Producers often use ex-Sherry, Madeira, Port, or even rum barrels to bring variety to the category. (Interestingly, the DO allows for the use of flavorless caramel coloring to provide visual consistency from batch to batch, a practice generally accepted across Europe.)

A Sense of Style and Place

Scotland is divided into five legally recognized whisky-producing regions—Highland, Lowlands, Speyside, Islay, and Campbeltown—with 130 operational distilleries. (A sixth region, Islands, is also commonly recognized today.) While each zone is known for its unique take on the spirit (Highland for its Sherry-forward flavor, Islay for peat, Islands for its maritime influence, etc.), these regional classifications have nothing to do with where the barley is sourced or grown. In fact, much of it is grown across Europe and the UK, with only a small portion coming from Scotland itself (though this has been changing recently with the resurgence of local farm distilleries). Overall, Scotch is less about terroir and more about style.

Highland	Lowlands	Speyside	Islay	Campbeltown	Islands
Wide range of flavor profiles	Soft, creamy, floral, toasted cereals	Sherry-driven, baking spice, dried fruits and nuts, baked apple	Peat-driven (smokey), medicinal, aromatic, maritime influence, savory	Brine, peat smoke, dried fruit and citrus peel, medicinal	Maritime influence, seaweed, lightly smokey, umami

Scotch whisky by region.

Kilchoman
Islay

MACHIR BAY

The first distillery founded on Islay in over a hundred years, 100% of the barley Kilchoman uses is grown on mainland Scotland and malted in Islay at Port Ellen Maltings. This single malt is sweet and savory, with a snappy finish that only younger peated malts can achieve.

A Sense of Place

Bruichladdich Distillery
Islay

BERE BARLEY

Bere Barley is a six-row variety, a type rarely seen in Europe. Barley for this Bruichladdich release is grown on Orkney Island by the Agronomy Institute. Unpeated and aged 10 years, this whisky showcases a forgotten grain, offering biscuity notes tempered by dried fruits and toasted coconut.

Farm Distillery

The Balvenie Distillery
Speyside

DOUBLEWOOD 12 YEAR

This is a classic single malt I go back to time and time again. Though the distillery opened in the late 1800s, the DoubleWood—which splits time between American oak and ex-Sherry barrels before being combined—debuted in 1993.

Tried and True

Deanston Distillery
Highland

2000 ORGANIC WHISKY

Once home to a former cotton mill along the River Teith, Deanston only uses Scottish barley and relies on water from the river—which flows over granite—to produce its whisky. Their yearly, limited-edition releases include a certified organic bottling or two, typically unpeated, with lots of clean honey and cereal notes.

Organic

Edradour
Highland

CALEDONIA 12 YEAR

Founded in 1825, Edradour is one of Scotland's smallest distilleries and uses time-honored equipment, including the smallest traditional pot stills in Scotland. The Caledonia bottling is finished in Oloroso Sherry casks, giving it notes of dried fruit and sticky toffee pudding.

Artisanal and Traditional

Arran
Islands (Isle of Arran)

10 YEAR

This bottle's label proudly boasts its "natural color" and "non-chill filtered" status. With notes of ripe stone fruit, candied citrus, and croissant dough, this introductory 10 Year is an example of a no bells and whistles whisky—relying instead on fine craftsmanship alone.

Off the Beaten Path

IRISH SINGLE MALT WHISKEY

IRISH SINGLE MALT

Plant: Barley (malted)

Place: Ireland (Republic of Ireland and Northern Ireland)

Production: Pot still; double or triple distillation allowed

Protection: DO

Like many, my first foray into Irish whiskey was Jameson, consumed in shot form or tastefully mixed with ginger ale and bitters. At the start of my bartending career, this 240-year-old brand was the industry drink of choice, and we drank a lot of it.

Jameson is not a single malt; it's a blended whiskey, which, as you may remember, means it's made from malt whiskey (meaning barley and a pot still) and grain whiskey (Jameson uses corn and a column still). Like most blends, it's much heavier on the grain— light, fruity, and approachable, excellent for folks just getting into the category. But the world of Irish whiskey is much broader than what we commonly see on most backbars.

Scotch vs. Irish Whiskey

Whiskey vs. Whisky

You may have noticed two different spellings of "whiskey," with the distinction usually coming down to the country of origin. To keep my spelling correct, I'm fond of author and distiller Heather Greene's trick: countries spelled without an "e" don't use one in their whisky either! (The US and Ireland generally use the "whiskey" spelling, while Scotland, Canada, Japan, and a few others use "whisky").

Irish single malt, like Scotch, has a recognized DO with many of the same rules as Scotch whisky and then some. It also has a long history full of political strife and economic setbacks. Though there is some debate about if whiskey was first made in Scotland or Ireland, as with Pisco, I'll stay out of it. Regardless, it's generally believed that whiskey was being produced in Ireland as early as the 6th century CE, though the claim is more anecdotal than evidence-based. The earliest documentation of whiskey in Ireland comes from the Annals of Clonmacnoise (aka Mageoghagan's Book), an Irish chronicle of events from prehistory up to the early 15th century, which mentions whiskey-making in 1405. At its inception, Irish whiskey would likely have been drunk unaged and infused with herbs and flavorings, not unlike early versions of Scotch. It would have also followed a similar rise in popularity, getting its big break during the outbreak of grape phylloxera. However, it wasn't until the invention of the Coffey still that it would adopt the expression we know today.

Irish single malt	100% malted barley	Pot still	Triple distillation is common but not mandatory	Aged a minimum of 3 years
Irish single pot still	A minimum of 30% each of malted and un-malted (green) barley	Pot still	Triple distillation is common but not mandatory	Aged a minimum of 3 years
Scottish single malt	100% malted barley	Pot still	Double distillation	Aged a minimum of 3 years

Comparing Scotch and Irish whiskey.

Ironically, Irishman Aeneas Coffey, inventor of the first patented continuous still (1830), had more initial success in Scotland than in his home country. At the time, some of the most prominent Irish distilleries, such as Jameson, were unimpressed with Coffey's newfangled technology. But as Scotland's blended whiskies (which relied on continuous distillation) gained in popularity, resistance toward the new method softened, and the style became accepted throughout Ireland.

By the mid 1800s, Dublin had four prominent distilleries, with two of the four owned by members of the Jameson family. (One of those two, John Powers & Son, was the first Irish distillery to bottle its whiskey rather than sell it to merchants or public houses.) Many smaller distilleries also operated throughout Ireland, but their contribution by volume was slight in comparison. By the late 1800s, Irish whiskey had reached peak popularity and accounted for roughly 70 percent of the international whiskey market.

It wasn't to last, though. Numerous setbacks—including a war of independence (which cut off access to the British market), US Prohibition, and world wars—took a devastating toll on years of progress. By the 1980s, only two whiskey distilleries remained. Fast forward to today, and Irish whiskey has completely turned a corner. In 2010, there were four whiskey distilleries in Ireland. Today, there are forty and counting—a true revival of the category.

Single Pot Still Whiskey

Single pot still whiskey, sometimes called "pure pot still whiskey," is missing one important word: malt. That's because this unique Irish style includes a small portion (minimum 30%) of un-malted barley (aka green malt) along with the malted barley.

BARLEY

SINGLE MALT

When Dingle Distillery launched in 2012, they were the first independent whiskey producer to open shop in Ireland in 150 years. Their core single malt, aged in ex-Bourbon and Pedro Ximénez Sherry casks, is complex, rich, and full of surprises.

Artisanal and Independent

SINGLE MALT

In 2022, the distillery was awarded "Sustainable Distillery of the Year" by *Whisky Magazine*. Their flagship single malt is aged in 5 different ex-wine casks: Sherry, Port, Madeira, white Burgundy, and Cabernet Sauvignon. It is well-rounded and fruit-forward, with vinous notes.

New Kid on the Block

12 YEAR

Part of the Midleton Distillery group (along with Jameson), this bottle is a gateway into Irish whiskey. A single pot still whiskey—which, as noted earlier, uses both malted and un-malted barley—this bottling is distilled 3 times before it's aged in ex-Bourbon and Sherry barrels for 12 years.

Tried and True

CONNEMARA 12 YEAR PEATED SINGLE MALT

You can get your peat fix in Ireland if you know where to look. Sweet and savory, this complex whiskey offers a long finish, taking you through chewy, dried fruits to a medicinal, herbal profile.

For the Adventurous Palate

AMERICAN SINGLE MALT

American single malt is a budding spirits category, but it's building momentum thanks to the advocacy of passionate distillers. In 2016, a group of more than seventy craft distillers banded together to create the American Single Malt Whiskey Commission (ASMWC) with the mission "to address the growing need for American-based producers to define the category—both domestically and internationally—in order to protect, educate, promote, and ultimately grow it." They successfully petitioned the TTB in 2022 for a standard of identity for American single malt whiskey, setting forth an agreed-upon set of rules for all US producers. The proposal is officially pending and will likely be officially approved any day now.

The proposed standard of identity set some quality and consistency measures without being as stringent as those of Scotch. The foundation of the proposed category rests on the whiskey being made from 100 percent malted barley mashed, distilled, and matured in the US. (However, the barley does not have to be grown or malted in the US.) And, like with Scotch, it should be distilled at a single distillery. Unlike with Scotch or Irish whiskey, there is no three-year minimum aging requirement, likely due to the wide temperature variances across the US. (For example, aging time would look different in Texas than in Washington state.) Another significant difference in the American single malt category compared to Scotch is that double distillation in pot stills is *not* required, allowing for hybrid stills, which are common in many smaller distilleries.

AMERICAN SINGLE MALT

Plant: Barley (malted)

Place: United States

Production: Any still type; produced entirely at one distillery

Protection: Soon to have a standard of identity from the TTB

Proposed Standard of Identity as Posted by ASMWC

- Made from 100% malted barley;

- Distilled at one distillery;

- Mashed, distilled, and matured in the US;

- Matured in oak barrels not exceeding 700L;

- Bottled at a minimum 40% ABV (80 proof); and

- Color correction and additives allowed.

Aging

Unlike in Scotland and Ireland, there are currently no age requirements for American single malts. Because the US is generally warmer than the UK, whiskeys will age much faster. For example, a 12 Year single malt, aged over a dozen hot Texas summers, won't have much leftover for drinking after the *angel's share* (i.e., the amount of the spirit that evaporates during aging).

Westland Distillery

Using a combination of 5 different malts from Washington state and the UK, Westland has one of the most unique and approachable American single malts. Their flagship is an ideal place for Scotch lovers to start their American single malt journey, as caramel, cacao, dried fruit, and subtle baking spices make this a well-rounded dram.

Their Outpost limited releases are outstanding in concept and execution, and they're always experimenting with ways to showcase terroir in a spirit category where it has yet to be recognized or sought. Sometimes, this means using what's around them in the Pacific Northwest: Garryana oak for barrels, peat sustainably harvested from the Skagit Valley, and locally grown Colere for malted barley.

Germinated barley, Admiral Maltings, photo by Nat Harry.

BOTTLED-IN-BOND AMERICAN SINGLE MALT

Bottled-in-bond (see the chapter on corn) and single malt are two terms you don't usually see in the same sentence, but here we are, and I'm not mad about it. This little distillery tucked into a warehouse district in West Oakland gives us a chewy dram with brown sugar, molasses, and baking spices.

Modern yet Artisanal

PRINCIPIUM

While I typically think of this distillery's more adventurous spirits like Absinthe, distiller Stephen Gould has whiskey in his sights. I'm often skeptical of young whiskey (less than 3 years), but this bottle proves you should keep an open mind when it comes to age.

Ages is Just a Number

BLUE PEAK SINGLE MALT

One of the first American single malts to hit the market, Stranahan's uses Rocky Mountain malted barley and large, charred American oak barrels, aging it for 4 years in a solera-style system. The final product is brought to proof with local spring water.

Tried and True

TEXAS 1 SINGLE MALT

While famous for their blue corn whisky, Balcones was determined to make a single malt. Their Texas 1 single malt is pot distilled, bottled at cask strength and aged at least 2 years. It's chewy, oily, and highly aromatic, with dark undertones of black walnut and dried cherry.

Big Flex

JAPANESE WHISKY

Over a decade ago, a spirits rep walked into the bar I worked at and poured me a Yamazaki 12 Year. At the time, the parent company, Suntory, was relatively unknown outside of Japan, so it was a hard sell, even in a cocktail-loving region like the San Francisco Bay Area. Buying a bottle for the back bar wasn't overly risky (the cost was relatively minimal), but there was an expectation that it would collect dust.

JAPANESE WHISKY

Plant: Cereal grains (malted)

Place: Japan

Production: Any still type

Protection: Japanese standard of identity as of 2024

A couple of years later, in 2015, the 2013 Yamazaki Sherry Cask would be named "World Whisky of the Year" by a well-known whiskey writer. And boy, look where we are today. Next to Bourbon, Japanese single malt has some of the most avid collectors out there. As the category took off, imports skyrocketed, and new and previously unseen brands emerged. In 2010, the US imported around $1.4 million worth of Japanese whisky. By 2015, it was closer to $18 million, and in 2020, it was nearly $67 million.

But what exactly is it about Japanese whisky that's captured the attention of whiskey aficionados? After all, it's not wholly unlike its single malt siblings and remains rooted in the spirit's traditional distilling methods that originated in Scotland. In fact, most of today's Japanese whisky distilleries use imported malted barley, both peated and unpeated, from Scotland or other parts of Europe. In other words, what makes Japanese whisky special isn't where the barley is grown, as it could be the same used in a Scotch or Irish single malt.

Importing the grain wasn't always the status quo. The first malting barley introduced to Japan, a two-row variety called Golden Melon, was imported from the US in 1873. It was primarily cultivated in Hokkaido—a prefecture (aka district) with a similar climate and environment to Scotland—the same region the "father of Japanese whisky," Masataka Taketsuru, would set up his independent distillery more than fifty years later. Golden Melon was used in brewing and distillation for nearly a century after its arrival despite its shortcomings: lower alcohol yields, rangy stalks, and late-season maturation. By the 1950s, barley breeding programs established by the Japanese government began working to improve the variety. Over the next several decades, major breweries (such as Sapporo and Asahi) would join in the quest, launching their own private breeding programs. Still, it wouldn't be enough to rescue Golden Melon from the brink of obscurity.

SPIRITS DISTILLED

In the early 1970s, Golden Melon began facing competition with the introduction of better-yielding varieties that had been bio-engineered overseas over the course of decades. By the 1980s, both Yamazaki and Nikka, Japan's two largest distilleries, had ceased malting and peating their grains in-house, preferring to use less expensive, imported malts. Japanese barley would continue to be used to a limited degree until 2004, thanks partly to an agreement between Japanese spirits makers and domestic barley farmers. However, Japanese whisky distillers, predominantly servicing a domestic market, struggled. Smaller distilleries shuttered, and the contracts were soon renegotiated so that the Brewers Association of Japan would purchase the grain instead. Today, the price of domestic barley in Japan remains high—almost four times as much as imported barley. It's another reason we no longer see it used in whisky or even the Japanese liquor, shochu.

Either way, a category's reliance on imported ingredients prompts reflection about what makes a spirit's sense of place and identity and challenges consumers to distinguish between convention and tradition. So, back to the question at hand: What makes Japanese whisky unique? The answer is multifaceted. Single malt is the product of different casks marrying together, and those used in Japan's whisky often impart an ephemeral quality. Japan's whisky is also heavily influenced by the country's "soft" water (meaning it's low in minerals such as calcium and magnesium), which is used to make the mash and to proof it down. Yeast is another player, and Suntory claims to have around 150 different strains, each capable of coaxing out a different set of flavors. For a spirit so closely resembling its Scottish muse, Japanese whisky still manages to retain its own style, showcasing the processes, blending, and craftsmanship of Japanese distillers and highlighting the concept of balance ingrained within Japan's culture of food and drink.

Secret, Secrets, are No Fun

Throughout the last half-century, the category of Japanese whisky has seen some profound changes, and today, the work continues as the spirit

---

The Beginnings of Japanese Whisky

If you have experience with any Japanese single malt, it's likely to be from one of two of the nation's largest and oldest distilleries: Suntory (producers of the coveted Yamazaki) and Nikka. Masataka Taketsuru traveled to Scotland in 1918 to learn the art of distillation, bringing the knowledge back with him 2 years later when he helped open the Yamazaki distillery. Venturing out on his own, he launched the Yoichi distillery in Hokkaido and, eventually, the Nikka brand. Today, Nikka has 2 operating distilleries, Yoichi and Miyagikyo; each makes a different style of single malt.

---

navigates what could be described as an identity crisis. In the last decade, a host of new distilleries have broken ground, putting out "newborn," or very young, expressions that are sometimes only months old. Even well-known distilleries have struggled to meet the demand and growing pains of the category. For example, not long after Japanese whisky soared to global success, age statements quietly started to disappear from popular bottlings, such as the Hibiki 12 Year—which became a blend called Japanese Harmony—and Nikka's Yoichi and Miyagikyo expressions. When that still wasn't enough to meet the demand, new brands began touting their own 12 Year whiskies. You might be asking: Where did these aged whiskies come from if the distillery selling them only recently opened? (For those familiar with Bourbon, this story will sound familiar.) Essentially, imported Scotch helped many distillers bridge the gap between supply and demand.

Anecdotes of Scottish bills of lading (a legal receipt for shipped goods) in Japanese distilleries began to float around, suggesting that some companies were simply importing their whisky pre-aged and ready to rebottle. Some distilleries, like Nikka, were transparent in their use of Scotch in some of their blends, but most others were quiet on the issue. In 2020, the *New York Times* published a story many in the industry knew as an open secret: a lot of "Japanese whisky" wasn't actually made in Japan. This article prompted a better-late-than-never response to define the category, and in 2021, a list of rules and a standard of identity were proposed. The most significant regulation was that whisky sold in Japan had to consist of at least 10 percent aged malt whisky. However, the remaining 90 percent could be any unaged spirit; it didn't even have to be made of grain.

The proposed rules for Japanese whisky came into compliance in 2024 and will undoubtedly offer some stability to a category that has experienced a high-speed ascent in popularity. Still, these regulations may not provide an instant fix, so I recommend careful consideration if you're just starting your Japanese whisky journey.

New Standard of Identity for Japanese Whisky (in effect as of 2024)

- Japanese whisky must be made with malted grains grown in Japan and use water extracted from Japan. (This excludes rice whisky, which uses *koji* (i.e., a cultured rice-based mold, see the chapter on rice) and not malt;

- "Saccharification, fermentation, and distillation" must take place at a distillery in Japan—this means no more importing pre-distilled whisky for blending or rebottling;

- The distillate must be aged in wooden casks of no more than 700L and matured in Japan for at least 3 years. (This echoes the standards of Scotch and Irish whisky);

- Bottling must also occur in Japan, with the minimum ABV set at 40%; and

- Caramel is allowed.

Kaiyō Whisky

Kaiyō Whisky came onto the scene just as age statements started disappearing from Japanese whisky labels. The brand has been shrouded in mystery since it first hit shelves, and I'll admit I, too, was suspicious of its "authenticity." Everyone I knew in the industry believed it was just another imported Scotch.

While working at Cask, I had the fortune of speaking with Kaiyō's founder and master blender, Jeffrey Karlovitch, who filled me in on some of the brand's secrets (though the rest remain protected through numerous NDAs). It turns out their whisky is indeed sourced, but from within Japan. By buying the spirit unaged, Kaiyō is essentially acting as an independent bottler, blending and maturing the whisky after purchase (not unlike what we see with blended Scotch).

The idea for Kaiyō came to Karlovitch when he worked as a blender and consultant for White Oak and Chichibu Distillery. He had a feeling early on that Japanese whisky would be big, so he began buying whisky from any distillery that would sell to him, which, he learned, was not many. Distilleries were reluctant to sell their aged whiskies, so Karlovitch began to buy *new make* whisky, or the unaged whisky fresh off the still. Then he waited . . . and waited, for the whisky to come of age.

Japanese Whisky Highball

The key to this simple, refreshing cocktail is the spirit to water ratio and using cold glassware and ingredients—yes, even the whisky.

- 2 oz. of Japanese whisky
- 5–6 oz. soda water
- lemon peel, for garnish

In a highball glass, add the ice and whisky. Stir a few times with a long-handled spoon. Top with soda water and gently agitate with your spoon to integrate. Garnish with a lemon twist.

Interestingly, Kaiyō has never labeled its whisky as explicitly "Japanese." As a result, they haven't needed to make any adjustments in the aftermath of the 2024 regulations, which would exclude them due to where the whisky is aged a portion of the time: at sea. So, while not falling under the new proposed standards for a Japanese whisky, Kaiyō's expressions are a unique way to taste creative blending and maturation in native Japanese oak without breaking your budget (for now).

MIYAGIKYO SINGLE MALT (NO-AGE-STATEMENT EXPRESSION)

This bottle is an excellent introduction to Japanese single malt. While Nikka does source from their sister distillery, Ben Nevis, in Scotland, for some of their expressions, this bottle is 100% Japanese-made, offering notes of dried fruit, nuts, and toasted coconut, with hints of cacao.

Age is Just a Number

HAKUSHU 12 YEAR SINGLE MALT

Harder to find, though not impossible, this is a classic example of what made the category a global success. Compared to its Sherry-forward sibling, Yamazaki 12 Year, Hakushu has not seen the same rabid fan base, partly because of its more complex herbal notes and lightly peated profile.

Tried and True

TAKETSURU PURE MALT

Relaunching this expression in 2020, likely with the foresight of the 2024 requirements, this blend from Yoichi and Miyagikyo distilleries delivers flavor without drowning your bank account. It presents notes of dried fruit and a hint of leather, though nothing too funky.

Most Bang for Your Buck

VARIOUS SINGLE MALT RELEASES

Founded in 2016, this new distillery is redefining what it means to make Japanese whisky. These bottles aren't cheap or plentiful, but neither is creating a brick-and-mortar and sourcing local barley. Inspired by Islay Scotch, the flavor profiles reflect their love of smoke and salinity.

A Sense of Place (and Adventure)

WORLD SINGLE MALT WHISKEY

Most world single malts—those made outside the historically producing regions of Scotland and Ireland—tend to follow the spirit's existing rules and traditions, typically using 100 percent malted barley double-distilled in copper pot stills. Aside from that, it's up to a region or country to define the category further (e.g., age requirements, barrel size, etc.) if they choose to do so at all.

SINGLE MALT

Plant: Barley

Place: Worldwide, outside of established DOs

Production: Pot still

Protection: None or may vary by region

French single malt

ESTATE CASK

Created with terroir in mind and crafted in the heart of Cognac country by a 3rd-generation Cognac maker, Brenne's single malt whiskies are distilled in traditional Charentais stills, using 2 types of estate-grown heirloom barley. It's also 100% organic!

Funky but Cool

Indian single malt

EDITED

Using peated, six-row barley grown in the foothills of the Himalayas, Paul John is known for choosing flavor over yield. The higher proteins and fatty acids in this particular barley variety lead to a richer, oily spirit, and this bottle (one of their many options) is savory with a touch of barbeque.

A Sense of Place

Australian single malt

NOVA

Made with Australian-malted barley and aged in ex-red wine barrels from the Yarra and Barossa valleys, this bottle is ridiculously approachable. With the warmer Melbourne climate, the whisky ages quickly. The result is reminiscent of a fruit and nuts Cadbury bar, with notes of port wine.

For the Adventurous Palate

Taiwanese single malt

CONCERTMASTER PORT CASK FINISH

Due to the hot summers that accelerate aging, it's rare to see a bottle of Kavalan with an age statement; this bottle is no exception. Their Concertmaster single malt is first aged in American oak and then finished in Port casks. Sweet and savory with a long finish, it's a great introduction to Taiwanese whisky.

Expect the Unexpected

GRAIN AND SINGLE GRAIN WHISKEY

The rules and practices around grain-based spirits can be confusing. Grain whiskey is typically, though not exclusively, made from cereal grains *other than* malted barley (unlike Scotch, Irish whiskey, or other single malts). Instead of the ingredient defining the category, in the case of grain whiskey, it's the type of still used to distill it: the column still, which we've learned allows for a much lighter and sometimes cheaper distillate and is easier to produce in larger quantities.

GRAIN AND SINGLE GRAIN

Plant: Any grain, particularly corn and wheat

Place: Anywhere, traditionally Scotland

Production: Column still

Protection: None

Each country has its down distillation rules for single grain whiskey. In Scotland, a single grain whisky must come from one distillery/producer and be aged at least three years (the aging rule for any Scotch). However, unlike single malt whiskies, which only use barley, single grain whiskies can be made from a mix of malted and unmalted grains. Because grain whisky is a key component of blended Scotch, it's usually produced in specialized distilleries that almost exclusively make distillates for blending. Cameronbridge, Loch Lomond, Girvan, and Strathclyde are also a few of the remaining distilleries producing grain whisky. Long story short, if you see a single grain whiskey as a standalone bottling, I highly recommend giving it a try.

Barley (malted)

SINGLE GRAIN WHISKY

An outlier for several reasons, Loch Lomond is one of the only distilleries I've come across that produces both grain whisky and single malt whisky at one distillery. They also use malted barley as their base, which is atypical of grain whisky, though their use of column stills makes for a lighter spirit.

Why Not Both?

Corn; Other grains

COFFEY GRAIN JAPANESE WHISKY

Predominantly corn-based (95%) and aged in used (re-filled), rather than new, charred casks, grain whiskies like this one are a major component in Japanese blends. This bottling showcases a lighter distillate that shines in a highball but is also easily sipped. A great introduction to Japanese whisky that won't break the bank.

Corn Dominant

Corn; Barley (malted)

SINGLE GRAIN IRISH WHISKEY

This 95% corn and 5% malted barley bottling is column-distilled and will taste nothing like an American corn whiskey. Bottled at 46% and non-chill filtered, it's matured in red wine casks, accentuating the fruity nature of the whiskey.

Luck of the Irish

Corn; Wheat

HEDONISM

From John Glaser's line of expertly blended whisky, the now annual release is a blend of grain whiskies from distillers like Cameronbridge, North British Distillery, and Port Dundas. While the flavor profile changes every year, expect notes of vanilla, crème brûlée, and dried fruits.

Blended Grain

CORN

My obsession with corn (aka maize) began with my first bite of a fresh, handmade masa tortilla in Oaxaca, Mexico. From its mythical creation story and deep cultural significance to its almost unfathomable array of modern uses—maize fascinates me. So naturally, when I had the opportunity to attend a corn whiskey master class at the American Distilling Institute in St. Louis in 2022, I eagerly accepted. The experience did not disappoint. I listened to corn grain breeders give their perspectives on genetic modification and flavor, learned about the importance of using quality ingredients from distillers, and, of course, I tasted a healthy amount of whiskey.

Endemic to the Americas, corn is one of the three most widely grown crops in the world, and that's in large part because it has seemingly endless applications. It can be eaten fresh off the cob, added to stews or salsas, milled into grits, ground into cornmeal or flour, used as a thickening agent, boiled down into syrups and sweeteners, and brewed into beverages like the traditional Mexican drink atole or the Andean beer chicha. And corn's usefulness extends beyond human sustenance in ways that aren't immediately obvious but that permeate our daily lives.

Chicomecóatl, Mexica maize diety, 15th–early 16th century, photo courtesy of the Metropolitan Museum of Art.

The Cultural Importance of Maize in Mesoamerica

By around 3,000 years ago, maize had become so important to its cultivators that it was appearing in Olmec art and iconography; there may have even been a maize deity in the Olmec pantheon. A few thousand years later, the Maya creation story, the Popol Vuh, recounted how humans were formed by the gods out of dough made of yellow and white corn flour. Similarly, the Mexica (Me-SHEE-ka) honored the life-giving crop in the form of Chicomecóatl, goddess of corn and nourishment.

On the botanical front, corn (scientific name: *Zea mays*) is a highly domesticated crop with tens of thousands of varieties. Like all cereal grains, it is a simple fruit and a member of the grass family, Poaceae. But this "grass" that we call a corn stalk doesn't occur in the wild. It's a domesticate of several species of tall, wild grasses known as *teosinte* (from the Nahuatl word *tosintli*, meaning "sacred corn"). These grasses are native to Mesoamerica and have been cultivated there for at least 9,000 years. Careful selection of teosinte's more attractive genetic traits over millennia transformed the wild grass into a crop, leading to more kernels per ear (early varieties only had about a dozen) and larger, softer kernels. The process also resulted in a tougher *rachis* (the central stem, or "cob," the kernels are attached to), which, over time, meant this grain became reliant on human intervention for seed dispersal.

An American Grain

The Americas have given the world around two hundred different species of maize, with Mexico alone providing sixty-four of those. This standout quantity is made possible thanks largely to the preservation of teosinte as a wild varietal, as this grass remains close enough in relation to maize to aid in its pollination. Today, Mexican farmers often plant it on crop borders to encourage biodiversity, and while natural cross-pollination does occur, hand pollination using teosinte ear "tassels" is more likely to guarantee a cross of genetic material. This cross-breeding, combined with societal respect for the crop's history and cultural importance, mitigates the impact of monocropping and allows the natural biodiversity of the region to thrive.

Traditionally, maize is planted alongside companion crops like beans and squash (as well as winter gourds and pumpkin). These plants have a symbiotic, mutually beneficial relationship: the squash vines suppress weeds, the beans provide nitrogen to the soil, and the maize's tall stalks provide a natural trellis for the beans' climb. This agricultural trifecta is sometimes called the "Three Sisters Garden," and for many Native communities, these remain their most vital crops. While this complementary agricultural strategy is used throughout the Americas, the name "Three Sisters" is thought to originate with the Haudenosaunee (aka the Iroquois).

Fermentation tubs at Maker's Mark, photo by Nat Harry.

Fermentation, Not Distillation

You may recall that fermentation is the breaking down of sugars into alcohol and that it occurs naturally—as any drunken bear who's raided a cache of fallen apples can attest. Distillation, however, is the use of heat to separate various liquids, including alcohol. There's a wide variety of tasty and traditional maize-based beverages that are fermented but not distilled, including *tejuino* (a cold drink made of *masa* [i.e., corn dough], unrefined whole cane sugar, water, and lime juice), *atole agrio* (a hot, creamy, acidic drink used medicinally and ceremonially), and *pozol* (a nixtamalized maize [see sidebar on page 104] and cocoa drink). Although fermentation can occur without human intervention, maize requires some help, as it lacks the enzymatic properties necessary for spontaneous fermentation. This is why most corn whiskeys have a small amount of barley added to the mash bill, or at the very least, some artificial enzymes to help it along.

The Etymology of Maize/Corn

Today, about 68 Indigenous words for maize remain. (The word "maize" stems from the Spanish *maíz,* adopted directly from the Caribbean Taíno word—*mahiz*). But when English speakers first encountered the cereal grain, the term "corn" was used to mean any grain, the way some folks call all sodas "Coke." To distinguish this new crop from those they were familiar with, English colonists began calling maize "Indian corn" and oats, barley, wheat, and pretty much any grain that wasn't maize, "British corn." Eventually, government regulations changed, and by the 1800s, the "Indian" descriptor for this American grain was dropped altogether.

Nixtamalization

Nixtamalization—a combination of the Nahuatl words *nextli* ("ashes") and *tamalli* ("corn dough")—is an ancient Mesoamerican process of preparing maize for human consumption. The dried kernels are cooked in water with a small amount of food-grade calcium hydroxide, typically called "Cal" or "pickling lime," and then rinsed thoroughly before grinding and forming into dough. Due to the alkaline nature of the Cal, the fruit's *pericarp* (the protective outer covering of a kernel) will easily rinse away. The process is now essential to over 300 foods and beverages, including tamales, tortillas, arepas, and whiskey.

Red flint corn, photo by Nat Harry.

POX

There aren't many maize-based spirits that originate from Mesoamerica, but Pox (pronounced *posh*) stands out as an exception. Made by the Tzotzil Maya using a combination of maize, wheat, and/or sugarcane/cane syrup (and sometimes all three), this distilled spirit blends Maya and Spanish Catholic methods and ingredients into a synthesized beverage that dates back as far as Mezcal (see the chapter on agave) and the introduction of Spanish distillation technology to Mesoamerica.

Used by the Maya people in ceremonies and rituals for the last four hundred years, the word Pox means "medicine" or "healing" in Tzotzil. (The Tzotzil language is still spoken in the Mexican state of Chiapas, where a quarter of the population speaks a Mayan dialect or related

POX

Plant: Blend of grains and cane sugar (or *piloncillo*)

Place: Chiapas, Mexico

Production: Ancestral methods favored by the Tzotzil Maya

Protection: None

language.) As a symbol of Indigenous cultural perseverance, the spirit, which the colonial government once outlawed, can still be seen in semi-autonomous places like the remote town of San Juan Chamula, where *curanderos* (shamans) continue their medicinal and restorative healing practices.

Originally made exclusively from maize as a sort of unaged whiskey, today, Pox is made from an assortment of ingredients. There is no "right way" to make it, and very few production rules exist. Each producer has their recipe, each varying in proof and style. Some producers use sugar cane during fermentation, while others use boiled cane syrup (you'll see similar variations like this in the sugarcane chapter where we discuss Clairin), and still others use *piloncillo* (i.e., blocks of unrefined cane sugar). Occasionally, Pox will be infused with herbs, fruit, or cacao. And while the spirit is relatively unknown outside of Mexico, it has been exported commercially since the early 2000s (though for a while, selling it outside Chiapas was prohibited). In Mexico, Pox's ABV can be as low as 19 percent or as high as 60 percent. However, the little Pox sold in the US—like most spirits—must be at least 40 percent ABV. At present, the spirit remains off most imbibers' radar.

POX

Siglo Cero's Pox is made from 44% heirloom maize (white, red, yellow, and black), 28% wheat, and 28% sugarcane, with fresh cane juice and piloncillo used in the distillation. It's sweet and savory, with notes of green pepper and toasted cornmeal.

For the Adventurous Palate

BOURBON

These days, Bourbon is perhaps the spirit most synonymous with corn. As with most spirits, no one person "invented" Bourbon, though plenty would influence its evolution. The epitome of an American spirit, it's a blend of Old and New World ingredients that, much like its birthplace, combines the knowledge and influence of a diverse range of people.

Compared to other corn-based spirits, Bourbon is just a baby. In fact, the laws defining it weren't codified by Congress until 1964. It took some time for colonists to distill corn in the first place, though a few in 1600s Virginia dabbled with it. The main reason for Bourbon's delayed takeoff was that the taste of corn distillate was considered too "aggressive." So, the settlers favored what they already knew: rum and brandy—ironic considering rum (nicknamed "Kill Devil") had a reputation for lacking subtlety and finesse.

BOURBON

Plant: Minimum 51% Corn (usually hard types like dent or flint) plus other cereal grains

Place: United States

Production: Any still type

Protection: Federally protected standard of identity (US)

By the time Europeans began settling the Kentucky "frontier" (in the early 1770s), they would have encountered lots and lots of corn. This access, combined with the fact that distilling was a common skill in the average homesteader's toolbox, led to an increase in corn distillation. By the 1820s, the word "Bourbon" came to mean whiskey from the Kentucky county of Bourbon, which was named after the dynastic family line, the House of Bourbon, in gratitude for King Louis XVI's assistance during the Revolutionary War.

Some of the first official Bourbon distilleries, like Buffalo Trace and Jim Beam, are still the biggest names in the category today—similar to the current landscape of Cognac and the "big four" (see the chapter on grapes). For example, Buffalo Trace—situated on the banks of Kentucky's Ohio River—was founded in 1775. At that time, the distillery shipped barrels down the river to New Orleans, a trip that could take weeks or months, allowing for a bit of aging to occur along the way.

Of course, this is just one aspect of Bourbon's history. Another, vital part, is how it was made (i.e., human labor). While written documentation on the topic is sparse, most, if not all, Antebellum Bourbon distilleries used slave labor, both in the field and in the distillery. In the 1830s, 28 percent of white Kentucky families held people in bondage; in Woodford County, home of the Oscar Pepper distillery (now Woodford Reserve), there were more enslaved people than free citizens. Oscar

106   SPIRITS DISTILLED

Pepper himself enslaved twenty-three people and trained at least one of them, a man named Albert, to fill the role of assistant distiller. As is the case with so many things we enjoy today, it's important to remember and respect the contribution of all and acknowledge that, for some, there was little agency or choice in the matter.

What's a Mash Bill?

The term "mash bill" gets thrown around a lot in American whiskey chatter, so it's good to have a little primer if you're just getting into the category. Simply put, a *mash bill* is the mix, or recipe, of different grains used to make whiskey, while the *mash* itself is a soupy mixture of milled grains, water, and yeast. Today, the term is used almost exclusively in American whiskey production, as mixed grains have been the norm for the category since colonial times, unlike most other modern styles of whiskey made outside of the US, like Scotch or Irish whiskey, which tend to be made either from a single grain or a blend of grains using separate distillates. But today's mash bill isn't just a hodgepodge of grains tossed together—each one plays a specific role.

By law, Bourbon *must* have a mash bill of at least 51 percent corn. The rest of the mash can consist of other grains—typically rye and barley for spice and mouthfeel (as well as for barley's enzymatic properties), and sometimes wheat for texture (these Bourbons are often called "wheaters"). Unless touted as "high rye" (which is exactly what it sounds like), most Bourbon mash bills will go well above the minimum percentage of corn, to sometimes as high as 65 or 70 percent. If you only remember one rule about Bourbon, remember that corn is king.

Most Bourbon distilleries make a specific house style of mash bill—that is, they strive toward a particular profile in their recipe. Some larger distillers will have more than one mash bill, such as Jim Beam, who makes both high- and low-rye Bourbon, and Buffalo Trace, who makes several brands on their massive campus but keeps the details of their mash bills close to the chest.

Sweet vs. Sour Mash

The difference between sweet mash and sour mash is akin to the difference between a loaf of sourdough from a starter vs. a loaf of plain white bread. Sour mash has long been the default for most Kentucky-made Bourbons and Tennessee whiskeys and involves the distiller leaving some of the mash behind from the most recent batch before adding the next. Before the implementation of sanitary processes, this practice helped regulate the mash's pH and ward off unwanted bacteria that could spoil the whiskey. It also aids in maintaining consistency between batches.

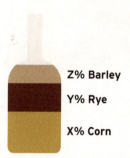

Z% Barley
Y% Rye
X% Corn

Producer	Spirit	% Corn	% Rye	% Barley	% Wheat
Maker's Mark	Bourbon	70	0	14	16
George Dickel	Tennessee Whiskey	84	8	8	0
Jim Beam	Bourbon	63	27	10	0
Wilderness Trail	Bourbon	64	12	0	24
Laws	Bourbon	60	10	10	20

Mash bills from American whiskey distilleries.

Not Your Grandpa's Whiskey

There's no shortage of Bourbon labels touting their "great-granpappy's recipe" passed down for generations. And while the mash bill proportions may not have changed, the ingredients sure have. Surprisingly, the food we grow evolves quickly, with different varieties and hybrids jockeying for the spotlight. The Yellow dent corn used by distillers just 5–10 years ago is different from what's used today and vastly different from what was used 50 years ago before the rise of GMOs. I have a bottle of W.L. Weller 12 Year I've been nursing for some time. I probably bought it close to a decade ago, and I swear, this bottling is rounder, sweeter, and more nuanced than any W.L. Weller 12 Year I've had since. So, start comparing the same bottles you drink over time (keeping in mind that oxygen will also play a role in changing the flavors)—if it seems like they've evolved or taste a little different, you might be right.

Yellow dent corn, photo by Nat Harry.

Lend Me Your Ears

Imagine if every restaurant could only cook with four ingredients, and they bought their ingredients from the same place. Sounds uninspired, doesn't it? Of course, you can use seasonings, but at the end of the day, the chef is working with a limited range. That's basically the current state of American whiskey. Sure, it's delicious, but there's a cap on what it can achieve, and it starts with the main ingredient—corn.

Corn is generally divided into six main types: dent, flint, flour, popping, sweet, and waxy. In the world of distilling, we deal almost exclusively with dent corn, a hard, dimpled variety very different from the kind you'd eat straight off the grill (that's sweet corn, and it accounts for less than 1 percent of corn crops). In fact, almost all of the corn grown in the US (which is overwhelmingly dent corn) isn't the kind humans typically eat at all, at least not fresh. If we do consume dent corn, it's in processed items like tortilla chips, breakfast cereals, grits, or cornmeal, all of which require additional steps to make the variety digestible and palatable.

While the US grows an enormous amount of corn (it's the world's largest single-country producer, growing 30 percent of the world's corn on roughly 400,000 farms), consumers don't have many choices on the commercial market. By now, this statement is unlikely to surprise you. Farmers today aren't as incentivized for crop variety as they are for yield, and this seems especially true for corn. Dr. Rob Arnold, author of *The Terroir of Whiskey*, believes that "flavor is not a reward for farmers, if anything, diversity became a nuisance." So, how did US-grown corn get so . . . boring?

Three major factors led to today's monotonous landscape: seed catalogs, Prohibition, and industrialization. In the US, up until the 1880s, farmers depended on landraces. They would propagate them, save their seeds, and trade them with other farmers at agricultural fairs—and where there was farmland of any kind, there were distilleries. According to Arnold, this meant that "whiskeys made from [landraces or local heirloom grains] would have carried the signature of terroir." While seed catalogs initially expanded agricultural possibilities, their widespread adoption changed how farmers sourced their seeds, eventually reducing the varieties grown throughout the country.

Landraces

A *landrace* is a domesticated crop that takes on specific characteristics as it adapts to its location or environment over time, like drought resistance or putting down sturdier roots in windy areas. Landraces differ from hybrids in that the method of selection is less formal, typically occurring over generations as farmers pick and choose the traits that work for their farms. They aren't quite the same as heirlooms either, which lack connection to a specific region.

USDA Grain Standards

The USDA's grain standards and quality grading system also contribute to the limited selection of corn varieties on the market today. Corn and wheat are graded on a scale of 1 to 5, with 1 being the highest and most valuable. The assessment considers the presence of foreign materials (bits that aren't corn), broken kernels, mold, and heat damage. According to Arnold, after grading by the USDA, "regardless of terroir—regardless of the variety or farm—a load of Grade 2 yellow dent corn is interchangeable with all other Grade 2 yellow dent corn loads." And that overgeneralization is how grades are treated by the majority of the American whiskey industry (though we'll see examples of how those attitudes are gradually changing).

Prohibition was the next critical blow, outlawing homestead liquor distillation, transportation, and sale and cleaving off a crucial secondary source of income for farmers. In effect for thirteen years before it was repealed in 1933, the legislation uncoupled the dual role of farmer and spirit producer (common at the time). Then came industrialization. Grain elevators, improved transportation, and synthetic fertilizers, combined with crop hybridization, made growing fewer types of corn *very* efficient, so much so that corn surpluses were turned into animal feed, which led to a boom in the meat industry and further entrenchment of a few varieties.

So, if we recognize the connection between a spirit's ingredients and its quality/flavor (as we do with grapes for brandy and agave for Mezcal), then why is corn treated as an afterthought in the Bourbon world? Why aren't more producers wielding their buying power to promote a better base for their distillate? After all, corn is the star of the Bourbon show; the entire category is built around it. Distillers tinker with mash bill, yeast strain, barrel size, and char type (see the chapter on wood), but the corn largely remains the same.

Cows, Pigs, and Genetically Modified Whiskey

In the late 19th century, Iowa teacher and agronomist P.G. Holden was so enthusiastic about maize that he created and promoted "corn shows"—essentially, beauty pageants for corn. In 1893, Holden, who had a penchant for pretty corn with long ears, awarded the grand prize at that year's World's Fair in Chicago to a hybrid called Reid's Yellow Dent. It was a cross between Gordon Hopkins, a reddish dent strain popular in Virginia, and Little Yellow, a landrace flint strain grown for centuries by Native Americans in the Northeast. This hybrid field corn would take the farming world by storm, becoming the most commonly grown variety in the US. But it wasn't grown for flavor.

I've mentioned that most of the corn produced in the US isn't bound for our plates (only about 15 percent of what's grown is consumed by humans). Most US-grown corn is turned into animal feed, the majority of which is genetically modified, a point of contention among a growing chorus of farmers and conservationists. Unfortunately, when sourcing corn, most large distilleries—the ones that make your recognizable brands of whiskey—are just following in the wake of the animal agriculture industry's choices. And these distilleries source *a lot* of corn, with the biggest ones consuming acres daily. Gary Hinegardner, an agronomist-turned-distiller, noted how frustrating this can be. "We're not even in charge of our main ingredient," the heirloom corn advocate told me, referring to the Bourbon industry.

While cows and pigs won't be leaving one-star reviews for their meals, the reliance on GM corn impacts the quality of corn-based spirits. Commercially introduced in the mid-1990s, GM corn rapidly won favor with large-scale farmers partly because of its ability to fight off a microorganism called *Bacillus thuringiensis*, or "Bt." The goal was that Bt-corn would, with its own built-in insecticide protein, "selectively" kill European corn borer larvae before they could become crop-damaging caterpillars. Though there was (and still is) concern about the threat of Bt-corn to non-target insects (such as several types of moths and, notably, Monarch butterflies), it was approved for use by the EPA in 1995. Fast forward to the present, and corn is one of the most GMO-dominant crops in the US.

Most major US whiskey distilleries use whatever corn gets delivered regardless of its GM status, focusing on grade above all else, which makes sense because, as of 2022, 92 percent of US-grown corn is genetically modified. Brown-Forman, the owner of Jack Daniel Distillery and Woodford Reserve, switched to non-GMO corn in the early aughts but changed back in 2014, releasing the following statement: "A rapidly shrinking supply of non-GMO corn in North America is making it increasingly more difficult to sustainably source the quantity of high-quality corn required for our Bourbons and whiskeys. . . . In light of no genetic material making it through the distillation process and into our whiskey, our desire not to add to our carbon footprint by sourcing non-

Gold Rush

A modern classic, this whiskey sour variation is simple and balanced.

- **2 oz. Elijah Craig Bourbon (originally made with 12 Year)**
- **1 oz. fresh lemon juice**
- **¾ oz. honey syrup**

Shake all ingredients with ice, about 20–30 seconds. Strain into a double rocks glass over fresh ice.

(recipe by T.J. Siegal, Milk and Honey, circa 2000)

GMO corn from more distant locations, and the long-term trend toward decreasing availability of non-GMO corn in North America, Brown-Forman has made the decision to use GMO corn in our distilleries."

Of course, some buck the trend. Buffalo Trace, Four Roses, and Wild Turkey all quietly purchase the harder-to-come-by and more expensive non-GMO grain. Smaller whiskey producers like Willet Distillery also skip the GMOs because they don't want GM grain going back to the livestock (many distilleries recycle their spent grain as animal feed). Some grow their own grains, like Michter's, a former contract-distilled brand (see sidebar) that now runs two brick-and-mortar facilities and plants non-GMO grains on 200+ acres of farmland in Springfield, Kentucky. Of course, any certified organic whiskey will be free from GMOs (see Introduction), but there's no labeling currently required by the TTB regarding GMOs.

Of all the elements that affect whiskey, the raw material should be the most important to invest in, grow, and diversify. But with the dominance of big agriculture, that is easier said than done. One would think that with the sheer acreage of corn purchased by high-production distilleries, they would have the leverage to source or command a better type of corn, and they might, but doing so is a financial gamble. Why pay more for a grain if the public is already satisfied with the product? It's the good old "if it ain't broke, don't fix it" approach. Hinegardner knows this challenge well and admits it was difficult to get farms to work with his distillery, so the first thing he did (before even setting up a still) was plant twelve acres of heirloom corn varieties on the property, including Missouri Shoepeg, Bloody Butcher, and Hopi Blue. By 2021, he was growing 129 different corn varieties, and the farmland attached to the distillery had become an agricultural research station in coordination with the USDA. Hinegardner now works closely with local farmers and uses roughly sixty-five acres of corn per year at his whiskey distillery, Wood Hat, showing that distillers can successfully gamble on heritage corn and variety.

Contract Distilling: MGP, Yea You Know Me

If you're stuck in a room full of whiskey nerds (yikes, sorry!), you'll hear the acronym "MGP" casually mentioned quite often. Formerly called LDI—for Lawrenceburg Distillers Indiana (and sometimes still used interchangeably with it)—MGP stands for Midwest Grain Products. As contract distillers, they make spirits for many brands that lack a brick-and-mortar space. Still something of an open secret, contract distillers like MGP play a significant role in the American spirits industry. It's highly likely one of your favorite brands is made at an MGP distillery, as over the years, they've distilled for over 130 labels. One way to see if MGP makes your whiskey is to check the label, which might read something like, "Produced/distilled in Indiana and bottled in Kentucky." Of course, the most important question to ask yourself is, "Does it taste good?"

Whiskey Sisters Supply

Felicia and Stephanie Ohnmacht, founders of Whiskey Sisters Supply, are helping distilleries reconnect with the farms in their home state of Colorado by buying raw grain directly from the source—the Ohnmacht's family farm. The idea for the business was the result of pure happenstance. In 2015, Stephanie, whose family owns a 2,000-acre farm that grows corn and other grains, attended a spirits tasting at Laws Whiskey House in Denver. At the time, Stephanie and her sister, Felicia, had separate careers in the corporate sector, but when Stephanie learned that Laws Whiskey House needed a corn supplier, she mentioned her family's farm, and the connection was made.

Like many small farms, theirs struggled to make ends meet (this struggle is often the reason many independent farmers eventually fold and sell to big agriculture). And yet, it took some convincing for their family to get on board with the proposal. The elders of the Ohnmacht family ran a dry household. Grandpa was a teetotaler, and they'd grown up without alcohol in the house, so the whiskey business wasn't exactly on their "Save the Farm" bingo card. However, after some convincing and a successful trial run, the partnership with Laws Whiskey House proved to be a viable source of income. The Ohnmacht sisters went on to create a sustainable business using nothing but word of mouth and reputation.

Despite challenges, including rising temperatures, drought, and the loss of local aquifers, the Ohnmacht family prevails by investing in and honoring the land. For example, they practice no-till farming to avoid disrupting the soil's microorganisms and releasing carbon into the atmosphere. Furthermore, rather than treating every acre the same, they zone sample the soil and monitor nitrogen levels so each area gets the right amount of fertilizer and water. This tailored approach isn't just good for

The Grand Chawhee

A cross between a Mint Julep and a Kentucky Buck, using Fernet Leopold's Highland Amaro is key here for the fresh mint profile.

- 2 oz. bourbon (90 to 100 proof)
- ½ oz. fresh lime juice
- ½ oz. simple or gomme syrup
- ½ oz. Fernet Leopold
- 2–3 oz. Q Mixers ginger beer
- 2 dashes Angostura bitters

Shake all ingredients (with ice) except ginger beer. Strain into a tall Collins glass over fresh ice. Top with ginger beer and garnish with a mint leaf or sprig.

(original recipe)

> the soil; it's also good for the wallet, as it prevents the overuse of resources.
>
> The sisters meet specific customer demands by growing heirloom and specialty grains like millet and triticale for particular batches. They also connect distillers to local farmers, acting as brokers for the raw ingredients of whiskey (namely corn, but also wheat and rye). This intentional grain-to-glass model can be a boon for smaller distilleries and a lifeline for small family farms. Not only does it ensure that a farm's crop will be sold, but the farmers also retain a deeper connection to their harvest—it doesn't just go to a processing plant or packing warehouse. A farmer can trace their hard work to the end of the line: a whiskey made from their grain.

Change is Coming

The good news is that attitudes toward corn by distillers are changing slowly but surely. Whether it be planting a few acres of corn themselves, experimenting with a new varietal in a mash bill, or seeking partnerships with local farmers, spirit makers are beginning to gamble on consumer palates. These days, you can find a variety of heirloom corn Bourbons at your local store, and more are coming down the pipeline.

In Petaluma, California, Spirit Works Distilling is focusing on sustainability and has moved to sourcing the raw ingredients for their core spirits line to within 100 miles of the distillery. In 2023, Spirit Works began experimenting with different corn varieties, including red and blue—and immediately noticed a difference. Distiller and production manager Tyler Burke said the following, "In both the fermentations and distillations, our blue corn had a beautiful berry fruit character. It was very pronounced. The red corn, on the other hand, started out with

---

Bottled-in-Bond

The Bottled-in-Bond Act of 1897 was introduced to improve the quality of whiskey and protect consumer health. Before its introduction, there was little industry oversight. Corners were frequently cut, and neutral grain spirits and other cheap distillates were often colored with whatever was on hand, from tobacco to iodine. The law required that bonded spirits come from a single distillation season and from one distiller; that it be bottled and stored in bonded warehouses under US government supervision for a minimum of 4 years; and that it be bottled at no less than 100 proof. Though today we have other standards to manage quality control and customer safety, Bottled-in-Bond brandy and whiskies are still made, though mostly as a nod to the past.

an almost smoky Mezcal quality during the distillation, which settled into a wonderfully complex, rounded Bourbon."

A few acres here and there start to add up. Buffalo Trace started an heirloom corn program after acquiring nearly 300 acres of farmland in 2015 and plans to release an estate whiskey in the future. They've grown a different varietal each year since launching the program, starting with Boone County white corn, an heirloom dating back to 1876. High Wire distilling in Charleston, South Carolina, has been using Jimmy Red corn in their Bourbon, working for the last nine years to rebuild a reliable seed supply for the future. And Widow Jane Distillery in New York is moving toward making a permanent addition to its whiskey line with a hybrid called Baby Jane, a cross between two heirloom varieties: Bloody Butcher and Wapsie. Meanwhile, the Whiskey Sisters in Colorado offer a blue and red varietal alongside their Grade 1 yellow dent. Acre by acre, the landscape is changing.

Red and purple corn, photo by Nat Harry.

KENTUCKY STRAIGHT BOURBON

♦

Many large whiskey distilleries make a wide variety of products, but Maker's Mark still relies on its flagship Bourbon. This easy-to-drink wheated mash bill remains the company's bread and butter, and even their other bottlings, such as the Cask Strength and Maker's 46, use this same base whiskey.

Tried and True

EAGLE RARE 10 YEAR

♦

When you get down to it, Buffalo Trace Distillery operates like a manufacturing plant; it has automated systems, huge continuous stills that run 24 hours a day, and a campus the size of a small village. This 10 Year (from their brand Eagle Rare) uses non-GMO corn and is a versatile bottle for sipping and mixing.

Big Industry That Gets It Right

SMALL BATCH SELECT KENTUCKY STRAIGHT BOURBON

♦

Four Roses uses 2 mash bills and 5 different yeasts at their distillery, resulting in 10 recipe combinations. Their 104-proof Small Batch Select Bourbon is a blend of recipes that are aged 6–7 years. It is a great intermediate whiskey, offering plenty of spice.

Non-GMO / Still Under the Radar

KENTUCKY STRAIGHT WHEATED BOURBON

♦

While the founders of Wilderness Trail once focused on the yeast side of the whiskey business, they now make their own line of rye and Bourbon from locally grown grains. Their small batch, bottled-in-bond Bourbon is aged 5-6 years and blended in 18-barrel lots. It's grain-forward with a long finish.

Next Generation

STRAIGHT BOURBON WHISKEY

♦

This "whiskey farm," run by 5th-generation farmers, is a hefty 1,500 acres. Using homegrown grains (including non-GMO corn and two-row barley malted on site), their flagship four-grain Bourbon is a balanced, grain-forward whiskey.

Farm Distillery

FOUR GRAIN STRAIGHT BOURBON

♦

Sourcing only Colorado grains and working closely with family farms like the Ohnmacht's, Laws Whiskey House uses heritage corn and wheat and an open-air mash, allowing native yeasts to interact with the whiskey. This bottle is heavy-handed with notes of brown sugar, candied orange peel, and tannic black tea.

A Sense of Place

CORN WHISKEY

Corn whiskey, like rye, is one of the oldest styles of whiskey in the US. Though unlike rye, it remains an underdog that's largely been neglected by "serious" whiskey drinkers. This is because historically, most corn whiskeys were unaged—intended to be drunk right off the still—and relatively high in ABV, giving them the moniker "white lightning" and the reputation as paint-thinning moonshine. However, these days, corn whiskey looks much more like Bourbon, at least from a distance.

Defined by the TTB as having a minimum of 80 percent corn in the mash, corn whiskeys are their own distinct category. One of the rules governing their production is the prohibition of charred oak during aging, which allows the grain to shine through. As a result, it's an excellent place for consumers and distillers alike to explore the potential flavors maize has to offer, which is why it's the first style many distillers use in their heirloom corn experiments. The lack of charred oak aging also means corn whiskey is free to reveal a wide variety of flavor profiles—from butterscotch candy and caramel popcorn to meaty umami—without interference from the strong flavors of the barrel's char.

Because corn provides a hefty dose of natural sugars to the mash bill, you'll find these whiskeys to be on the sweeter side, lingering on the front palate. They're gaining popularity among whiskey aficionados, and I believe we're about to see a corn whiskey renaissance in the coming years thanks to the budding grain-to-glass revival and varietal-focused outlook on the category.

CORN WHISKEY

Plant: Minimum 80% corn

Place: Anywhere

Production: Any still type

Protection: Federally protected standard of identity (US)

CORN

Destilería y Bodega Abasolo

While there's not much corn whiskey made in Mexico currently, that is poised to change, thanks in part to Destilería y Bodega Abasolo. As one of the highest elevation distilleries in the world, it's perched at 7,800 ft. above sea level in the city of Jilotepec de Molina Enríquez—about 2 hours north of Mexico City. (Keep in mind higher elevations are not uncommon in Mexico, and many *palenques* [Mezcal distilleries] in Oaxaca are situated 4,000-6,000 ft. above sea level.) It may seem like an odd place to find a whiskey distillery, but Jilotepec—Nahuatl for a "place of the tender corn"—is the perfect spot for such an endeavor. The area is rich in agricultural history, with the distillery founded on land previously used for farming and drying maize. Additionally, the owners restored many of the original buildings on the property—including a stable and storage cellar—intending to revitalize the area and keep tradition alive.

Their corn whiskey is made from a 100% heirloom varietal called Cacahuazintle. Similar to hominy, Cacahuazintle is often used in *pozole* (a traditional soup/stew) and cornbread. However, in this case, the large kernels are dried in the field on the stalk, and the *wort* (i.e., the sweet liquid extracted from the mashing process) is nixtamalized, dried, and ground in a tortilla mill. A portion of the Cacahuazintle is also malted. Destilería y Bodega Abasolo doesn't just make corn whiskey; it also produces a *licor de elote* (corn liquor) called Nixta, made by macerating the Cacahuazintle in a corn distillate (double the corn!) and then sweetening it with a clarified wort made from ripe Cacahuazintle kernels.

Yellow dent corn growing near Wood Hat Spirits in Missouri, photo by Nat Harry.

White dent (food grade)

STILL AND BARREL PROOF KENTUCKY STRAIGHT CORN WHISKEY

The folks at MB Roland are nowhere near the Kentucky Bourbon Trail, but they do make a mighty fine spirit. Their corn whiskey is made with 95% food-grade white corn (the same kind you'd mill into grits) grown locally in Christian County. It offers notes of salted kettle corn, roasted peanuts, and tahini.

The Proof is in the Glass

Bloody Butcher

CASK STRENGTH BLOODY BUTCHER CORN WHISKEY

Wood Hat's cask strength corn whiskey, made with Bloody Butcher red corn, is aged in Chinkapin white oak (*Quercus muehlenbergii*) in warehouses fashioned from box cars. This is a big flex of a whiskey—the Chinkapin oak is earthy, the corn is meaty, and the ABV is a whopping 62.8%.

A Sense of Place

Blue flint

BABY BLUE CORN WHISKY

Made from a hybridized Blue flint corn grown in West Texas (typically used to make tortillas and chips), the kernels used in this whisky are roasted, adding a nutty, vegetal flavor. It's a rich dram bursting with caramel corn and buttery toffee.

Trailblazers

Rotating selection of heirloom corn

MODERN ANCIENT GRAINS PROJECT

This bottling offers a rotating collection of whiskeys made from heirloom grain varietals and sustainably-farmed ingredients. Batches are very small, and notable expressions include a corn whiskey made of 100% Bolita Belatove—a nearly extinct pink varietal grown in Oaxaca.

Worth the Splurge

Blend of heritage corn (black, purple, yellow, and red)

OAXACAN BLACK CORN WHISKEY

Distilled by Douglas French—best known for his brand Scorpion Mezcal—the corn for this bottling is dried on the stalk and hand-picked and shucked by local farmers. The black corn is earthy and savory, lending the bottle notes of baking spice and even a bit of banana bread.

Funky but Cool

Yellow Dent

MELLOW CORN

Light, playful, and fun in cocktails, this bottling is ideal for a flask or to take camping. With its retro label and pale-yellow liquid, you may feel some uncertainty at first sight, but this corn whiskey is a favorite among bartenders for its pleasant sweetness and inexpensive price point.

Tried and True

RYE
&
WHEAT

I remember first reading about rye whiskey in the up-and-coming cocktail and drinks magazine Imbibe back in 2007 when I was a young bartender. At the time, the only rye whiskey I could get my hands on in the small, upstate New York town where I lived was a bottle of Old Overholt, and while it's one of the oldest brands of rye whiskey, it's not the sort of bottle that will knock your socks off. Fast forward to today, and visiting a whiskey specialty shop may provoke choice paralysis. Talk about a revival.

Rye (Secale cereale), or winter rye, is a grass, meaning it's a member of the Poaceae family, and as a close relative of barley and wheat, it also belongs to the Triticeae sub-family. Historically, it's been an underdog in the world of grains. Not adopted quite as readily by early Neolithic cultivators as its cereal siblings, rye snuck into the agriculture party as a weed. (It shows up in trace amounts in archaeological contexts alongside wheat and barley as early as 11,000 years ago.) By nature, weeds have a strong survival instinct and are skilled at adaptation, undergoing genetic shifts that deter their eradication. Essentially, unruly rye kept showing up in early agricultural fields until it, too, was discovered to be a useful grain several millennia later. Rye is nothing if not persistent.

RYE

Rye's long existence as a wild, foraged grass has made its taxonomy difficult to nail down. Typically, humans select favorable qualities in plant cultivation over time. Scientists are then able to determine a domestication timeline by observing these shifts. But because rye essentially adapted itself (indirectly via the domestication of other related crops), it's nearly impossible to tell the difference between wild and domesticated species. While today rye is often associated with Eastern European baking and American whiskey, the crop originated in Southwestern Asia, where it was likely first domesticated around 6000 BCE from the wild species *Secale vavilovii*. Other wild species, such as *Secale montanum*, native to high-elevation areas like Turkey and northern Iran, are thought to never have been domesticated and still grow alongside their domesticated siblings.

By about 600 BCE, rye was commonly grown across the Balkans and Central Europe, though it was primarily planted as a "starvation" crop for when times were tough. But ever-determined, it continued tagging along with other crops like wheat (some wild varieties were even mistaken for wheat) and barley, proving itself time and time again, until farmers finally took notice.

Today, rye is widely recognized as a beneficial grain. In addition to being a valuable product, it is also a vital cover crop, as it preserves nutrients in the soil, particularly nitrogen; prevents erosion with its extremely deep roots that can penetrate the soil at a depth of over four feet (or one and a half meters); outcompetes (other) weeds; requires about 30 percent less water than wheat; discourages some pests; and is exceptionally cold-hearty (winter rye varieties can germinate at temperatures in the low thirties Fahrenheit). It is also used for grazing, and the straw can be used for livestock bedding, thatching, paper, and even particle board. Naturally a favorite in colder northern latitude regions, rye is most commonly grown in the EU, Russia, Belarus, Ukraine, and Canada.

Roggenbier

While not nearly as popular as barley, malted rye can be used to make beer and was widely used in Bavarian brewing to make *roggenbier,* or "rye beer" (usually made with 60% rye malt). However, this changed in 1516, when the German *Reinheitsgebot,* commonly known in English as the German Beer Purity Law, formally regulated the ingredients used in brewing after a series of poor harvests led to a shortage of rye and wheat for bakers. As a result, rye would be reserved for bread, and only barley, water, and hops were allowed in beer.

RYE WHISKEY

In the wake of Bourbon's increasing popularity, some misconceptions have followed, including the idea that Bourbon was America's "original spirit." Setting aside applejack, the first spirit produced in the US (see the chapter on apples), rye was the plant that got the whiskey party started, and not just as a supporting actor in a mash bill—the first recorded whiskey made in the American colonies was in 1640, and it was made of rye. As one of the first distillates made by colonial farm distillers, rye whiskey, as a category, actually predates Bourbon by several decades! That said, it wasn't too long ago that this truly American spirit was on the verge of extinction.

Though rye whiskey is predominantly associated with British America's original thirteen colonies (and sometimes Canada), German and Dutch distillation practices created the foundation for its legacy. This influence is documented in correspondences like a 1648 letter found by drinks historian David Wondrich in which the Massachusetts colony requests "the German receipt [recipe] for making strong water with rye meal." By that time, rye had been a staple of Germany's agricultural landscape since the medieval period and was a popular grain used for bread flour—while the Dutch used rye combined with malted barley as the base for their Holland-style gin (the predecessor of genever gin).

The Rise and Fall of American Rye

In 1776 America, successful agriculture and cattle breeding ventures were still mostly trial by fire, meaning the livestock business was often a losing investment, and a cruel one at that. It was commonplace to grow crops on a single parcel of land until it went fallow and then move on to the next parcel. This practice eventually rendered soil dead and useless, a reality that would later be exemplified by the entirely

---

RYE WHISKEY

Plant: 51% minimum rye plus other grains

Place: Anywhere

Production: Any still type

Protection: Federally protected US standard of identity

Genever

The predecessor to modern gin, the Dutch spirit genever (juh-*nee*-vur), was developed for medicinal purposes and macerated with various botanicals, most notably juniper. Genever, made with a portion of "malt wine," has been given a new lease on life in the classic cocktail revival of the last few decades. Malt wine is essentially a white whiskey. It is distilled 3 times and is distinct in that it lacks the neutrality of gin or vodka. Today, genever is typically a blend of malt wine and a more neutral, column distilled spirit, tempering the intense flavors of the grain.

human-made disaster we now call the Dust Bowl (during the Great Depression to boot).

During this period of early settlement, much of the colonists' starchy diet came from a mix of American and European crops like corn and potatoes and rye and barley, respectively. After much trial and error, rye became the most widely grown grain in the newly established US. It succeeded in places where wheat had failed, particularly in sandy and acidic soils. In the tobacco-growing states of Virginia and Maryland, rye actually improved the soil quality and subsequent tobacco harvest when grown as a rotation crop. In arid regions, its hearty root system made it drought-resistant, and in the Northeast, its cold tolerance was even more impressive than barley's.

At this time, the fruits of the earth were consumed not far from where they were grown. In "The Rise and Fall of Rye," the late whiskey icon and distiller Dave Pickerell wrote, "Since the distillery was essentially a piece of farm equipment, it should be no surprise that by the late 1700s, there were literally thousands of small grain distilleries." This number continued to grow, and it's estimated that from 1810 to 1840, between 14,000 and 20,000 stills were in operation. With the large-scale transportation of grain and other goods by railway still far off, distillation also offered convenience. For example, when the Scotch and Irish farmers of Western Pennsylvania wanted to barter their surplus grain, they had to trek over the Allegheny mountains via horse or mule. Each animal could carry only four bushels, a severe limitation. But distilled into whiskey, they could transport exponentially more. An unknown farmer quoted in Benson John Lossing's *History of American Industries and Arts* recalled the journey, saying: "Many a horse was seen going eastward over the [Alleghenies], with twenty-five bushels of rye on his back."

So, with all this going for it, what put the nail in the rye whiskey coffin? Rye began to fade into the background as a staple crop as access to other agriculture-producing regions grew. The arrival of wheat shipments

---

Kvass

No beer, no problem! A bit of rye bread can be used to make *kvass*, a fermented beverage dating back to at least 989 CE in Russia. (Linguistically, the word *kvass* may have many antecedents, including the Sumerian word *KAŠ*, meaning "emmer beer.") Long associated with the lower classes, commercially produced kvass is now lumped into the health food and soda market as it has a low alcohol content and is rich in Vitamin B (think kombucha and other probiotic and naturally carbonated beverages).

Merced rye from Corbin Cash's farm distillery, photo by Nat Harry.

Earl Brown with Merced rye from his family's ranch, at Wright & Brown Distilling Co., photo by Nat Harry.

via railroad, along with shifting agricultural practices brought about by modernizations such as the grain elevator, decreased its demand. However, it would continue to find success via farm distilleries until Prohibition, when distilleries were shuttered en masse (save for those able to secure a medicinal license, akin to today's cannabis laws).

When distilleries finally opened again, aged whiskey stocks were perilously low, and most American distillers had a tough time competing with the literal boatloads of imports waiting for repeal day on the shores. Additionally, by the end of Prohibition, American tastes had changed considerably. Due to its often intense, spice-forward flavor profile, rye wasn't embraced as readily as corn-forward Bourbon or European brandy.

In recent decades, we've seen rye reverse course, coming back from near eradication and becoming a burgeoning American category. So, how did it happen? A significant factor is the influence of bartenders and bar programs. The end of the aughts marked the start of a major craft cocktail movement in the US, and all boozy boats would rise with the tide. Additionally, in 2006, a relatively unknown rye whiskey called Rittenhouse 100 Proof won Top North American Whiskey and a Double Gold medal at the San Francisco Spirits Competition, rocketing the once overlooked thirteen-dollar bottle to immediate cult status for only a modest jump in price. The following year, rye whiskey options grew by 30 percent. From there, rye whiskey gradually got back on track, picking up momentum at the decade's end to the point that between 2009 and 2015, consumer sales skyrocketed a mind-boggling 600 percent.

Rye Whiskey Mash Bills and Styles

Rye whiskey mash bills are a reverse mirror of Bourbon; rather than containing a minimum of 51 percent corn, they must contain a minimum of 51 percent rye. As with Bourbon, the rest of the mash bill can be made up of other grains—typically, barley or corn, though some distillers boast high-rye mash bills that are 95 percent or even 100 percent rye. But is having more rye in the mash bill a sign of a "better" rye whiskey? Not necessarily. The answer is subjective and depends on what you want from the drinking experience.

Historically, popular rye whiskey regions in the US developed their own particular style, and while no official definitions of these styles were ever formalized, each has a distinct personality. Despite the diversity, one thing remains true across styles: rye carries a spice-forward profile that adds a peppery or grassy note compared to its cereal siblings.

Maryland Rye

Historically known as "Maryland Whiskey," this rye whiskey style originated with Irish Catholic settlers and was often distilled three

---

Pentosan

Rye is a notoriously fussy grain for distillers because it contains additional starches, including *pentosan*, that other grains don't have. This is great for baking but not so much for distilling. Pentosan results in more water retention, increasing viscosity and making it difficult to drain solids when making beer. These extra starches also lead to production issues like foaming, which can cause distillation equipment to malfunction.

Producer	Spirit	% Rye	% Corn	% Barley	% Wheat
FEW Spirits	Rye	70	20	10	16
Rittenhouse	Rye	51	37	12	0
Wilderness Trail	Rye	56	33	11	0
MGP	Rye	95	0	5	24

Mash bills from American whiskey distilleries.

times, as was customary with Irish whiskey. As the name implies, rye was the primary grain, along with a healthy dose of corn (to soften the profile). A third grain, such as malted barley, was also likely used. Compared to Pennsylvania rye, Maryland rye had a reputation for a sweeter, more subdued profile, and not just from the corn-heavy mash bill or the barrel. Some whiskey historians argue that much of Maryland rye was not the romanticized, farm-to-table product it's remembered as, noting that it was often a *rectified* spirit, that is, blended with a more neutral spirit and enhanced with flavorings like prune juice, Sherry, or port wine. These little tricks would soon be banned, however, by the 1906 Food and Drug Act that gave whiskey its legal definition and put many Maryland rye whiskey brands out of business.

Pennsylvania "Old Monongahela" Rye

Meanwhile, in Western Pennsylvania, colonists had been cooking up their own style of rye whiskey in the Monongahela Valley. Theirs was a high-rye mash bill, commonly four parts rye to one part barley (though sometimes as high as 95 percent rye). In other words, rye played a huge role in the spirit's unique, bold, and spice-driven profile. Using sweet mash, as was typical in the Northeast during this time (unlike the sour mash popular in Kentucky [see the chapter on corn]), each batch of Monongahela rye started with fresh yeast.

In 1780, there were around 5,000 stills in production, and by the late 1800s, Pennsylvania was the largest rye-whiskey-making region in the world! As whiskey production increased, so did the delivery radius, which created longer transportation journeys and inevitable delays that required producers to sit on empty barrels for longer periods of time. This led to some producers "cleaning" emptied barrels by toasting or charring them over open fire to remove any unwanted flavors between uses. "Cleaning" wasn't necessarily a new phenomenon in barrel- and cask-making; however, because a fresh, intense char on a barrel imparts more color to the finished spirit, this is likely how Old Monongahela earned the moniker "Red Whiskey." The purposeful aging of rye whiskey in this manner soon spread to Maryland, where it combined with the rectification practices mentioned earlier.

Toronto Cocktail

A 1920s-era classic cocktail revived by Jamie Boudreau of Seattle bar Canon.

- 2 oz. Canadian rye whisky
- ½ oz. Fernet Branca
- ¼ oz. rich simple or gomme syrup
- 2 dashes Angostura or aromatic bitters

Stir all ingredients in a mixing glass with ice for 20–30 seconds. Strain into a chilled cocktail glass or coupe and garnish with an orange peel (after expressing the oils).

Canadian Rye Whisky

While we often consider rye whiskey a uniquely American spirit, it can technically be made anywhere and be sold as rye, provided the country of origin is stated on the label. This brings us to Canada. At some point, "Canadian whisky" and "rye" became somewhat synonymous, leading to much confusion. While Canada makes plenty of rye whisky, not all Canadian whisky is considered rye or even uses the grain. Initially, whisky distillation in colonial Canada used grain surpluses (mostly wheat), and operations ran on a large scale. However, with a little nudge from their Dutch and German friends, millers discovered that consumers responded well to adding a bit of rye grain, and soon, any Canadian whisky of this type was referred to as a "rye whisky" rather than as "a whisky that has rye in it."

Given the strong association between rye and Canadian whiskey, it seems odd that in Canada today, the standard of identity for whisky, including rye, is rather loose. It need only be made from cereal grains (no specified amount or type listed), aged for a minimum of three years, and "possess the aroma, taste, and character generally attributed to Canadian whisky" (something we can all agree is not particularly helpful). Canadian rye imported to the US, however, must still follow the rules set forth by the TTB, meaning that if "rye" is printed on the label, it must comply with the 51 percent rye rule as well as other listed standards.

The Real Story of George Washington's Distillery

When it comes to issues of heritage, official narratives often overlook the people who played pivotal roles in order to accommodate a privileged few, and spirits distillation is no different. In the spirit of truth and transparency, it's important to remember that enslaved people, predominantly of African descent, were responsible for the upkeep of nearly every aspect of distillation in the US, from the fields to the whiskey production floor and each step in between. For example, the grains for George Washington's Maryland-style rye whiskey (made up of 60 percent rye, 30 percent corn, and 10 percent barley) were farmed and milled on his Mount Vernon plantation. Run by 317 enslaved people, the distillery was the largest spirit producer of any US distillery in the late 1700s, recording 11,000 gallons of spirit sold in 1799, including Maryland-style rye and fruit brandy. Of those enslaved, roughly fifty were trained in a "skilled" trade (as if farm labor is unskilled), among them three coopers who made the whiskey barrels and six distillers who

Close-up of George Green (left) and Jack Daniel (right), circa 1904, photo courtesy of Jack Daniel Distillery.

Nathan Green

Nathan "Nearest" Green is considered the first African American master distiller in the US. After the Civil War, Green was hired as a distiller for the recently opened Jack Daniel Distillery, where he mentored Jasper "Jack" Daniel, teaching him many of the distilling techniques that would help make Daniel's brand a lasting success. However, history would see Green's story fade into the background until, over 125 years later, author Fawn Weaver stumbled upon a photo of Jack Daniel and George Green (Nearest's son). After tireless research and connecting with the Green family, Weaver launched the Nearest Green Foundation and the Nearest Green Distillery to honor Green and his legacy. Today, descendants of Green continue to work at the Jack Daniel Distillery, and in recent years, the the distillery and its brands have found ways to acknowledge and celebrate Green's vital contributions, including supporting the Foundation and collaborating on the Nearest and Jack Advancement Initiative.

likely slept among the sweltering machinery during peak season, as distillation takes hours and runs would have required constant attention.

In sum, Washington's famous rye whiskey was shaped, at every stage, by the many hands held in bondage as they planted the seeds; harvested, threshed, and milled the grain; and toiled in the fields for fourteen hours straight, six days a week, during long summer days when wheat, corn, and rye were harvested. Without the generational knowledge and hard labor of those individuals who suffered and resisted oppression, the current spirits industry would look very different. Moving forward, the industry would do well to remember, respect, listen to, and learn from those whose histories and stories have been lost or overshadowed.

Corbin Cash

David Souza, a 4th-generation farmer-turned-distiller, has roughly 2,000 acres of almonds, sweet potatoes, and rye growing in Atwater, California—a farming town in the San Joaquin Valley named after wheat farmer Marshall Atwater. The raw materials for Corbin Cash's spirits fall into two categories: sweet potatoes (the base of their clear spirits) and rye (grown as a cover crop and distilled for whiskey). While most rye varieties prefer cooler temperatures, Merced rye, an heirloom variety from the county of the same name, likes the California heat just fine. The variety has been grown by Souza's family since 1917, and it appears to be either a landrace or heritage variety unique to Merced County, though it also grows in pockets of Washington and Oregon.

While Merced rye performs well in this warm, dry environment and has a knack for disease resistance, from a modern agricultural standpoint, the grain underperforms due to its comparatively lower starch content and yield. This is true of many heirloom and heritage variety grains (see the chapter on corn). Merced rye's lower starch means less sugar, and less sugar means less alcohol. If you weren't already growing Merced rye for other purposes—in this case, as a cover crop for sweet potatoes—it would be considered a poor investment for a whiskey maker. Luckily, the distillery is a secondary source of income for the working farm, and since they are growing the grain already, distilling it turns a "weed" into a profitable whiskey-destined heritage grain.

STRAIGHT RYE WHISKEY

A combination of unmalted Merced rye grown on the family farm in Humboldt County, malted rye from Germany, and a big helping of malted barley from both Ireland and California gives this whiskey significant structure and balance.

A Well-Traveled Mash Bill

ROKNAR MINNESOTA RYE WHISKEY

Situated on a former wheat field belonging to the Swanson family farm, Far North distills its whiskey using 80% Hazlet Winter rye, 10% heirloom corn, and 10% barley, then ages the spirit in small (15-gallon) barrels before finishing it in Cognac casks.

Farm Distillery

THREE CHAMBER RYE

Todd Leopold's fascination with historical production methods led him to build a special three-chamber still just to make this whiskey historically accurate! Working from old manuscripts, he designed this pre-Prohibition-era still and uses heritage Abruzzi rye for the distillation.

Worth the Splurge

1910 RYE

Many folks hear "Canadian rye" and immediately think of Crown Royal or other budget blends. If that's your only association, it's time to find out what you've been missing. This Canadian rye (imported and bottled in Oregon) has a 100% rye mash bill and is aged for 12 years. This easy drinker offers lots of maple, dried fruit, and a touch of baking spice.

The Underdog

100 PROOF STRAIGHT RYE WHISKY

Heaven Hill helped change the course of rye whiskey with its brand Rittenhouse, putting it back on the spirit industry's radar. This bottle is a cocktail workhorse often found in bar wells. It's spicy and aggressive and gets bonus points for being relatively inexpensive.

Tried and True

MERCED RYE

This whiskey is crafted from the rare California rye variety Merced and aged in American white oak barrels for 6 years. Its flavor profile is full of brown sugar and intense spice.

Farm Distillery

WHEAT

Common wheat (*Triticum aestivum*) is one of the world's most important staple crops, a significant part of the Western diet, and the key to some of our most prized carbs—bread and pasta. Its use as a base for spirits, however, is a relatively recent development, precisely because of its value as a food crop. But once it entered the distillation scene, it took its unique place among spirit-making grains. The texture, or mouthfeel, is where wheat shows off its assets—soft yet with plenty of body. Where rye whiskey is all hard edges and spice, wheat whiskey offers smooth planes and subtle sweetness. Where corn vodka can sometimes prove astringent and too straightforward, wheat vodka is often savory and silky.

One of the principal cereal grains of the Neolithic Period, along with barley and rye, wheat was domesticated around 10,000 years ago in the Fertile Crescent. By this time, humans had already been collecting and consuming wheat berries (whole wheat kernels) for 7,000 years, though some scientists suggest wild wheat was snacked on as far back as 100,000 years ago! Still, early consumption of wheat berries was no Michelin-style affair— the seeds were gathered, the hulls rubbed away, and the wheat berries either chewed raw or cooked with water to make a basic porridge. The earliest cultivars—einkorn, emmer, and spelt—would later play a fundamental role in the transition to widespread agriculture in the Middle East and Europe.

Categories of Wheat

	Wheat Type	Uses	Location Grown in US
HARD ↑	Durum	pasta and couscous	North Dakota, Montana, Arizona, and California
	Hard Red Winter	all-purpose flours, simple breads, and flatbreads	Great Plains Region
	Soft Red Winter	Crackers, pastries, flatbreads, and rolls	Texas and Kansas up through the Midwest and central, Eastern states
	Hard Red Spring	specialty flours for croissants, pizza crust, and bagels	Northern Plains Region, Minnesota, and parts of Pacific Northwest
	Hard White	whole wheat breads that are softer in texture and light color	Kansas, Nebraska, Colorado, and California
SOFT ↓	Soft White	specialty flours used in cakes, pastries, and confections; Middle Eastern flatbreads	Idaho, Michigan, New York, and the Pacific Northwest

Unlike rye or corn, wheat is categorized by planting season, kernel hardness, and color. Regarding its planting season, wheat can either be sown in the fall or spring. As the name suggests, spring wheat is planted in the spring and harvested in the summer. Unlike winter wheat, it matures quickly and has the accidental benefit of disease resistance, as it simply has less time to become infected. Conversely, winter wheat—planted in the fall and harvested in the spring—is typically higher in proteins, making it the more desirable option for bread-making. More than 80 percent of the wheat grown worldwide is classified as winter wheat, which is largely why it is most often used in distilling.

Hard Wheat vs. Soft Wheat

Hard wheat is known to have strong gluten proteins and is therefore used for chewier, yeasty breads and rolls. Soft wheat, by comparison, is preferred for more delicate baked goods like cakes or biscuits.

Like corn, the bulk of wheat used in commercial distillation isn't grown for that purpose. Typically, wheat is grown as a commodity grain destined to be milled into flour for human consumption. As such, you won't find many brands or producers showcasing or highlighting specific wheat varietals in their spirits. Of course, there are always exceptions, particularly among small distilleries working directly with farmers, such as Laws Whiskey House in Denver—they use a landrace called Centennial—and Dry Land Distillers in Longmont—which makes two different wheat expressions showcasing the Sonora and Antero varietals.

As a Base for Spirits

The truth is, in the spirits industry, wheat typically exists in the background and with little fanfare. It's commonly a base for vodka and gin, occasionally the third or fourth ingredient in Bourbon, and sometimes made into a high-proof, grain neutral spirit. So why, of all the major cereal grains, is wheat one of the least showcased in the world of distilling?

First, wheat is one of the most well-rounded grains in terms of nutritional value. It contains essential starches and proteins and is particularly high in one specific protein you're probably already familiar with—gluten. This high gluten content is what gives dough its elasticity and makes wheat a favorite among bakers. As a grain so well suited for making bread and providing nourishment, wheat has often been considered too valuable to use for spirit-making.

Not until the post-WWII-era would wheat allocation for spirits become a subject of discussion. Wartime controls over most American industries were slowly being rolled back. At one hearing before the House of Representatives, A.P. Fenderson of Publicker Industries spoke on behalf of the company and its whiskey-making subsidiaries. Surprisingly, he noted that Publicker and other grain distillers supported keeping some of the restrictions in place, recognizing that "the price of wheat makes the price of bread, and the price of corn makes the price of meat, eggs, poultry, and milk." In other words, grain demand from distillers could put undue pressure on food prices in times of shortage. (At the time, corn and wheat were selling "pound for pound" at the same price, and American distilleries used between 6 and 10 percent of the commodity

Gluten in Spirits

As the public's awareness of food allergies and Celiac disease has improved, distillers have begun labeling bottles "gluten-free." But all distilled spirits, no matter the grain they're made from, will emerge from the still a gluten-free product. (Gluten proteins aren't volatile and therefore can't withstand the evaporation process.) However, small amounts of gluten can make its way back into a spirit in other sneaky ways. Caramel coloring, flavorings, and other additives, such as those going into flavored whiskeys or spiced rums, are some possible gluten sources. (These ingredients aren't required to appear on the label if they comply with TTB amount standards.) Cross-contamination with the bottling line is another. That said, even a "gluten-free" label is no surefire guarantee. Producers that market their spirits as gluten-free are responsible for their own lab analysis and must use their own discretion when meeting the FDA's standard of having a gluten content below 20 ppm.

corn grown.) This is just one example of how what we eat and drink is shaped over time—during times of crop failure and food insecurity, government intervention has historically been a common practice.

Aside from being over-endowed with gluten (which must be broken down to access starches), wheat also lacks certain fermentation-friendly enzymes. As a result, it's not easy to ferment compared to other grains and, therefore, not at the top of most distillers' ingredient lists.

In American whiskey, wheat is more often used to complement a mash bill, imbuing the spirit with a floral or citrusy note. Meanwhile, in Scotch grain whiskey, wheat is typically favored over corn. Overall, wheat is comparatively softer and quieter than other grains, lending texture and nuance without hogging the spotlight. In fact, vodkas and the wheat-based spirits used for some gins often present with a soft, silky texture, which some describe as "smooth"—a word generally despised in the wine and spirits industry for its lack of flavor specificity. However, the place wheat shines brightest is in wheat whiskey, which, despite the whiskey boom, is still not on the radar of the average Bourbon and rye consumer.

WHEAT WHISKEY

Bourbon fans, slow down and take notice. As you might have guessed based on the other American whiskey mash bills we've seen, wheat whiskey requires a mash bill of at least 51 percent wheat. (The rest of the mash bill can be made from other grains like rye, corn, or barley.) Wheat whiskey must also be aged in charred, new oak barrels, and, unlike Bourbon, it does not need to be made in the US (though most are). Like rye, wheat whiskeys are considered an American style. And though its prospects have improved over

WHEAT WHISKEY

Plant: 51% minimum wheat plus other grains

Place: Anywhere, though the US is the biggest producer

Production: Any still type

Protection: Federally protected US standard of identity

**Wheated Bourbon
(aka "Wheaters")**

One of the most coveted Bourbons is appreciated, in part, because of its wheated mash bill: W.L. Weller. While I don't necessarily recommend tracking down this high-demand, pricey bottling, a few other equally tasty wheated options are hiding in plain sight, including Maker's Mark, Larceny, and 1792's Sweet Wheat (limited release).

the past decade, there still aren't many examples of straight wheat whiskeys on the market. It's a category that has yet to catch the eye of most whiskey drinkers, but one that certainly deserves more attention.

My first taste of wheat whiskey was a Berheim Original 7 Year—an underdog bottling by Heaven Hill—and, after that initial taste, I couldn't for the life of me figure out why everyone wasn't drinking this whiskey. It was a hard bottle to sell (one that required a bit of convincing for the customer) and couldn't compete as consumers sought out the next big Bourbon brand.

Heaven Hill claims the Bernheim bottling was the first new variety of "American straight whiskey" since Prohibition and the first American whiskey to use winter wheat as its primary grain. If true, its appearance in 2005 would make this category a very late bloomer. However, one would assume that, historically, some type of wheat whiskey was distilled at a modest scale prior to Heaven Hill's bottling, as a proper definition of the spirit appeared in the 1935 Federal Alcohol Administrative Act alongside definitions for rye and Bourbon. Still, as a commercially recognized category, wheat whiskey, specifically American-made, remains in its infancy.

Colorado wheat harvest, photo courtesy of Whiskey Sisters Supply.

BERNHEIM ORIGINAL STRAIGHT WHEAT WHISKEY

This 7 Year whiskey remains one of my favorites. With notes of orange and vanilla, honey, and buttered toast, this approachable bottle ought to be on every American whiskey drinker's radar.

Tried and True

STRAIGHT WHEAT WHISKEY

This grain-to-glass whiskey from wine country distiller Spirits Works showcases a savory, grain-forward, yet well-rounded profile. This nuanced whiskey will have you scratching your head, wondering why more people aren't obsessed with this category.

Artisanal

WASHINGTON WHEAT WHISKEY

Dry Fly's wheat whiskey has been around for some time and is ready for some overdue appreciation. Made with 100% wheat (sourced from small farmers located 30 miles away) and aged for 3 years, this whiskey is truly a unique expression.

Farm Connection

CENTENNIAL WHEAT (BOTTLED-IN-BOND)

Many distillers prefer winter wheat, but Laws favors Centennial, an heirloom variety of soft white spring wheat grown by a family farm in Colorado's San Luis Valley. This limited release is aged for 7 years and is the first Colorado wheat whiskey to be bottled-in-bond.

Bottled-in-Bond

"ODDBALL" GRAIN AMERICAN WHISKEYS

When I say whiskey can be made from *any* grain, I mean any of them. Smaller whiskey distillers have been trying their hand at several specialty grains like triticale—a hybrid cross between rye and wheat—or those not frequently seen in the world of alcoholic beverages, such as oats (*Avena sativa*). Here are four distilleries that provide an alternative view of whiskey culture.

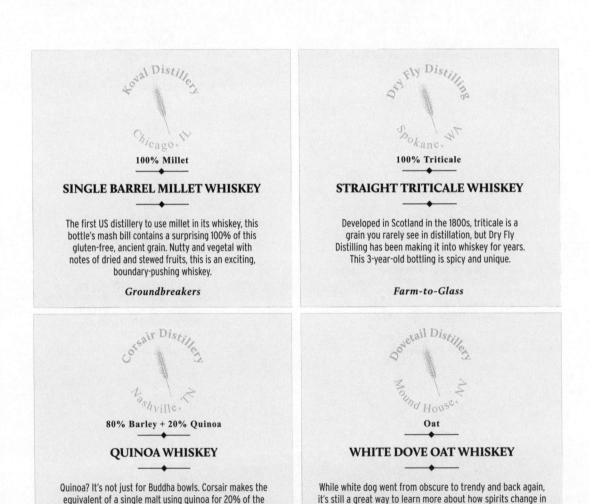

Koval Distillery — Chicago, IL

100% Millet

SINGLE BARREL MILLET WHISKEY

The first US distillery to use millet in its whiskey, this bottle's mash bill contains a surprising 100% of this gluten-free, ancient grain. Nutty and vegetal with notes of dried and stewed fruits, this is an exciting, boundary-pushing whiskey.

Groundbreakers

Dry Fly Distilling — Spokane, WA

100% Triticale

STRAIGHT TRITICALE WHISKEY

Developed in Scotland in the 1800s, triticale is a grain you rarely see in distillation, but Dry Fly Distilling has been making it into whiskey for years. This 3-year-old bottling is spicy and unique.

Farm-to-Glass

Corsair Distillery — Nashville, TN

80% Barley + 20% Quinoa

QUINOA WHISKEY

Quinoa? It's not just for Buddha bowls. Corsair makes the equivalent of a single malt using quinoa for 20% of the mash bill. Interestingly, they label it a "Quinoa Whiskey" rather than a malt, which bucks the trend of having the 51% minimum grain represented on the label.

For the Adventurous Palate

Dovetail Distillery — Mound House, NV

Oat

WHITE DOVE OAT WHISKEY

While white dog went from obscure to trendy and back again, it's still a great way to learn more about how spirits change in the barrel. Nevada-based distiller Dovetail created a mash bill inspired by his childhood favorite—oatmeal cookies. Expect peppery, vegetal notes followed by raw cookie dough.

Like Mom Used to Make

POLUGAR (BREAD WINE)

Polugar, or bread wine, is an obscure spirit largely unknown outside of Eastern Europe, unless you're someone with a keen interest in spirits history. Essentially meaning "half burned," polugar was a precursor to vodka and provides a glimpse into an earlier tradition of spirit-making—similar to how gin evolved from genever but with a much more convoluted path. Polugar likely originated in the 1400s, around the time distillation technology first arrived in the region, and was traditionally made in copper or other rustic stills.

POLUGAR

Plant: Rye, wheat, and other grains

Place: Present-day, Poland; historically, Russia

Production: Pot still or other traditional method (not column still)

Protection: None

There are a couple of theories on the origin of polugar and how it got its name. In his book *A History of Vodka*, Soviet historian William Pokhlebkin describes polugar as a "simple wine" that was "half-burned." However, this burning was not referencing how the distillate was made but rather the quality-testing process used, in which three "buckets" of spirit were diluted with one bucket of water and then "set alight." (Buckets being an early measurement of volume between 12 and 14 liters, and fire being the scientific instrument to determine proof, as this predated any modern methods to determine alcohol content—so, no doubt a perfectly safe experiment.) According to Pokhlebkin, "if the spirit burned down to the line—that is, halfway—it was considered fit for use." Retired Russian scientist-turned-vodka historian Boris Rodionov documented a similar historical "test" for alcohol purity: boiling the distilled spirit until only half of the liquid remained (though he didn't mention adding water). Either way, it appears that polugar traditionally involved fire either through direct contact or heat source, thereby earning its name.

What Happened to Polugar?

So, how is it that polugar seems to have dropped off the earth? For one, distillation techniques leaped forward in the late 19th century, and this

Horilka

In Ukraine, a polugar-like spirit called *horilka* followed a similar path. Infused with ingredients like honey, pepper, and other spices, horilka is still commercially available and is sold as a type of Ukrainian vodka. Traditionally, these "bread wines" and their ilk were paired with meals and were much lower in proof than today (perhaps 23% or 25% ABV)—akin to Japanese shochu (see the chapter on rice).

homely little bread wine was soon portrayed as a rustic, old-fashioned, and unfinished product—essentially moonshine. Perhaps more importantly, Russian Tsar Alexander III made distillation in pot stills illegal in 1895, hailing the arrival of shiny, efficient, "modern" column stills purchased and operated by the government to produce vodka. Imperial Russia took full control over this new, profitable market and outlawed any distillation that wasn't state-run, even going so far as to order all pot stills be dismantled. It proved a very lucrative (though unpopular) decision. As with rye whiskey during American Prohibition, banning these traditional spirits pushed them into obscurity.

Today's iteration of the historical spirit, revived by Rodionov and his two sons, gives us a bit of history through a much more refined, finished product—no fire needed. They researched and revived this mostly forgotten category, rediscovering more than 300 different polugar recipes and going so far as to recreate 1800s-era stills from drawings found in their distillery. Compared to modern vodka, poulgar is lower in alcohol. Furthermore, copper pot stills and production methods allow for better oil retention and significantly more flavor than spirits distilled in a modern column still (similar to white whiskey).

Today, the Rodionovs offer a variety of single grain and flavored bottlings, adding some life back into the category along with historically accurate details. Some recipes are infused with garlic, caraway (think aquavit), and even honey and allspice. But one thing *has* changed: today's polugar production takes place in Poland, not Russia, as state-unaffiliated commercial spirit production remains illegal.

VODKA

Vodka is a tricky spirit to discuss in terms of agriculture because, by today's standards, it can be made from just about any ingredient with enough fermentable sugars (except in regions like Poland with stricter production rules). It's also a spirit with a long history in Eastern Europe and Russia, though its global popularity would not spread for centuries, only catching fire in the 1970s.

VODKA

Plant: Grain is most common (though any fermentable plant can be used, including grapes and potatoes)

Place: Anywhere

Production: Column still (typical), though any still type is allowed

Protection: EU-recognized DOs for Poland, Sweden, Estonia, and other countries, otherwise variable by region

While vodka was born a grain spirit, its current identity is as fluid as ever. Pineapples, honey, strawberries, sweet potatoes, and olives are just a few of the primary ingredients that have been used as a base for vodka in the last few decades. There's seemingly no end to the creativity. Honey? Bee-lieve it. Whey—the byproduct of cheesemaking? Yep, there's a vodka made from that, too. While more than a handful of vodkas are made from grapes, potatoes, and other unexpected ingredients, grain remains the dominant raw material for most of the world's vodka. (And for those wondering why we're introducing vodka in the context of grains, and not potatoes . . . let's just say spuds must have some pretty good PR because they've somehow established themselves as a star player in the vodka scene when they only account for a small percentage of the world's vodka.)

As is the case with most spirits, the etymology of the word vodka, leads us back to the concept of water. We've seen spirits first described as the "water of life:" eau de vie, Uisge Beatha, and aqua vitae; "burning water," aguardiente and aqua ardens; and now we have "little water" derived from Russian or Polish. In Poland, *wódki* or *wódka*, meaning "little water," would first show up in court documents dating back to

RYE & WHEAT

1405, likely in specific reference to a spirit used medicinally at the time. However, the name vodka wouldn't catch on among the masses until after Russia took an interest in popularizing it (i.e., after it seized spirits manufacturing operations for the "benefit of the country").

Like many spirits, vodka evolved gradually and simultaneously across regions. As a result, while it's most strongly associated with Russia, a number of Slavic and Eastern European countries, including Estonia, Lithuania, and especially Poland, also have strong cultural ties to the spirit.

A variety of endemic grains would be used—often hardy rye, but also wheat and molasses made from beet sugar. Potatoes were actually one of the last to make an appearance in vodka, as they weren't widely cultivated in Europe until the mid-19th century, partly due to the public's skepticism around the gnarly looking (and foreign) tubers that some called "devil's apples." And while potatoes were quicker to catch on in Eastern rather than Western Europe, grain remained the primary base used across Europe, particularly in Poland.

While Russia is closely associated with the creation of vodka and continues to anecdotally take a lot of credit for brands that "sound" Russian, vodka in the US is from just about everywhere except Russia. This was the case even before the conflict with Ukraine, partly because vodka can be made with any fruit or vegetable and has no regional limitations, and also because the chaotic, political side of the Russian vodka industry would likely play too large a role in the importing of said vodka.

The mere threat of annexation by the Russian government has undoubtedly scared off many enterprising brands. One such example is the now-popular brand Smirnoff. Originally founded in Russia in 1864 by P.A. Smirnov, P.A.'s son, Vladimir, relocated the brand to the US after the Russian Revolution. (The name was also changed to what we know today as "Smirnoff.") In 1934, Smirnoff would become the first vodka on

---

Neutral Grain Spirit vs. Vodka: What's the Difference?

Defined as any grain spirit distilled to 95% purity (190 proof), neutral spirits are sometimes referred to as "rectified" alcohol, of which Everclear would be a popular example. They represent just about the purest form of a potable spirit—a higher proof would require a laboratory and result in 100% pure ethanol, which would be volatile and definitely not recommended for human consumption. Most vodkas begin as neutral spirits and are proofed down with water, though some are re-distilled (occasionally with flavorings or botanicals; hello, gin!). Many liqueur producers use neutral grain spirits (NGS) or other neutral spirits (like beet or grape) as a base.

SPIRITS DISTILLED

the US market. (At the time, the brand's vodka was distilled in Bethel, Connecticut, but production has since moved to Illinois.)

Vodka imported from Russia wouldn't hit American shelves until the 1970s, and even still, most of the imagery surrounding Russian vodka is just that. The Moscow Mule was invented in Los Angeles with an American-made vodka (Smirnoff) that the company was marketing as "white whiskey." The current best-selling vodka in the US? Tito's from Texas. Grey Goose is French. Sobieski and Chopin are from Poland. You get the idea.

Spotlight on Poland

Poland, another country with a rich history of vodka production and culture, takes its clear spirits very seriously, yet it gets little to no recognition, at least compared with Russia. Historical documents indicate commercial-style distilleries were operating in Gdaÿsk as early as 1454 CE and that there was large-scale vodka production in Krakow by 1550. Today, Poland has a DO recognized in the EU to regulate vodka production, and in contrast to the wide variety of raw ingredients used to make vodka worldwide, Poland continues to stick with the basics: cereal grains (rye, wheat, barley, oats, triticale) and potatoes.

Under the DO, Polish vodka (unflavored) cannot contain any additives, including sugar. The rationale is not just to have bragging rights for purity but to ensure distillers produce a better, cleaner product that doesn't need extras to cover up flaws or cut corners. (The exception is for flavored vodka, which must take on the character of the listed flavor profile.)

Production is Key, but Tastes Are Changing

When it comes to vodka, we usually look to production methods, not raw ingredients, as the foremost defining aspect of the spirit and its pursuit of neutrality. One of vodka's universally recognized qualities

Moscow Mule

- 2 oz. vodka
- ½ oz. fresh lime juice
- 4-5 oz. chilled ginger beer

Building in the glass or copper cup, fill the cup with ice, then add vodka and lime juice. Top with chilled ginger beer, stir gently, and garnish with a lime wheel.

is distillation to a high proof, specifically 190 proof—essentially pure alcohol. From here, it can be diluted or further rectified. The most effective way to reach 190 typically involves utilizing a column still and stripping the spirit down plate by plate—that's what it does best. That said, you *can* make vodka in a pot still. However, doing so requires a lot of time and effort to get that relatively neutral profile that persists and is expected of the spirit. For example, Irish producer Dingle Distillery distills their pot still vodka five times to get the desired result. Some distillers also use hybrid stills, providing the best of both worlds.

Distilling to such a pure form of ethanol is a process that also strips flavor and other chemical compounds that contribute to the character of a spirit, and up until the last decade or so, a key characteristic of vodka (in most markets) was to get it as neutral (i.e., flavorless, odorless, colorless) as possible. But with the craft movement going mainstream, producers have begun to take risks, and mainstream vodka has been getting a lot more expressive. While distillation methods largely haven't changed, the treatment of the distillate has become more adventurous, such as less filtration post-distillation, which makes for a less neutralized spirit.

The old adage "it all tastes the same" couldn't be further from the truth these days. So much so that in 2020, the TTB adjusted their standard of identity for vodka to "align with changes in the industry and modern tastes," announcing that "the requirement that vodka be without distinctive character, aroma, taste, or color no longer reflects consumer expectations and should be eliminated. Vodka, [henceforth, it proclaimed] will continue to be distinguished by its specific production standards: Vodka may not be labeled as aged, and unlike other neutral spirits, it may contain limited amounts of sugar and citric acid." That said, the new US allowance of sugar and citric acid may open up another host of complications in terms of "purity."

A Note About Flavored Vodkas

With all this talk of neutrality and sugar limits, you may be wondering about how these rules above apply to your favorite blue raspberry or marshmallow fluff vodka. Flavored vodkas have their own set of rules, including lower ABV allowances (minimum 30%), and the name of the most prominent flavor must appear on the label.

Wheat

ELYX

Push past the shiny marketing, and you'll find a wheat-based vodka sourced from a single estate in Sweden that has grown the crop since the 1400s. This vodka is distilled in a vintage column still made in 1921, and will satisfy both the old and new schools of vodka drinkers.

Farm Chic

Wheat

KETEL ONE

Produced by Dutch distillers with a history of making genever, this non-GMO wheat vodka is on the unconventional side as both column and pot stills are used in production, and the two distillates are then blended with water. Classic and reliable, this bottle is ready to be put to work in cocktails.

Tried and True

Corn and barley

NIKKA COFFEY VODKA

I haven't found a 100% corn vodka that's knocked my socks off. But this corn and barley vodka from whisky maker Nikka comes pretty close. This crisp and light expression makes for a versatile cocktail base.

Expect the Unexpected

Rye

POTOCKI WÓDKA

Potocki's Wódka gave me my first real eye-opening vodka experience. It is clean without being stripped down to neutral, has no additives, and offers subtle spice thanks to the Polish-grown rye. This is my top vodka of choice when it comes to sipping neat or mixing in a Martini.

Traditional and Artisanal

Wheat and Pomegranate

VODKA

A leader in the American organic spirits movement since 2004, Greenbar focuses on sustainable practices, like using lightweight glass bottles. Their vodka is made with wheat and California-grown pomegranate, and crafted to showcase exceptional texture and body. Made without added sugars or additives.

Certified Organic

Rye

BOTANICAL VODKA

One of the first producers of organic vodka in the US, this rye-based vodka is made from Montana-grown grain. Redefining what it means to be a flavored vodka, the base is clean and crisp with the botanicals adding a fresh burst of citrus and herbs for those who might stray more toward gin.

For the Gin Drinker

RICE

Rice is an unassuming little grass with a massive presence—grown in 95 of 195 countries, it's a staple crop for over 3.5. billion people worldwide. A semi-aquatic plant, it thrives in marshy and flood-prone areas like river valleys, and though independently domesticated on three different continents (Asia, Africa, and South America), it was in China's Yangtze Valley that a key domesticate was cultivated. Here, through careful human manipulation spanning millennia, wild rice (Oryza rufipogon) was cultivated into Oryza sativa, one of only two domesticated species encompassing about 110,000 varieties (the other, Oryza glaberrima, continues to be heavily used across Africa). Today, Oryza sativa accounts for around 90 percent of the global rice supply and almost 100 percent of rice-based spirits.

Many East Asian countries have particularly strong cultural ties to the grain, with several millennia-old fermented beverages to show for it. While most people are familiar with saké, Japan's brewed rice beverage that dates back to around 300 BCE, there's also Chinese Shaoxing rice wine, which dates back to around 700 BCE. (Like Sherry, one version of this tart rice wine can be sipped on its own, and another is used in regional Zhejiang cuisine.) Archaeologists have also uncovered another spirit from Northern China—an unnamed 9,000-year-old rice brew made with spices, honey, and fruit. In sum, the historical connection to rice goes way back.

Rice, Rice, Baby!

Oryza sativa is a thirsty plant compared to other grasses we've covered, which is why it's so often portrayed as growing in a rice paddy. But this isn't the only way rice is grown. The domesticated plant is divided into two subspecies: *japonica* and *indica*, short- and long-grain types, respectively. *Japonica* contains more amylopectin (a component of starch that's not water soluble), giving this grain a stickier texture (think varieties of sushi rice or arborio). In comparison, *indica* has less amylopectin, allowing the longer grains to remain separate as they cook (types include basmati or jasmine). The two sub-species also grow differently depending on climate and generally prefer different amounts of water.

Japonica is the less thirsty of the two and—when grown in more tropical growing regions—tends to be planted *upland*, or at higher elevations. It's also favored in more temperate climates and performs well in places like Japan, parts of northern China, Australia, and the southern US. (*Japonica* rice actually grows well in southern Arkansas, which shares the same latitude as the rice-growing areas of Japan, along with other favorable environmental conditions for growing sushi and saké rice.) Upland farming is sometimes called "rainfed," a nod to the crops getting their water solely from Mother Nature. It is also the more labor-intensive of the two farming styles, as the absence of weed-drowning, seasonal flood waters means farmers must weed by hand. To compensate, upland rice farmers tend to grow multiple crops at once or in rotation, allowing for improved soil health. For example, rice farmers in the Philippines may harvest rice in one season and then plant peanuts or pigeon peas in the next.

Indica, on the other hand, is mostly limited to the lowlands. It loves the water and is, therefore, favored in the wetter climates of India, the Philippines, and Southern China. *Lowland*—or irrigated—farming is the planting style most of us are familiar with. This "paddy"-grown rice often requires submerging a field in water—the most efficient watering method for large-scale farming (which accounts for about 75 percent of commercial rice farming worldwide). In the US, most rice is farmed this way because it facilitates aerial seeding, a very popular and efficient method of planting. Still, no matter the subspecies planted or the techniques used, these tiny grains require tremendous effort and resources.

Sustainability and Climate Change

Despite their purported efficiency, lowland rice farms account for nearly 8 percent of global methane emissions, but the reason may surprise you. Flooded fields are breeding grounds for methane-releasing bacteria, and many rice farms leave their fields saturated year-round. Though their impact is relatively small compared to the methane output created by fossil fuels, there is hope these farms will adapt, if not for any other reason than to brace for the economic impacts of climate change. For example, to save on water and the cost of keeping fields saturated, farmers are drying their fields between planting seasons, thereby decreasing methane outputs. Some are also experimenting with new drip irrigation techniques and more drought-tolerant hybrid seeds that require less water.

In traditional rice-growing regions of Vietnam, farmers are reverting to tough landraces and heirloom varieties that may have a lower yield but are less dependent on synthetic fertilizers and better suited for the changing environment. In Arkansas—which produces roughly 40 percent of the US's commodity rice—farmers are shifting to more modern practices such as zero-grade farming. In this method, the land is leveled off, and a crop border is created to manage drainage and prevent erosion. As a result, farmers have more control over water levels and don't need to flood the fields or rely on sloped levees. Though the up-front costs can be high, the long-term savings on water and fertilizer combined with the environmental benefits are leading many farmers to make the change.

Rice Distillation in the US

Rice hasn't had the same dietary or cultural importance in North America as in Asia and Africa (it can only be grown in 6 US states), so it hasn't been used as a primary distillation starch. But that's beginning to change. Led partly by global enthusiasm for Japanese whisky, rice has started popping up in more recipes than you'd expect. Craft distilleries in the US are now incorporating locally-grown rice in Asian-style lagers, sakés, and shochu, and even Anheuser-Busch has gotten in on it, with rice making up almost 30% of Budweiser's recipe.

Arkansas rice farming at Isbell Farms, photos courtesy of Sara Reeves.

Koji: A Mold of Many Colors

As with barley, extra steps must be taken during rice fermentation to access the sugars trapped in the starch; it's here that *koji* (*Aspergillus oryzae*) enters the chat. On paper, koji may not sound terribly appealing—it's essentially a moldy starch used to achieve *saccharification*, which is the process of turning a carbohydrate into a sugar. Koji is essential to rice fermentation, and its preparation is a traditional Japanese process unlike anything in the West. Because koji must be prepared separately from the brewing or distilling process, making fermented rice beverages requires advanced planning.

There are three types of koji (black, white, and yellow), and each is essential to a specific kind of fermented product, from saké and shochu to soy sauce. Made in what is basically a rice sauna called a *muro*, koji needs a hot and humid environment to develop. The process starts with the *koji-kin*, a powdered form of the mold, which is then added to freshly steamed rice and cultivated in the muro for no fewer than forty hours and up to several days. In a process referred to as *multiple parallel fermentation*, the koji fungus creates enzymes that convert starch to sugar, while the yeast converts sugar into alcohol (meaning the saccharification and fermentation processes happen simultaneously). This process is essentially an alternative to malting the grain, which, though possible, is less effective in accessing rice's fermentable sugars.

	Flavor & Aroma	Character	Uses
Shiro (white)	Mild, sweet, balanced; reminiscent of sake aromas	More efficient enzymatic properties; mutation of kuro koji	Shochu, saké
Kuro (black)	Strong, earthy, mushroomy	Produces more citric acids that are excellent preservatives	Awamori
Ki (yellow)	Delicate, fruity, floral; lychee and honeysuckle aromas/flavors	Temperature-sensitive; does not produce strong acids and is prone to spoilage	Saké, miso, soy sauce

Japanese koji types.

Fermentation of Thai rice for Awamori, photo by Tokio Marine Life.

HONKAKU SHOCHU

HONKAKU SHOCHU

Plant: Rice, barley, and sweet potato as well as other starches and cereals grains

Place: Japan

Production: Pot still (single distillation), with vacuum distillation increasingly common; koji-based fermentation

Protection: It's complicated! 4 shochu DOs (recognized by the WTO but not the TTB)

Shochu can be made from almost any starch, and while there are up to fifty legally permitted ingredients, including sesame, shiso, and brown sugar, 99 percent of production consists of just five: rice (*kome*), barley (*mugi*), sweet potato (*imo*), buckwheat (*soba*), and sugarcane (*kokuto*). While it's common for producers to highlight one ingredient in their bottlings, the vast majority of shochu is a blend of two or more of these starches. Still, different primary ingredients appeal to different consumers. For example, barley-based shochu is the most widely consumed and available in the US, while sweet potato shochu gets the popular vote in Japan. Still, rice was likely the earliest primary ingredient used to make shochu, as many believe the spirit was first made using rice lees of saké (aka kasu, see sidebar). So, shochu and its connection to this vital grain is where we'll begin our exploration of rice distillation.

Category	Distillation	Rules
Honkaku	Single-distilled	Bottled under 45% ABV, no additives post-distillation, restricted to approved raw materials
Korui	Multiple or continuous distillation	Bottled under 35% ABV, barrel aging longer than a year is prohibited, few restrictions of raw materials
Otsurui	Single-distilled	Fewer restrictions of raw materials, additives allowed, bottled under 45% ABV
Konwa	Blend of Korui and Otsurui	The spirit making up the greater part of the blend is listed first on the label

Categories of shochu.

KUMA SHOCHU	IKI SHOCHU	AWAMORI	SATSUMA SHOCHU
—	—	—	—
RICE SHOCHU FROM SOUTHERN KUMAMOTO	BARLEY SHOCHU FROM IKI ISLAND	RICE SHOCHU FROM OKINAWA	SWEET POTATO SHOCHU

Varieties of Honkaku shochu.

A Brief History of Shochu

There are two main shochu categories in Japan: Honkaku and Korui. Honkaku, which essentially means "traditional" or "authentic," is considered to be the more artisanal of the two. Per Japanese regulation, Honkaku shochu is single-distilled, ensuring the final spirit retains more of the raw ingredient's flavor and aroma, which ranges from savory notes of steamed rice to sweet, tropical fruit. It's typically sipped with water added or over ice (if you're a fan of saké, you'll likely enjoy Honkaku shochu). Conversely, Korui shochu—which was once referred to as simply "white liquor"—came into existence after the introduction of the column still. The continuous distillation gives the spirit a more subtle—sometimes verging on neutral—profile. While this makes Korui an excellent choice for mixing in cocktails, it tends to have a reputation for being mass-produced and having less character.

Like many ancient spirits, we can only speculate about shochu's roots. It's generally believed to have begun as a rudimentary spirit made by farmers and fishermen soon after the arrival of distillation technology to Japan. After all, distillers in Okinawa, the birthplace of *Awamori* (see the section on Awamori), were distilling by 1477 CE. However, the characters for the word "shochu" only first appeared in 1559 CE as graffiti on the rafter of a Shinto shrine. It's also unclear how distillation technology arrived in the Land of the Rising Sun in the first place. It's possible the practice was introduced from Thailand, based on the steady flow of Thai rice into Japan around the time Japanese spirits were

Kasutori Shochu

Like Grappa, Kasutori shochu is made from the byproduct of another drink and once had a less-than-stellar reputation. The base for Kasutori is *kasu,* or the rice lees left over from saké production. This ingredient made for a potent distillate and a spirit known for not being the highest quality. Nevertheless, Kasutori shochu was relatively common from as early as the Edo period until WWII, when saké became a luxury. Today, the style is making a comeback as distillers seek cost-saving and waste-reduction measures. (The distillation process also strips the leftover kasu of any remaining alcohol, allowing the spent grain to be used as fertilizer.)

Shochu or Soju? What's the Difference?

Soju is the national spirit of Korea, and while the name may look and sound similar to Japan's shochu, the two have little else in common. Like shochu, soju was originally made with rice as the primary ingredient. However, the grain was officially banned from distillation during the Korean War owing to food insecurity, leading distillers to use other crops and flavor additives. Today, most soju continues to be made from inexpensive starches like barley, tapioca, and sweet potato.

Another key difference between shochu and soju is the number of distillations. Where Honkaku shochu is distilled once, soju is typically distilled multiple times. To make matters more confusing for American consumers, since the 1990s, laws in NY and CA have allowed for Japanese shochu with an ABV of 24% or less to be sold in restaurants with only a beer and wine license; but with a caveat—it had to be labeled (incorrectly) as soju. Amendments in 2022 in NY and 2023 in CA now allow it to be sold as shochu.

born and on the older Thai tradition of Awamori production. Another hypothesis is that distillation arrived via illicit maritime trade with Korea or Okinawa (which didn't come under the control of mainland Japan until the early 1600s). Whichever route distillation took to Japan, it's undeniable that rice became a critical Japanese distillation ingredient. In the 17th-century, Edo-period rulers in Nagasaki even had to outlaw its use in shochu production to protect the crop as a food staple and tribute method (tax payments were made in rice and some rates could be as steep as 40 percent of a farmer's annual crop).

Despite its antiquity, shochu was slow to gain mainstream traction, even within Japan. Consumed primarily in rural areas, it was saddled with an unfavorable reputation as a blue-collar and lower-class drink. But times have changed. Shochu finally slid into the spotlight as a respectable beverage in the late 1970s, and today, it is made in all forty-seven of Japan's prefectures—though most production is centered on southern Kyushu Island (the Kumamoto Prefecture is renowned for its rice-based shochu) and Okinawa.

A Diamond in the Rough

With the exception of Awamori—a specific, regional shochu favoring Thai-grown rice—shochu producers don't usually seek out specific rice varieties like they do for saké. In fact, shochu can use imported rice, unlike Japanese saké, which must be made with domestic (Japanese) rice. In both cases, the rice must first be "polished," meaning further milled, to remove the outer layers of the rice kernel, which contain impurities. For a basic polish, the hull and bran are removed, reducing the rice to 85–90 percent of its original size, which for most shochu producers, is suitable for distillation. (This range is much higher than the polishing ratio used in saké production.) Added polish translates into added cost, but generally, shochu distillers look to retain more proteins and flavor compounds anyway—too much polish can strip away "impurities" integral to the spirit's complexity and flavor.

But there's another step before alcohol can be made: a process called *shikomi* (meaning "preparation"), which creates the koji. As mentioned earlier, this mold is crucial to fermentation, both for its saccharification of starch and unique flavor-enhancing qualities. While complicated, and done differently depending on the end product (saké or Awamori versus shochu), shikomi is a bit like activating or feeding a dormant sourdough starter. Then, before distilling, a "mash" called *moromi* is made combining the prepared koji, water, and the main ingredient, rice. Most Honkaku shochus undergo two separate moromi preparations (the first using a smaller amount of raw ingredients, as its job is to kickstart fermentation.)

Next is distillation, which brings us to a new technique: *vacuum distillation*. While not all shochu involves this process (developed in the 1970s), many producers today are choosing it over traditional, or "atmospheric," distillation, as it allows for distilling at reduced pressures and lower temperatures, thereby reducing the boiling point of the liquid and preserving the spirit's delicate fruity, floral flavors. Because of the increased popularity of vacuum distillation for shochu production, you'll commonly see either "vacuum" or "atmospheric" noted on labels or a store's "shelf talker" cards when shopping for a bottle.

Most shochu are proofed down to 38 percent (EU) or 40 percent (US) ABV. However, Japanese Honkaku shochu is typically proofed much lower (20 to 35 percent ABV), making it not just approachable on its own but also popular in cocktails or diluted in a Mizuwari highball. (*Mizuari*, meaning to "cut with water," refers not to a specific shochu cocktail, but the act of diluting the spirit.) In their popularity, shochu highballs have gained the moniker "Chu-Hi" or "Chuhai." While a classic Mizuwari highball might use a ratio of 3 parts shochu to 2 parts water or soda water, a Chu-Hi may have a little something extra, like a splash of juice.

Dealer's Choice Chu-Hi

- 1 part shochu
- 1 part fresh fruit juice of your choice
- 3 parts chilled soda water

Fill a Collins glass with ice, add spirit, juice, and soda. Stir gently to agitate. Strong carbonation is key, so make sure to chill your soda.

Akita Seishu · Akita, Japan

Kasutori Shochu

NAMAHAGE "DEVIL'S MASK"

Since 1983, this bottling has been made with blocks of lees (kasu)—containing 8% ABV—left over from the brewery's various saké productions. Currently my favorite shochu, this bottling is nuanced, leans savory, and finishes clean.

Sustainable

Osuzuyama Distillery · Miyazaki, Japan

Kome Shochu

YAMASEMI

Made with 100% estate grown Hanakagura rice—a variety popular with saké brewers—this bottling uses black koji during fermentation, similar to Awamori. The shochu is aged in clay pots, resulting in a complex, herbaceous spirit with a long finish and notes of minerality.

Farm-to-Table

St. George Spirits · Alameda, CA

Kome Shochu

SHOCHU

Originally a special one-off project for Oakland's Ramen Shop restaurant, this bottle is now a mainstay in the distillery line-up. Using Sacramento-grown Calrose rice and bottled at a full strength of 40% ABV, this is an umami bomb brimming with character.

Artisanal in the US

Sengetsu Shuzo · Kumamoto, Japan

Kome Shochu

MUGON HONKAKU SHOCHU

This shochu is aged for over a decade in barrels made of Japanese evergreen oak, a rarity as most shochu is traditionally aged in clay. The result is a unique aroma and flavor profile, with notes of vanilla, tropical fruit, and a subtle, nutty quality.

For the Adventurous Palate

Arkansas rice at Isbell Farms, photo courtesy of Sara Reeves.

AWAMORI

Awamori, or the "Spirit of Okinawa," is likely the oldest distilled spirit in Japan. In fact, it is considered shochu's predecessor and was referred to as "saki" when it debuted—a term still used in modern Okinawan dialect to refer to spirits or liquor in general. Essentially a type of shochu, Awamori is typically made from Thai rice—an *indica*, long-grain style— using multiple parallel fermentation. Compared to Honkaku shochu, Awamori tends to have a fuller body and mouthfeel due to its higher ABV (between 30 and 40 percent) and rich flavor profile. Like many spirits, its higher proof made it popular for medicinal purposes, though today, it's usually enjoyed on ice with a splash of water.

So, why the Thailand connection? From the mid-15th through the 19th century, the southernmost Ryukyu islands (of which Okinawa is a part) did not belong to Japan. Instead, they were unified under the independent Ryukyu Kingdom, and a long trade history existed between Okinawa and Thailand—which, as mentioned earlier, might have been the source of Japanese distillation technology. Thai rice eventually became a spirit industry standard for Awamori, partly because distillers felt that koji responded more favorably to it.

However, the special ingredient setting Awamori apart from other shochu categories is black koji (*Aspergillus luchuensis*). This native mold is well-suited for breaking down starch and acting as a preservative in the humid island climate, thanks to its high levels of bacteria-resistant citric acid. An added benefit is that the mold allows for open-top fermentation of the mash, which invites natural yeasts in from the environment and leads to more complex flavors. A key requirement of the DO that sets Awamori apart from Honkaku shochu is that saccharification and alcohol conversion must occur simultaneously, meaning that all ingredients are added at once.

AWAMORI

Plant: Rice (usually Thai rice or *indica*)

Place: Okinawa, Japan

Production: Pot still; black koji; multiple parallel fermentation

Protection: DO (recognized by the WTO but not the TTB)

In other words, similar to saké production, Awamori undergoes multiple parallel fermentation. This process takes about fourteen to twenty days; then distillation can begin.

Awamori can be aged or unaged, and aged Awamori is labeled "kusu" if 50 percent or more of the spirit is aged three or more years. (In Okinawa, this aging period is called "letting it sleep.") Unaged Awamori is typically rested in stainless steel before bottling, while traditionally aged Awamori is left to mature in earthenware vessels. Fractional blending—better known in the world of Sherry as solera aging (see the chapter on grapes)—is also a common practice for aging the spirit. Porous earthenware vessels like clay and ceramic allow for oxygenation while aging, giving the spirit time to mellow and imparting a nutty or vanilla-like quality. Still, some producers are moving toward more modern, Western-style wooden vessels like barrels or oak containers, especially those looking to enter the American market as a whiskey.

Prior to the Allied bombing campaigns of the Japanese countryside during WWII, Awamori as old as 200 years still existed in storage (a very long nap indeed). However, the spirit's popularity declined in post-war Japan, taking a back seat to drinks like saké. Today, there are only about forty-five Awamori distilleries left on Okinawa, and Awamori remains relatively unknown outside of Japan. But that may be about to change. Some Okinawan distilleries are trying their hand at less traditional spirit adaptations like Awamori-based gin and rice (koji) whiskies. These Awamori-in-disguise are already proving successful at expanding Awamori's footprint.

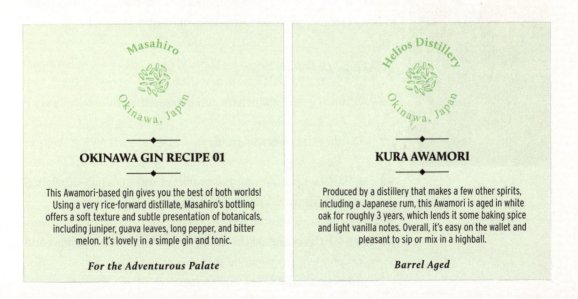

JAPANESE RICE WHISKY (AKA KOJI WHISKY)

JAPANESE RICE WHISKY

Plant: Rice

Place: Japan

Production: Any still type; koji fermentation; oak barrel aged

Protection: None

Surprisingly, rice whisky (aka koji whisky) isn't actually whisky in the eyes of Japanese regulators. As far as they're concerned, the spirit doesn't exist. That's because, historically, any Japanese koji-distilled rice spirit was called shochu (or Awamori), meaning that a shochu aged in oak (what we're calling "Japanese rice whisky") is technically considered a barrel-aged shochu. Still, koji whiskies have made their way into the Japanese whisky craze of the last decade, adding some new whisky shelf mates that taste different from what you'd expect.

Rice whiskies have a different profile than whiskies made from barley, rye, and corn. They tend to be lighter and fruitier than their counterparts, and I find them very food-friendly, especially when served alongside spicy dishes. These spirits evoke the essence of the raw ingredient coaxed out by the koji fermentation. Interestingly, there is little demand for rice whisky (or barrel-aged shochu) in Japan. However, in the US, the TTB considers them whiskies since they satisfy all requirements under the standard of identity (see below). This ostensible promotion in the US within the whiskey category means this misfit spirit has found a second home.

TTB Legal Definition of Whiskey

- Distilled from a grain mash (any grain satisfies this requirement);

- Distilled to below 190 proof;

- Have "the taste, aroma, and characteristics generally attributed to whisky," which, as we know, is quite subjective;

- Aged in oak containers (resulting in the above characteristics); and

- Bottled at 80 proof (40% ABV) or above.

Ohishi-san with barrels, photo courtesy of Ohishi Whisky and Impex Beverages.

Stainless steel pot still at Fukano Distillery, photo courtesy of Fukano Distillery and Impex Beverages.

Conversely, in Japan, these spirits have no designation unless they meet the requirements of shochu. This is difficult, as their extended aging, higher proof, and oak barrel treatment are a vast departure from traditional shochu, which is often aged for shorter periods in earthenware and proofed down to a much lower ABV. In short, these bottles are destined for international markets, and if, by chance, they are sold in Japan, they're never labeled as "whisky." For this reason, rice whisky can be a polarizing subject, though that might not have been the case if history had followed a different timeline.

Many in the industry argue that rice whisky's appearance on the "traditional" whiskey market makes too many concessions to help shore up increasingly frequent Japanese whisky shortages (see the chapter on barley), while others say that major distillers like Nikka and Yamazaki just don't like the competition. However, the rice whisky versus traditional whisky debate would likely not even be an issue had Jokichi Takamine's endeavor to use koji in place of traditional malting (see sidebar) proved successful. In an alternative timeline, koji whisky would indeed be considered a traditional whiskey.

The Takamine Process

In 1891, Dr. Jokichi Takamine left Japan for Chicago with his American wife and their two sons. He took with him an interest in science, agriculture, and distillation—and a particular knowledge of koji as a fermentation powerhouse. By 1894, Takamine secured a US patent for what he'd called "the Takamine Process," which uses koji in place of traditional malting techniques. Shortly after, the *Chicago Tribune* reported that the Takamine Process would shake up the whiskey business and reduce production costs by as much as 20%. This was likely unwelcome news to the old guard of American distillers, and 2 weeks later, a suspicious fire destroyed Takamine's lab. Yet he persisted and later registered his patent with a major distilling and cattle feed trust company in Peoria (the equivalent of a distiller like MGP today). A limited amount of koji-fermented corn whiskey was made under the brand name "Bonzai," but the government soon shut down the operation in a trust-busting move.

For my part, I'm of the opinion that rice whisky provides a window of opportunity to experiment and explore old concepts in new ways. And whether or not they align with the flavor profile of traditional Japanese whiskies, these spirits are fun, interesting, and unique—and certainly fill a void in a very thirsty market. The trick to having a positive experience with them is setting your expectations before purchasing a bottle. Remember, these are nothing like the classic expressions from Hakushu or Yamazaki, which reflect traditional Scottish distillation.

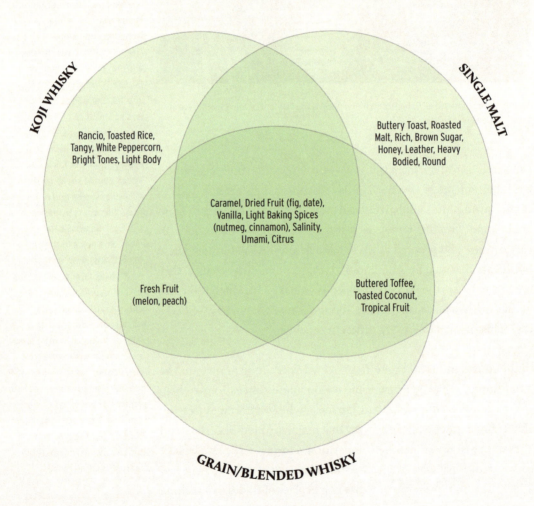

Koji vs. single malt vs. grain whisky: more in common than you might think.

KIKORI RICE WHISKEY

An excellent entry-level rice whiskey, this bottling is aged at least 3 years, with most of that time spent in new American oak before it's moved to ex-Oloroso Sherry and new French oak casks. Light and fruity, with notes of melon, this bottling will appeal to a wide range of palates and is exceptionally food friendly.

Tried and True

FUKANO SELECT

Fukano favors limited releases that vary from batch to batch. They also experiment with barrel finishes and are the first distillery in the Kumamoto region to mature shochu in oak. This stainless-steel pot still whisky is light and fruity, while also notably nutty, rich, and oxidized.

For the Adventurous Palate

8 YEAR SHERRY CASK

Founded in 1872, Ohishi has made a name for itself making saké and shochu. The distillery sources all of its rice from the Kumamoto region (even growing some of it themselves) and, in an effort to go more natural, uses koi fish as "weed killer" rather than synthetic herbicides.

Locavore

10 YEAR SINGLE GRAIN BOURBON CASK

This Okinawan distillery barrel ages their Awamori, which is made with *indica* rice and distilled just once in stainless steel pot stills. This bottling is sold as single grain whisky, and the ex-Bourbon barrels it's aged in impart a classic profile of baking spice, vanilla, and brown sugar.

Awamori in Sheep's Clothing

BAIJIU

BAIJIU

Plant: Sorghum (primary), as well as rice and various other grains

Place: China

Production: Solid-state fermentation and distillation

Protection: Some regional protections in place; no TTB standard of identity

---

Geographical Indications (or Lack Thereof)

The TTB currently has no standard of identity listed for shochu, soju, or baijiu, meaning the US doesn't recognize or enforce any related DOs. In other words, these categories remain at a disadvantage outside their home countries. According to author Christopher Pelligrini, everything outside of TTB categories falls in the "spirits specialty" category and requires more effort to get approval, and if the TTB has questions, it could delay bottling and importing for months.

Trivia time! What is the world's most consumed liquor? If you answered anything other than China's national spirit, *baijiu* (pronounced *bye-geo* or *bye-j'yo*), I'm sorry to say you've guessed incorrectly. Like whiskey, baijiu is a category with as many components as possibilities. It has regional variations, can be made from a variety of grains (though sorghum is most common), and contains around a dozen unique sub-categories and styles.

A vital element element of the Chinese social fabric since the Ming Dynasty (1368–1644), baijiu needs no special occasion (though a celebration usually isn't complete without it). It's also a staple at Chinese business meetings and political gatherings, and gifting a bottle of the spirit can be a sign of respect for the recipient. "No other spirit has the cultural significance of baijiu," says baijiu educator and author Derek Sandhaus.

However, this spirit may not be for everyone, and those accustomed to the profiles of Western spirits may not immediately take to its unfamiliar and intense flavors, which range from umami-driven mushroom and dark soy sauce to overripe melon and canned lychee. "Most people don't understand that [baijiu is] a nebulous universe of spirits rather than a solitary well-defined planet," explains Sandhaus. In fact, baijiu (which essentially means "white alcohol") usually offers a polarizing experience for those new to the category—people tend to either love it or hate it on their first attempt. If you find yourself in the latter camp, I recommend you keep trying it, as this spirit class is large and varied.

Unfamiliar Territory

While baijiu can be made from just about any available grain, sorghum (aka broomcorn) is the raw ingredient most often used, with rice

164   SPIRITS DISTILLED

coming in a very distant second. According to Sandhaus, "baijiu is highly associated with agrarian and working-class communities in a country that has been historically plagued by famine, and thus was rarely made from products widely used as food sources. That's why most baijiu is made from sorghum (cheap, rarely eaten by humans) rather than rice (expensive, a dietary staple) and other prized food products."

Sorghum isn't often used as a distillation base outside of China, so we won't do a deep dive into this particular grain, but the need-to-know bits are that sorghum is a cereal grain originally hailing from the heart of Africa (Ethiopia and Sudan, around 8000 BCE), and it can be milled into flour or made into a molasses-like syrup. And though sorghum has been malted and used in numerous fermented and unfermented beverages in Africa for eons, in China (a major producer and importer of the grain), sorghum is mainly used for feedstock and baijiu production.

In many ways, baijiu production follows steps and processes that we are familiar with by now—relying on yeast for fermentation and later adding that to some kind of fruit or grain slurry. However, baijiu then departs from this fermentation style by using *solid-state fermentation* (which grows the microorganisms cultivated during fermentation on solid materials without the use of free-moving water).

As the central building block of baijiu production, qu, like yeast, contributes to and even guides the flavor profile of a wine or spirit. Its role is akin to that of koji (i.e., it causes saccharification), but qu is much more complex. This microbial wonderland is created from a grain base that hosts various bacteria, yeast, mold, and fungi, and it requires a lot of labor and preparation. In doing so, qu also reflects a sense of place and even changes with the time of year it's made. (A distiller's qu recipe is usually better guarded than a prized Kentucky mash bill and is the key to coaxing out unique flavors during fermentation.) And while a myriad of recipes and techniques for making qu exist, this fermentation starter can be divided into two categories: "big" and "small" qu.

Huangjiu

China has an impressively long history of fermenting (both foods and drinks) and began tinkering with alcoholic beverages some 9,000 years ago. By around 220 BCE, a brewed, grain-based wine known as huangjiu had become today's Western cultural equivalent of beer. Huangjiu's unique flavor and aroma can be partially attributed to the use of qu, a yeast and fungi combo responsible for saccharification and fermentation processes, which result in the volatile compounds and esters that

Qu

Koji isn't the only fermentation helper used in Chinese cuisine. Qu (pronounced chew), a solid-state fermentation starter dating back at least 5,000 years, is also used for spirits. It's similar to koji in that it's a catalyst for saccharification, but the process and flavor profile are vastly different. Qu is a crucial building block of the traditional Chinese spirit baijiu and is used to make several different styles of Chinese rice wine.

"Big qu" (*daqu*)—made of wheat, barley, and sometimes peas—is the go-to starter for sorghum-based baijiu. The grains are soaked, ground, and pressed into large bricks (traditionally by foot but nowadays more often with machine pressing). The outside of the bricks are then dried in sunlight before being moved to a dark "incubation chamber." This is where the microbial activity occurs—our magic ticket to Flavortown. The process can take several weeks, and the bricks can be cured or aged further to develop more complex flavors.

"Small qu" (*xiaoqu*), on the other hand, is typically made from rice (or glutinous rice flour), hand-formed into balls or paste, and used in rice-based baijiu and traditional huangjiu. Medicinal herbs are occasionally added to small qu, offering an element of traditional Chinese medicine into the mix.

Organization by Aroma

Like whiskey, baijiu is made of fermented and distilled grains and can be subdivided into a variety of categories and styles. But that's where the similarities end. Baijiu is intentionally expressive (some might say strong), and its flavors provoke equally potent smells. Based on these intense olfactory experiences, it is primarily classified by "aroma" (and by the type of qu used in fermentation). My first experience with the spirit was a record-scratch moment that forced me to stop and re-evaluate what I looked for in a tasting. It wasn't until I'd had about a dozen styles that I started to make sense of baijiu and identify my preferences. (I'm team sauce aroma!) I recommend you do the same, try

Style	Qu Base	Primary Ingredient	Flavor and Aroma Profile
Light	Wheat bran, barley, peas	Sorghum, rice husks	Floral, fruity, lychee, tangy, cooked fruit
Strong	Wheat	Simple grain (sorghum), mixed grain (sorghum, corn, wheat, rice)	Mushroomy, umami, medicinal, overripe tropical fruit
Sauce	Wheat	Sorghum	Pungent, umami, soy sauce, miso
Rice	Rice, medicinal herbs	Long grain, glutinous rice	Mild, floral, saké-like, steamed rice

Baijiu flavor and aroma categories.

a range of styles and see what you like best. The (non-exhaustive) chart below will give you a crash course on what to expect from the major categories.

Despite its numerous producers and long history, a relatively small amount of baijiu is imported into the US, though that has gradually begun to change as interest grows. Recommending baijiu to Western palates is tricky, and each bottle below could arguably fall under the For the Adventurous Palate heading. It's also important to note that these bottlings lean toward the higher end of the ABV spectrum (between 45 and 58 percent).

Kinmen Kaoliang
Taiwan
Sorghum

KAOLIANG

This distillery–built during wartime in 1952 to help support struggling farmers–once utilized underground tunnels to help its workers avoid being fired upon. Their baijiu is a light aroma style that's funky, floral, and mushroomy, with a long finish and a high ABV of 58%.

High Proof, Light Aroma

Kweichow Moutai
China
Sorghum and wheat

YINGBIN

One of the most well-known brands in China and throughout the world, this state-owned and operated distillery's entry-level bottle takes 2 years to produce. It's a pungent and tangy sauce aroma style, complete with miso notes and a lingering finish.

For the Adventurous Palate

Luzhou Laojiao
China
Sorghum

ZISHA DAQU

Luzhou Laojiao has a 400-year history–in fact, this bottling is said to have created the strong aroma category in 1573. Made with Sichuan-grown red sorghum, it's intense on the nose and palate, offering medicinal notes, overripe fruit flavors, and earthy undertones.

Tried and True

Luzhou Laojiao
China
Sorghum

MING RIVER SICHUAN BAIJIU

A gentle introduction to the category (and widely available in the US), this Sichuan-made baijiu is produced using local red sorghum and fermented in earthen pits for 2 months before distillation. It's packed with notes of overripe tropical fruit and offers a rich, lactic mouthfeel.

Baby's First Baijiu

AGAVE

In 2016, I ventured to Oaxaca, Mexico, for the first time. I was on a quest to immerse myself in the world of Mezcal and soon found myself bouncing around the dirt roads of San Luis del Rio and Zoquitlán, touring palenques (the regional term for Mezcal distilleries) with an enthusiastic group of bartenders-turned-Mezcal tour guides known as the Puro Burros. We were there to explore the different forms agave drinks can take—fresh aguamiel (agave nectar) straight from the plant, fermented pulque, and, of course, Mezcal. The experience was transformative, opening my eyes to the intersection of culture and spirits and inspiring a deep appreciation for the craft.

Maguey, metl, the "century plant," the "tree of wonders," the "plant of a thousand uses,"—agave has gone by many names in many languages. For centuries (if not millennia), the heart, or piña, has provided nourishment; the leaf tips have been used as sewing needles; the fibers have been turned into thread and building material; and the pulp has been manufactured into paper. Agave is also one of the few plants capable of preventing soil erosion in arid environments, and it comes with the added bonus of making an effective natural fence to mark boundaries or corral livestock. Given its variety of applications in relatively inhospitable lands, it's become an iconic symbol of Mexico's physical and cultural landscape—a reputation suddenly amplified by the recent global fascination with agave spirits.

Just Don't Call Me Late for Dinner

Considering the word for agave varies from region to region and that there are currently 63 nationally recognized Indigenous languages in Mexico alone, the number of monikers for this unique plant is almost too high to count. For example, the Zapotec call it *tobá,* the Mixtec call it *yagui,* the Purépecha call it *papalometl,* and the Mayans call it *k'il*. Later, the Spanish introduced more names, like maguey, aloe, and pita. In the Anglosphere, it's colloquially known as "the century plant" after a common misconception that it blooms once every hundred years (despite only living for ~30 years).

No, It's Not a Cactus

The agave plant is a member of the family Asparagaceae (yes, asparagus) and belongs to the same subfamily as yuccas and Joshua trees (Agavoideae). Native to the Americas (chiefly Mexico), 200 officially documented species exist (though there may be as many as 270), and they all thrive in hot, arid, and semi-arid climates. And while they're prolific throughout Mexico, the states of Oaxaca, Durango, and Chihuahua harbor the most diversity, with about 150 species endemic to those regions.

Because they're adorned with thick, leathery "leaves," or *pencas*, agaves do not meet the criteria for cacti. Instead, they're considered a sweet succulent, and that distinction makes all the difference when it comes to distilling. Arranged in a rosette shape and lined with spikes along the edges, agave has a notoriously tough exterior. The plant's outer membrane (aka the epidermis) is covered in a waxy layer called the *mixiote*, which prevents the pores—responsible for exchanging gasses like carbon dioxide—from releasing too much moisture. This adaptation allows the agave to store water during extended dry seasons in drought-prone environments. And because everything about these plants seems to be a little *extra*, they're also *monocarpic*, meaning they bloom just once in their lifetime.

Spiny pencas of Jabalí agave in Oaxaca, photo by Nat Harry.

While agave's hardiness, resourcefulness, and relative ease of cultivation have all contributed to its success, the plant has always demanded one thing in return: patience. Unlike most other crops, which mature in a single season, agave takes six to thirty years to reach maturity, depending on the variety. To signal that they're nearing the end of their lifecycle and are, therefore, ready for harvest, they sprout a tall, majestic flower from their center called a *quiote* (derived from Nahuatl, it's pronounced *kee-oh-teh*).

A powerful symbol of the plant's fertility, the quiote provides a range of benefits to the local ecosystem—serving as a food source to hummingbirds, moths, and long-nosed bats and maintaining the plant's genetic diversity by allowing for reproduction via seed. However, it also saps the plant of energy and, thus, sugar content (which, as we know from previous chapters, is vital for fermentation/distillation). The quick solution is to chop off the quiote before it begins to drain the plant of its sugar reserves—well before it goes to seed—but this means less-than-ideal outcomes for ecosystems.

You may wonder how reproduction occurs if no seeds are left over to do the job. Agave has the unique ability to reproduce in multiple ways and is commonly cultivated (especially in the Tequila industry) using rhizomes referred to as *hijuelos*—essentially clones of a plant that emerge from the root system near its base. These little "pups" are favored in the industry because it's far more efficient to replant them than to plant from seed in a nursery (plus, that would require allowing the plants to go to seed in the first place).

Given cyclical agave shortages and the time and effort it takes to cultivate from seed, efficiency seems like the ideal route. But there's more to life than efficiency, and focusing on it above all else carries its own cost. Mass cultivation from hijuelos severely limits genetic diversity. In healthy ecosystems, agave plants are surrounded by close relatives that are similar but not identical in their genetic makeup.

Agave in the mountains of Zoquitlán, Oaxaca, photo by Nat Harry.

This allows for a wider gene pool for reproduction, meaning a greater capacity for adaptation and an increased likelihood of species survival. However, industrial-scale farming relies on genetic copies, meaning there is less genetic variation to aid in adaptation to environmental changes or disease resistance. This use of clones, combined with the regulatory requirement that Tequila be made from a single type of agave, means many agave varieties are at great risk of decline and extinction.

The Mexican Long-Nosed Bat

The hard truth is that as the Mezcal and Tequila industries thrive, fewer plants are going to seed. That's not great news for biodiversity in general, but it's especially bad for the Mexican long-nosed bat, which relies on agave nectar as one of its main food sources. These bats, which have been on the endangered list since 1988, are the primary pollinators for three of the most important agaves in the agave spirits industry: *angustifolia, salmiana*, and *tequilana*. As they migrate, these bats sip on the nectar, pollinating the agaves and ridding them of pesky insects. However, they can only do so at night when the agaves bloom, meaning the bats don't receive the sugar and protein they need unless quiotes are allowed to flower. Given that most commercial agave farmers cut the quiote to redirect the sugars back into the plant, the long-nosed bat's food source has been nearly annihilated.

Common Species of Agave Used in Spirits

Much the same way not all grapes are suited for winemaking, only a fraction of the 200+ species of agave are suited for making spirits. And while Mezcal can be crafted from about thirty species, Tequila, as mentioned above, can only be made with one. Still, the reality is that only about a dozen species account for almost 99 percent of certified Mezcal and Tequila. And similar to wine grapes, different agaves thrive in different climates and soil types, meaning certain regions and villages in Mexico have made a name for themselves producing a particular type of Mezcal from a particular species of agave.

The Tequila Interchange Project

The cutting of quiotes before they are allowed to flower hasn't just been a blow to the Mexican long-nosed bat but also to the diversity of agave species (and not just those used for spirits production). In 2010, the Tequila Interchange Project was founded to combat this dilemma. It launched an initiative encouraging agave spirit producers to allow 5% of their fields to go to seed. But with the recent boom in agave spirits—agave has gone from $8 to $30 a kilogram in the last 15 years—the program has faced membership challenges.

Common Species of Agave Used in Spirits

ESPADÍN

Additional Common Names: Espadilla; Castilla; Tepemete (in Durango); Pelón Verde; Cimarrón; Doba-Yej (Zapotec)
Scientific Name: *Agave angustifolia*
Time to Maturity: 5–12 years
Region(s) Grown: Oaxaca; Michoacán; Durango

Espadín—the genetic parent to Blue Weber—is the foundation of Oaxacan Mezcal production. Easy to cultivate and quick to grow (as far as agaves are concerned), with high sugar concentrations that lead to higher yields, Espadín accounts for roughly 70% of all certified Mezcal production.

MADRECUIXE/CUIXE

Additional Common Names: Bicuixe; Cenizo; Tobaziche; Verde; Largo; Cirial
Scientific Name: *Agave karwinskii*
Time to Maturity: 12–18 years for most
Region(s) Grown: Oaxaca and other parts of southern Mexico

The Karwinskiis are a diverse group of agaves that include several subspecies, all of which can be identified by their tall trunks and unique, treelike appearance. (Think the trees from *The Lorax*.) The leaves create a more cylindrical shape, and the piñas (which can grow quite large and weigh 60–120 lb.) tend to be fibrous and have less sugar content than other species. Madrecuixe, which is often used interchangeably with Cuixe despite being two subspecies, is named for its tendency to cross-pollinate (thanks to long-nosed bats!) when allowed to go to seed—hence the name "madre" (mother). Most Karwinskii bottlings on American shelves are Madrecuixe or Cuixe (with the "x" sometimes appearing as a "sh").

BARRIL

Additional Common Names: Karwinskii
Scientific Name: *Agave karwinskii*
Time to Maturity: 12–15 years; Up to 30 for wild varieties
Region(s) Grown: Oaxaca and other parts of southern Mexico

Another subspecies of the Karwinskii group, Barril is slightly different than its cousins, though it sometimes gets lumped in with them. Due to their shape and size (Barril agaves are more "barrel"-shaped and with shorter leaves), they are often used as natural fencing for pastures. They're also more difficult to grow, as they are less prone to rhizome growth and are primarily cultivated by seed.

TOBALÁ

Additional Common Names: Papalomé; Papalométl
Scientific Name: *Agave potatorum*
Time to Maturity: 12–15 years
Region(s) Grown: Oaxaca; Puebla

Aromatic, complex, and slow to grow, this small agave proved extremely popular during Mezcal's rise to fame in the early 2000s, leading to overharvesting and the near eradication of the species in the wild. Unlike other agaves, Tobalá can only reproduce from seed, and is usually grown in greenhouses or nurseries and later transplanted into fields.

BLUE WEBER/TEQUILANA

Additional Common Names: Tequila Azul
Scientific Name: *Agave tequilana*
Time to Maturity: 6–10 years
Region(s) Grown: Jalisco

If you've ever had Tequila, you've had Blue Weber agave, as it's the only varietal permitted in the making of this famous spirit. Time to maturity depends on weather and subregion, but some producers will harvest plants as young as 4 years old when grown for the diffuser process (see the section on Tequila). Mezcal producers occasionally use Blue Weber as well, though not nearly as often as they should. Drinking Mezcal made with Blue Weber is a great way to experience what Tequila might have been like pre-industrialization.

TEPEZTATE

Additional Common Names: Pichomel; Pichorra; Pizorra
Scientific Name: *Agave marmorata*
Time to Maturity: Up to 25–30 years
Region(s) Grown: Oaxaca

Plentiful until the wild agave boom wiped out the surplus, Tepeztate spirits are the stuff of legend. This is partly because it takes an incredibly long time to grow (done exclusively from seed) and because of the complexity of its flavors, which can be earthy or have strong notes of caramelized tropical fruit. A glutton for punishment, Tepeztate also prefers high elevations, steep grades, and rocky soils.

CUPREATA

Additional Common Names: Chino; Ancho; Papalote; Papalometl (Nahuatl); Papalomé; Yaabendisi (Mixteco); Cimarrón
Scientific Name: *Agave cupreata*
Time to Maturity: 10–15 years
Region(s) Grown: Michoacán; Guerrero

Cupreata, also referred to as *tuchi* (a name given by the Huichol), is a great window into Mezcal production outside of Oaxaca. Endemic to Michoacán and Guerrero, it grows at elevations of 4,000–6,000 feet. This is one of my favorite subspecies, and there are endless flavor variations. (My first sip of a wild harvest Cupreata Mezcal tasted like roasted garlic!)

SALMIANA

Additional Common Names: Verde; In some regions, it's still called Pulquero, though Pulquero is now considered a separate agave species
Scientific Name: *Agave salmiana*
Time to Maturity: 12–25 years
Region(s) Grown: San Luis Potosí; Durango; Parts of Central Mexico

Known as the "green giant," Salmiana Mezcal is becoming an increasingly common sight in US liquor stores—though it's quite the style departure from its more popular cousin, Espadín. It leans heavier on the vegetal side, with a tangy, almost lactic quality. Despite its large size, Salmiana yields a low amount of fermentable sugar, sometimes taking up to four times the plant matter to match the yield of Espadín or Tequilana.

A Labor of Love

Of all the skilled laborers that craft agave spirits, chief among them is the *jimador*, or the farmer/field worker who tends, selects, harvests, and roasts agave piñas to a desired quality (*jima* means "to harvest" or "prune" in Nahuatl). This role is so central to the production process that it hasn't been replaced by modern technology and continues to be passed down over generations, most often from father to son.

Farm work generally requires specialized knowledge and demands physical strength, but in the case of agave, jimadores also impact the end spirit's flavor profile. Using a unique tool called a *coa*, they carefully trim the pencas of the 100–300 pound plants down to a desirable size. The more leafy material the jimador leaves on the piña, the greater its bitterness and vegetal quality. Agave spirits are so dependent on the highly skilled shaping of piñas that it is always done manually, no matter how sophisticated or large-scale the operation.

In Oaxaca, as in other prolific Mezcal-producing areas, the roles of farmer and distiller are even more intertwined, especially for the many small family operations still in existence. For this reason, farmer-distillers are usually just referred to as *mezcaleros* or *maestro mezcaleros*, depending on their status and level of knowledge.

Jimador working in Michoacán (left); coa used to cut pencas (right); photos by Nat Harry.

First, There Was Pulque

The fermented beverages of Mesoamerica have a long and well-documented past, and though they're made from a range of ingredients—including but not limited to corn and cactus fruit—the agave-based drink pulque is perhaps the most famous. Pulque is made by removing the quiote and scraping the remaining cavity to release a water-like sap called *aguamiel*, which is then fermented. The beverage dates back at least a thousand years and has persisted through the ravages of colonialism so successfully that today, it's nearly impossible to visit a palenque without being offered a glass or two of this milk-colored, fizzy beverage.

In antiquity, pulque held tremendous religious and cultural importance, so much so that it was consumed almost exclusively during ceremonies and rituals. However, these days, you can order pulque at the market or bring a vessel—growler style—to be filled at a *pulqueria* (a Mexican tavern specializing in serving pulque), where it's served by the liter and sometimes flavored. This bright, tangy drink ranges from 3 to 7 percent ABV, though it's typically on the lower end of the spectrum, not unlike a session beer. That being said, it's quite unlike beer or other fermented beverages that rely solely on yeast, as microorganisms and lactic acid found naturally in the aguamiel are key to pulque's fermentation. As a result, it's much more delicate and would be more accurate to compare pulque to kombucha or other probiotic drinks.

Removing the quiote to release aguamiel, photo by Nat Harry.

MEZCAL

MEZCAL (CERTIFIED)

Plant: Agave (30+ species)

Place: Mexico (primarily Oaxaca, Guerrero, and Michoacán)

Production: Favors traditional methods such as earthen oven cooking and manual or tahona crushing

Protection: DO

"Mezcal" derives from the Nahuatl word *mexcalli*, a combination of *métl*, meaning "agave," and *ixcalli*, meaning "cooked." Specialized knowledge of its many production methods and ingredients has existed for over 500 years, but the term became a catch-all for any Mexican spirit distilled from agave. However, that changed in 1994, when Mezcal received its own DO, and the category skyrocketed in popularity outside of Mexico. Today, "Mezcal" (spelled with a capital *M*) refers to the category protected by the 1994 DO, while "mezcal" (lowercase *m*) refers to a general agave-based spirit. Still, due to their intertwined past, it's challenging to discuss the two separately. (So, for our purposes, we'll refer to both with a capital M.)

Traditionally, Mezcal was made for friends and family, special occasions, or trade at the local market. In fact, most Mezcal never traveled outside the village where it was made (this is still very much the case today). This began to change in the 1990s thanks in part to the actions of a determined American artist named Ron Cooper, whose love for the spirit is a big reason for the current Mezcal renaissance. A California native, Cooper started the iconic brand Del Maguey by "smuggling" (his words) liters of Mezcal from tiny, unknown palenques across the border. He was so successful that in 2016, he partnered with liquor powerhouse Pernod Ricard, marking the end of Mezcal's underdog status in the US. Since then, the spirit has come a long way on the international market, outgrowing its early association with a worm in a bottle and a wicked hangover.

Slow and Low

Like many raw ingredients used in distilling, agave is cooked and processed before it's fermented. In the case of agave, that means "hydrolyzing the inulin into fructose." So, what the heck is inulin? (Or hydrolysis, for that matter?) *Inulin* is a starchy substance made of glucose and fructose molecules found naturally in fruits, vegetables, herbs, and roots. And *hydrolysis* is the process of using water to break down a chemical bond and unlock stored sugars—sometimes without even using heat (more on that in Tequila). Cooking, or more accurately, roasting, is the most common way to achieve this.

Cooked agave cooling at the Rey Campero palenque, photo by Nat Harry.

There are a few ways to cook agave for fermentation, though the most common is in an underground, earthen oven. This method is also the simplest in terms of the technology used: fire. These massive conical ovens are filled with large rocks that absorb heat from the fuel source—a mixture of dried *bagasse* (agave fibers) and local timber such as mesquite or pine. This roasting is a significant part of what makes Mezcal production unique—and what sets it apart from Tequila—because it imparts the smoky flavors people associate with the spirit. Cooking this way may look simple, but it requires specific considerations and methods. For example, to keep the rocks from burning or charring the

The Double-Edged Sword of the World's Largest DO

Of all the spirits covered in this book, Mezcal is perhaps the most fraught. After officially receiving a protected status, its international profile rose so sharply it fostered continual changes to the category, including the expansion of states authorized to produce Mezcal and allowances for more industrial producers to get certified. As such, the DO (which is now the largest in the world by territory and includes 10 Mexican states and various municipalities) struggles with being a victim of its own success by "diluting the brand," so to speak. If not careful, the industry may undo all its hard-earned success of the last 2 decades.

Fermentation

Traditional Mezcal is unique in two ways: 1) fermentation occurs along with the cooked agave fibers, and 2) it is typically fermented in open wood vats, which allow native and/or wild yeasts into the fermentation process. Both practices invite more complexity of flavor, and the use of native yeasts guarantees no two bottlings are ever identical, even if all other factors remain constant.

The fermentation vessels can also be quite eclectic. Ancestral ones (still used occasionally) include hollowed-out logs, cured animal hides, and stone cavities, though the most common practice is to ferment in large pine vats called *tinas* (Spanish for "tubs"). As the tina remains open, agave fibers form a dense layer or crust on the top, bubbling as alcohol is created.

piñas, bagasse is used to line the pits and separate the layers of agave. Then, to preserve even more humidity, the final layer of bagasse is covered with woven materials like burlap sacks or blankets before dirt is piled on top to prevent the heat from escaping. Techniques vary slightly depending on the producer and region, with some producers adding water to the oven before covering it to create even more steam.

Agave can also be cooked using an above-ground oven, an autoclave, or even a diffuser, depending on how the Mezcal is labeled. The above-ground oven (*horno*) can be made of brick, stone, or ceramic, and like an earthen oven, it uses steam to cook the piñas. This is the slowest industrialized cooking method and arguably one of the best for preserving complex flavors without having to dig a pit. Conversely, an autoclave is essentially a giant stainless-steel tube resembling a small submarine. Its purpose is to use steam—usually at high pressure—to shorten the cooking time (though industry veterans use low pressure with better results). A diffuser, on the other hand, uses hydrolysis to break down the agave. It's rarely seen in the world of Mezcal, though it may become increasingly common as restrictions on traditionally made Mezcal are chipped away by larger, profit-driven companies.

Horse-powered tahona crushing cooked agave, Oaxaca, photo by Nat Harry.

Fermentation vessels (tinas) at Mezcal Unión co-op palenque, photo by Nat Harry.

Crush

After cooking the agave, it must be crushed to break down the fibers and help release the juice and sugar for fermentation. While Mezcal and Tequila share some crushing methods, including the use of a *tahona* (a large heavy stone wheel), Mezcal producers favor more traditional approaches.

Technique/Style	Tool	Labor	Pros and Cons
Ancestral	Wooden Club/Mallet/Axe (hand processing)	Most intense manual labor requirements	Most ideal for preserving flavor and complexity
Traditional	Tahona/Large Stone Wheel	Pulled by burros (donkeys), horses, or tractor	Complexity and flavor maintained whilst reducing human impact
Modern	Roller Mill/Shredder	Mechanical efficiency reduces physical labor	Potential to release or create compounds that lead to unwanted flavors or methanol

Certified Mezcal Production by Subcategory

AGAVE

Traditional Mezcal stills, Santa María Ixcatlan, Oaxaca, photo by Nat Harry.

The Question of Origin and Distillation

Distillation's initial journey to Mexico remains a topic of debate. The most widely accepted belief is that the technology was introduced by the Spanish during colonization. However, some historians say it arrived from the Philippines via Spain—a result of the "Manila Galleon" trade that opened up a connection from Manila to Colima (a volcanic region just outside Tequila). In support of this theory, the traditional, rustic stills commonly used throughout Mexico today are more similar to Filipino stills than typical European, alembic style stills. And the most recent theory, put forward by ethnobotanist Patricia Colunga García-Marín and her colleagues, suggests that distillation in Mexico wasn't imported at all and that the practice developed independently in Mexico as early as 1500 BCE.

JOVEN	MADURADO EN VIDRIO	REPOSADO	AÑEJO	ABOCADO CON	DESTILADO CON
UNAGED (NOT THE SAME AS JOVEN TEQUILA)	AGED A MINIMUM OF 12 MONTHS IN GLASS	AGED A MINIMUM OF 2 MONTHS IN OAK	AGED A MINIMUM OF 12 MONTHS IN OAK	INDICATES A FLAVORING OR INFUSION ADDED AFTER DISTILLATION, SUCH AS CITRUS OR OTHER FRUIT AND SPICES	INDICATES A FLAVORING OR ADDITIONAL RAW MATERIAL ADDED DURING DISTILLATION

Mezcal by type.

Overharvesting and Exploitation

As Mezcal skyrocketed in popularity, farmers and producers scrambled to keep up. It was exciting to have money suddenly flowing into parts of Mexico that needed it, but unexpected consumer demand (and unchecked supply) also led to undesired outcomes. Crops were harvested by those with no farming experience, agaves were poached from other mezcaleros, and the situation became a free-for-all. Wild agave that had been maturing for decades were suddenly gone—a sort of mass deforestation, seemingly overnight. As it became clear Mezcal would be more than a flash in the pan, established producers started planning and organizing for the future. They put the brakes on aggressive harvesting, intentionally replanted and cultivated agave, and changed agricultural methods to meet demand in ways that respected the ecosystem. But the unfortunate truth is that wild agave at the abundance and scale that existed for eons is now a thing of the past.

To add insult to injury, many larger companies take advantage of sharp inequalities in rural Mexico, contracting with farmers for far below market price. These communities—many of them traditional, with deep cultural connections to the spirit—very often receive less than their fair share of the profits, to put it lightly. Meanwhile, self-styled entrepreneurs with little experience or industry knowledge seek out "rare" or wild varietals only to slap fancy labels on bottlings and upsell them with little regard for the community or sustainability. Ulises Torrentera wrote about this noxious trend in his 2012 book *Mezcalería:*

Field Blends (aka Ensembles)

Simply put, a *field blend* (aka ensemble) is the product of a mezcalero scanning their land, assessing which plants are ready to harvest (regardless of the species), and processing them for distillation. These mixed species are then roasted, mashed, and fermented together. Field blends lend themselves to more sustainable agave cultivation, and the results from these combinations can be transcendent. Still, despite being a traditional way to harvest and drink Mezcal, blends have fallen to the wayside in favor of single village and single varietal offerings—yet another product of vulture capitalism. Now that everyone's calmed down a little at the sight of a bottle of Mezcal, we can hopefully give them more attention.

Terms to Know

- Single Varietal – Made with one type of agave
- Single Village – Agave made from one village, though not necessarily a single producer
- Ensembles (Field Blends) – A blend of agave species; A traditional way of producing Mezcal using whichever types are mature at the time of harvest
- Pechuga – A celebratory style of Mezcal, traditionally made with a chicken breast or other protein along with local seasonal fruits and spices in the distillation chamber

Cultura del Mezcal, noting that "adventurers dressed as businessmen, both national and foreigner, arrive at the communities to acquire their product at laughable prices before signing an agreement which is prolonged five, ten, even twenty years without the possibility of adjustment that benefits those who manufacture or cultivate maguey." So, if all this degradation is to satisfy demand, the question becomes: how does the conscientious consumer get their Mezcal and drink it, too?

Rest assured, you don't have to compromise sustainability for quality Mezcal, and just a little bit of intentionality can go a long way. Overall, you'll want to look into the brand you're buying. Do they recognize the significance of Mezcal and agave in the cultures and places they originate from? Does the label list the producer and village, or otherwise imply a sense of transparency? Or seek out "ancestral" or "artisanal" products (see graphic on page 181). While these terms are usually buzzwords, in the case of Mezcal, they're regulated by the DO. Lastly, the most sustainable Mezcal option may depend on the drink. For example, if you want some wild agave, drink an ensemble (see sidebar on page 183), and if you're craving a Margarita, try using a cultivated or semi-cultivated agave or a split base of Tequila and Mezcal.

Because bottlings of Mezcal vary from batch to batch, recommendations here are for producers.

Oaxaca

Expressions: Pulquero; Chato; Jabalí

REY CAMPERO

In the tiny mountain village of Candelaria Yegolé, this family collective distillery makes a raw and beautifully simple distillate. They grow Jabalí (*Agave convallis*) and Tepextate (*Agave marmorata*) side by side, allowing a portion to go to seed and helping to sustain biodiversity.

A Family Affair

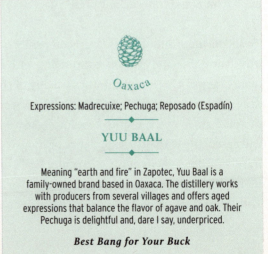

Oaxaca

Expressions: Madrecuixe; Pechuga; Reposado (Espadín)

YUU BAAL

Meaning "earth and fire" in Zapotec, Yuu Baal is a family-owned brand based in Oaxaca. The distillery works with producers from several villages and offers aged expressions that balance the flavor of agave and oak. Their Pechuga is delightful and, dare I say, underpriced.

Best Bang for Your Buck

Michoacán

Expressions: Cupreata; Tequilana; Seasonal limited releases

LA LUNA

A lovely introduction to Mezcal made outside of Oaxaca in Etúcaro, La Luna uses the prehistoric-looking *Agave cupreata*, and grows it amongst pine forests that are harvested for their sap. This 4th-generation producer has been making Mezcal with a strong sense of place and terroir since 1910.

Off the Beaten Path

Oaxaca

Expressions: Ejutla; San Luis del Río

NUESTRA SOLEDAD

Each Mezcal in Nuestra Soledad's line of single village bottlings comes from one of six different villages. Made using traditional production methods, these lovely expressions prove Espadín can be a great way to explore terroir and craftsmanship.

A Taste of Terroir

Oaxaca

Expressions: San Baltazar; Aniversario releases; San Miguel (Sola de Vega)

ALIPUS

A traditional brand developed for the US market, each bottling is from a different Oaxacan village and mezcalero. Most producers use Espadín as their base, though some incorporate a small amount of other varietals.

Single Village

Guerrero

Expressions: Cupreata

MEZCAL AMARÁS

Founded in 2010 with a focus on sustainable farming practices, including reforestation, this distiller has planted over 150,000 agaves grown from seed. The Cupreata is fresh but funky—light on smoke profile and heavy on jalapeño.

Sustainably Farmed

San Luis Potosí

Expressions: Salmiana

METICHE

Metiche's wild agave is regulated by the Ministry of Environmental and Natural Resources to prevent overharvesting, guaranteeing that each plant matures for at least 13 years. Since timber isn't native to the region, the agave is cooked above ground.

Harvested with Care

Oaxaca

Expressions: Elote; Ensemble; Pechuga; Tobalá

MEZCAL VAGO

With an emphasis on tradition and sustainability, Mezcal Vago recycles spent agave fibers and uses natural, regional dyes to make their bottle labels. While the Sola de Vega region is renowned for Tobalá, their Elote Mezcal, distilled with toasted maize, has long been one of my favorite bottles.

Tried and True

DESTILADO DE AGAVE

Destilados de agave are made using the same traditional methods as Mezcal, but they either don't meet the requirements of the Mezcal DO or the distilleries choose not to participate in certification—an increasingly popular choice among small producers. As the politics and identity around Mezcal continue to shift (there's so much drama surrounding certification that it could fill an entire book), in some ways, embracing spirits labeled "destilado de agave" or "aguardiente" signals that the category has come full circle, back to the days when mezcaleros distilled just for friends, family, and their local community and didn't have to follow rules or a checklist.

DESTILADO DE AGAVE

Plant: Minimum 51% agave (30+ varieties)

Place: Anywhere (predominantly Mexico)

Production: Favors traditional methods such as earthen oven cooking and manual or tahona crushing

Protection: Recognized by the TTB as "agave spirits"

The Consejo Regulador del Mezcal—often referred to as the CRM—is (technically) a private, not-for-profit organization established to enforce Mexico's Mezcal DO. They certify producers by processing and testing distillate samples and charging producer fees, and until recently, they were the only certification option available. Critics say the organization is too political, that they play favorites, and that the fees they charge (and the sample sizes required for certification) prevent the smallest producers from getting certified. The process costs producers anywhere from $3,000 to $10,000 (USD), which is pretty steep, considering the daily minimum wage in Oaxaca is currently 173 pesos, or about $8. The CRM was even fined in 2020 by Mexico's Secretary of Economy for "deceptive and abusive" practices, including running a campaign that stated if a bottle didn't have the CRM's signature holographic logo, then it wasn't "real" Mezcal, falsely implying they are the sole determiner of certification. The fine was a reminder from the government that the CRM does not "own" the DO of Mezcal. Still, the certification process remains complicated, leading some producers to forgo it altogether.

Nonetheless, thanks to the DO's successful marketing and Mezcal's popularity, plenty of consumers outside of Mexico have acquired enough understanding of agave spirits that they don't need such hyper-specific language on a bottle. If it looks, smells, and tastes like Mezcal, do you really need to see the word to make it legitimate? Many long-standing brands and producers have established trust through years of hard work. Ironically, this allows many long-time producers of Mezcal to skip the certification process (though it must still go through TTB testing and basic alcohol regulation to be imported to the US) and simply bottle under the label "destilado de agave" or "agave spirit"—a term that could refer to any spirit made from agave, regardless of the region or methods.

Oaxaca

Expressions: Arroqueño; Barril; Limited release ensembles

REAL MINERO

Any ancestrally produced Mezcal is worth the splurge, but I'm particularly fond of Real Minero's ethos and dedication to farming agave from seed. Real Minero is also one of the few women-operated palenques, with Graciela Ángeles Carreño running the show.

Worth the Splurge

Various villages

Expressions: Reina Sánchez; Berta Vasquez

REZPIRAL

There aren't many women distillers in the world of Mezcal, but two of my favorites produce very small batches of agave spirit for Rezpiral. The brand works with traditional "farmer artisans," using a profit-sharing model to support producers and their communities.

Sustainable and Fair

Oaxaca and Puebla

Expressions: Amando Alvarez (Papalometl); Delfino Tobón Mejía (Pechuga de Mole Poblano)

CINCO SENTIDOS

Founded by translator-turned-restaurateur Jason Cox, Cinco Sentidos celebrates uncertified spirits from five remote producers, employing the motto "drink with respect." The producers often use ancestral methods like fermenting in cowhide, stone, or tree bark, which lead to unique results.

Worth the Splurge

Various villages

Expressions: Ángel Cruz Robles; Maximiliano "Serafin" García Gerónimo

CUENTACUENTOS

Self-described as a "business development platform that helps traditional Mezcal families get their products to market," their bottlings are a mix of certified Mezcal and uncertified agave spirit focused on producers and traditional methods.

Modern Marketplace

TEQUILA

Though Mezcal predates it by centuries, Tequila reigns supreme in the world of agave distillates, and that doesn't seem to be changing anytime soon. But not many people know that Tequila is a kind of Mezcal: mezcal de Tequila. By modern standards, this is a misnomer, of course, with Mezcal now having its own rules, regulations, and DO. Still, for educational purposes, let's maintain that Tequila is a specific kind of Mezcal, the way Cognac is a specific kind of brandy with its unique identity linked to a place.

TEQUILA

Plant: *Agave tequilana* (aka Blue Weber)

Place: Mexico (Jalisco and municipalities in Nayarit, Guanajuato, Michoacán, and Tamaulipas)

Production: Favors modern, industrialized methods and above-ground ovens

Protection: DO

Tequila began claiming an identity separate from Mezcal around the mid-19th century, with the division occurring mainly along class lines. At the time, imported wine, Sherry, and liquor were the default preferences among wealthy Europeans living in Mexico. However, these elites (and their *criollo* and *mestizo* descendants) also ran their own distillation experiments with native plants whenever possible. Before long, "vino de mezcal" began popping up in regions with sizable European populations, like Guadalajara.

In time, agave came to be farmed exclusively for spirit production, and Mezcal from the Tequila region ("mezcal de Tequila") gained a reputation as a superior product, at least in colonial circles. Industrialization and the arrival of the railroad further entrenched divisions and extended Tequila's reach, making it more plentiful, accessible, and popular than ever before, especially in export markets.

Afraid of losing out on their own national patrimony, in 1978, the Mexican government registered Tequila under the Lisbon Agreement for the Protection of Appellations (AO), which protects products from the effects of globalization and reinforces their cultural and national associations. Fast forward to the present, and the spirit is a source of national pride, recognized worldwide as uniquely Mexican and dutifully protected by a DO. By law and under the regulation of the Consejo Regulador del Tequila (CRT), it can only be produced in 180 municipalities within five Mexican states: the entirety of Jalisco (the birthplace of Tequila), and various municipalities within Michoacán, Guanajuato, Tamaulipas, and Nayarit (whose Tequilas are rarely available outside of Mexico).

Tequila producing states in Mexico.

Certified Mezcal	Tequila
30+ species of agave	*Agave tequilana*
100% agave	Minimum 51% agave
10 Mexican states and various municipalities	5 Mexican states, primarily Jalisco, Michoacán, and various municipalities
Traditional methods, underground wood-fired ovens	Modern, industrialized methods, brick or steam ovens, diffusers
Distillation and fermentation typically include fibers	Distillation and fermentation rarely include fibers, only juice
Typically uses indigenous yeast, open fermentation, and batch variation	Typically uses closed fermentation, with the controlled addition of yeast for consistency

Certified Mezcal vs. Tequila.

Siembra Valles

You've probably caught on by now that Mezcal and Tequila exist in separate spheres, and we don't see much crossover between the two practices or their makers. Of course, there are always exceptions, and Siembra Valles Traditional Tequila is just that: a collaborative project between a long-time Mezcal-producing family and a Tequila-producing family that share similar goals and ideals.

Why is this significant? Not only do these two spirit industries rarely collide, but there remains an underlying tension between them, one rooted in classism. The Tequila industry has been working dutifully to distance itself from its rustic (and more Native) Mezcal ancestor since the day producers stripped "vino de mezcal" from their labels many years ago. Therefore, the willingness of two families to come together and share *generations* of family knowledge with each other to produce this Tequila is nothing short of amazing.

The process starts with Blue Weber agave grown in Jalisco, so business as usual there. However, after harvesting, the piñas are roasted underground in an earthen pit like traditional Mezcal, marking the first time in more than 100 years that agave has been cooked this way in Jalisco (producers moved away from the practice when developing more modern production methods for Tequila). The pit is filled with wood and lava rocks and roasted for nearly five days before being crushed with clubs, a method that predates even the use of a tahona. And I can tell you from experience it's a task that requires superhuman strength—those dense wooden bats are *heavy*, and though cooked, the agave does not yield easily.

Fermentation takes place in oak barrels and, distinctively, in brick containers, a technique not used since the early 1900s. The first distillation occurs in a 300-liter traditional Tequila copper pot alembic still. On the second run, the juice is transferred to a Filipino alembic still crafted from pine. It goes without saying that there are no additives here, and it's also worth noting that the Tequila is distilled at a higher proof than the industry standard, bottled at 50% ABV (100 proof).

Blue agave field, Jalisco, photo by Nat Harry.

Blue Weber Tequila and the Boom-Bust Cycle

Perhaps the most defining aspect of Tequila is its primary ingredient; it can only be made with one species of agave—Blue Weber (*Agave tequilana*). But this unique characteristic is also the spirit's Achilles' heel. On average, it takes 5–9 years (depending on climate and region) for the Blue Weber plant to reach maturity, meaning it's nearly a decade before it can be harvested for Tequila. Between the plant's time to maturity, the spirit's reliance on a single varietal, and the market's inconsistency, growing regions experience deep and recurrent agave shortages.

These shortages tend to trigger a series of chain reactions, one of the first being an increase in agave prices, which leads to distilleries taking shortcuts in craftsmanship and passing some of the cost down to consumers. (Thankfully, a Blue Weber shortage of around 30%–40% in 2018–2019 affected price tags by only a few dollars per bottle for most brands.)

Shortages also pressure producers to use young and unripe plants to meet consumer demand. To shore up the quality of a distillate made from a three- or four-year-old underdeveloped agave, producers use additives, like sugar, during fermentation as well as flavorings and aromas post-distillation. Additionally, many switch to using a diffuser to facilitate a quick turnaround and rarely revert back to traditional methods. In this scenario, flavor and sustainability become secondary to hedging against market instability and the famously mercurial whims of spirit trends.

Unfortunately, this economic imperative leaves small, independent agave farmers to fend for themselves, even as they become the last safeguard of quality. For example, two years ago, the market was starved for mature agave. Today, there's a surplus, yet many distillers continue buying from larger farms that sell young agave at better market prices than independent growers can offer. Jake Lustig, a long-time agave industry veteran and owner of Terranova Spirits, explains that it's a tough time for small farmers "whose worlds have turned upside down in the past few years. [They] converted to agave from beans, corn, tomatoes, and chilies, so are now without a short-term crop, and no market for their long-term crop." Unless, of course, consumers demand something better.

Tommy's Margarita

Created by Julio Bermejo in San Francisco for Tommy's Mexican restaurant (1995), this recipe uses agave nectar instead of an orange liqueur like Triple Sec.

- 2 oz. 100% agave Tequila
- 1 oz. fresh lime juice
- ½ oz. agave nectar (undiluted) or use 1:1 dilution agave simple syrup

Shake all ingredients with ice, strain into a rocks glass with fresh ice, and garnish with a lime wedge or wheel.

Fuenteseca

Long before launching a career as a Tequila producer, Enrique Fonseca's family were exclusively agave farmers in Jalisco. It was only after a break with two of their biggest clients—Jose Cuervo and Sauza Tequila—that they found themselves with tons of agave and no buyer. The following year, Fonseca pivoted: the family estate incorporated production to become grower-producers.

Though challenging, entering the world of production offered a key benefit: total control over every aspect of production—a fact Fonseca now proudly states on their estate grown *Huerta Singular* bottlings. For Fonseca, proper ripeness not only yields high sugar content but is vital to quality, adding to the spirit's complexity, flavor, and nuance. He refers to his agave fields as "orchards," *huertas* or *potreros* in Spanish. (Fuenteseca's importer Jake Lustig cheekily explained that only gringos refer to agave farms as "fields.")

Diffuser Tequila

Like the topic of GMOs, the conversation around diffuser Tequila can be tricky. On its face, the method may not seem problematic. We live in the modern era, and the diffuser is by far the most efficient way to extract sugars from agave at a whopping 95 percent or higher (compared with around 70 percent for traditional methods). Maximizing material output means less agave needed per bottle and more bang for your buck. But the problematic issues arise when we look at the big picture.

First, the diffuser was created to shave off harvest time, meaning it *exclusively* uses underripe, underdeveloped agave plants—the antithesis of what we've been taught to value in Tequila and Mezcal production. In this case, the unripe piña is considered little more than a vehicle for

---

Monoculture Problems

In the past, agave shortages have led to companies sourcing agave outside of their designated region or DO, a practice that would technically negate the distillate's official status. This practice seems to be an open secret in the Tequila industry, implying the CRT is either unable to keep up with enforcement or looks the other way.

saccharification, with the raw ingredient used more like a giant sugar beet to create alcohol. The result is a fermented product essentially robbed of everything that gives agave spirits character, leaving additives to substitute for flavor and body.

The diffuser process begins with a machine roughly the size of a basketball court, capable of quickly processing literal tons of agave at a time. I use "processing" here, not "cooking," because the "cooking" occurs with a cocktail of chemicals in a sexy little chemical reaction called acid-thermal hydrolysis. With a one-two punch of high-pressure water blasts followed by a treatment of hydrochloric acid, the starches in these young plants are chemically converted into fermentable sugar. (This is also how most agave syrups are processed.)

The Batanga

- 1 ½ oz. El Tequileño Blanco
- ½ oz. fresh lime juice
- 4 oz. chilled Mexican Coke

Rim a Collins glass with a quality salt, add Tequila and lime, and fill with ice (being mindful of the rim). Top with chilled cola and stir gently.

Personal flavor preference aside, the biggest problem with diffuser Tequilas is their effect on the surrounding ecosystem. Frequent crop rotations mean that roots don't stick around long enough to develop, and shade grasses (and other native flora) don't get the chance to grow alongside maturing agave—a critical attribute to their healthy growth. Lustig stresses that grower-producers and small farmers "tend to leave their agave orchards with weeds to compete with the agave for increased stressing, to host native insects, to attract birds which controls beetle outbreaks, and to prevent topsoil runoff in the rainy season." Constant disruption and tillage exhaust the soil and cause topsoil erosion. This, combined with the diseases that result from squeezing plants too close together, leads to a vicious cycle that harms the agave's ecosystem and, ultimately, the agave itself.

Still, trying to hurry nature along isn't exactly a new concept. (For example, companies are now creating "aged" whiskey and rum without the barrel, relying instead on chemical processes or vibration technology.) And while I hesitate to make value judgments in a complex and nuanced industry, steering clear of diffuser Tequila is a hill I'm happy to die on. If Tequila is meant to evoke a sense of place and identity, why would producers settle for a homogenized flavor? The short answer: profit. Making diffuser Tequila is cheap and fast (the entire process from diffuser to distillation could hypothetically happen in 24 hours), and many people don't seem to mind. But if they did, even just a little, they could get a reactive global Tequila market (valued at 16.5 billion US dollars in 2023) to pay attention.

Aging Tequila and Mezcal: The Difference Between Blanco, Reposado, Añejo, and Extra Añejo

After distillation, Tequila can be bottled as is, rested in glass, or aged in barrels. Reposado (rested), añejo (aged), and extra añejo (extra aged) are most commonly aged in oak barrels formerly used for Bourbon or Tennessee whiskey (see the chapter on wood). However, some distillers use ex-wine barrels or even *pipones* (known colloquially as *toneles*)—enormous wood vats ranging from 200 to 600 liters in size (the average being 200 liters, or fifty-three gallons).

BLANCO/JOVEN	REPOSADO	AÑEJO	EXTRA AÑEJO
SEES NO WOOD AGING BUT CAN BE RESTED IN STAINLESS STEEL OR GLASS BEFORE BOTTLING	AGED IN OAK FOR AT LEAST 2 MONTHS BUT LESS THAN A YEAR	AGED IN OAK FROM 1 TO 3 YEARS	AGED A MINIMUM OF 3 YEARS, NO MAX; MOST RECENT CATEGORY ADDED

Tequila age statements.

The Issue with Mixtos

There are two main types, or subcategories, of Tequila: 100% agave and mixtos. As the name indicates, 100% agave Tequila is made solely from agave (Blue Weber, of course). Mixtos, on the other hand, can be made from as little as 51 percent agave. The remaining fermentable sugars can come from other ingredients like sugar syrup or grain sugars (e.g., corn syrup). And while a mix of fresh cane and agave would be a delight, mixtos aren't usually made with much care. Some say they're too sweet or have a chemical aftertaste, and the added colorings, flavorings, and thickeners have given them a reputation as a hangover spirit. Indeed, using non-agave base ingredients offers a cost-benefit to producers, but they also lead to lower quality, causing mixtos to typically fall short of the craftsmanship and prestige of 100% agave Tequilas. (There are some rare exceptions, such as El Tequileño, featured in the Batanga cocktail.)

Unsurprisingly, many consumers are unaware of the existence of the two subcategories, thanks, in part, to the CRT. (Mixtos are easily identifiable by the absence of "Made from 100% agave" on the label). In Chantal Martineau's book *How the Gringos Stole Tequila*, she explains that the CRT prefers not to even use the word "mixto," instead opting to call the two types 100% agave Tequila and the other . . . Tequila.

On the surface, the "just call me Tequila" branding doesn't seem terribly problematic. Even 100% agave Tequilas can have additives post-distillation and aren't guaranteed to have quality ingredients or production methods. And in mixer-driven cocktails like the Batanga, the subtle flavor differences aren't discernable. Still, lower quality aside, the biggest concern with mixtos is that consumers often don't know about all of the ingredients being used. With these issues in mind, just know that when referring to Tequila throughout the remainder of this section, I'm referring to 100% agave Tequila.

Hiding in Plain Sight

As we've covered, additives are widely used in commercially produced wine and spirits, and like boisé in Cognac, they're allowed in Tequila in moderation. In fact, they're present in well over half the Tequila on the shelves today, including the 100% agave stuff, not just mixtos. For some, this may be shocking, but to most large producers, and even Mexican consumers, it's business as usual. If anything, the absence of additives goes against the grain.

Aged Tequila, in particular, is chock full of these sneaky ingredients. The CRT allows them without disclosure as long as they don't exceed 1 percent of the weight of the spirit. Even if purists don't love the idea, the regulations are pretty straightforward—well, sort of. Language is

---

What's in a NOM?

Akin to the FDA in the US, the *Norma Oficial Mexicana*, or the NOM, maintains the quality control of Mexican products across various industries. Their reach is exceptionally expansive and includes food, drink, appliances, textiles, and electronics. Certified Tequila (and Mezcal) distilleries within the DO label their bottles with "NOM," followed by a four-digit code corresponding to the brick-and-mortar distiller.

tricky, and because the NOM is a legal document, when you play fast and loose with words or, say, the absence of words, loopholes open up. For example, "abocante" is a term used in the NOM to describe four types of "mellowing" ingredients: glycerin (mouthfeel and texture), caramel coloring (color correction and aesthetics), oak extract (flavor, texture, color), and *jarabe* (sweetener, e.g., agave syrup). Though the word "abocante" is sometimes used interchangeably with "additive," according to the educational organization Tequila International Academy, not only are these two words not synonymous, but the word "additive" is never actually defined in the document, leaving it up to interpretation.

As mentioned above, if producers exceed the 1 percent limit of the four defined additives, the label has to disclose that information. But what about the other additives? Those left undefined by the CRT are up to the discretion and self-disclosure of the distiller. And then there's the CRT's 2013 decision to restrict blanco Tequilas from using abocantes but not necessarily from using a myriad of other sweeteners, aromatizers, and flavorings—the "no, but actually maybe yes" loophole.

Since the CRT doesn't currently offer "additive-free" labeling, producers that want the distinction get their bottles tested and "certified" free of additives from a third party. One such third party is Tequila Matchmaker, started by Grover and Scarlet Sanschagrin. Out of a passion for recognizing and celebrating craftsmanship, they started a testing service similar to the CRM's Mezcal certification. However, because they're independent and have no obvious conflicts of interest—suggesting no other motivations other than to inform consumers of what's in their bottles—"Big Tequila" is not a fan. In fact, the CRT has publicly spoken out against Tequila Matchmaker without naming names, potentially hinting that they may soon develop their own certification process.

NOM examples on certified agave spirits labels.

Don't Underestimate Tequila Blanco

Tequila has the unfortunate distinction of being associated with nights filled with less-than-stellar decisions. Perhaps it has to do with Tequila's most common method of consumption (shots) or imbibers' lack of knowledge about the spirit, leading to a poor-quality selection, but its reputation as a party drink and social lubricant discounts the fact that Tequila can be every bit as refined and interesting as a single malt or Cognac. Additionally, since most of the public's understanding of what makes a spirit "premium" comes from marketing, casual consumers over-value age, leaning toward reposado or añejo Tequilas. This leaves many sippable blancos (i.e., unaged Tequilas) underappreciated despite holding the full, complex flavor of the agave in its most unaltered state.

Spotlight on ArteNOM Selección

I met Jake Lustig about a decade ago while running the bar program at Revival Bar & Kitchen in Berkeley. He opened my eyes to the producer-centered concept of Tequila with his ArteNOM Series, which is bottled not by brand but by distillery and producer, hence the "NOM." Labeling according to NOM—which, as mentioned earlier, are each assigned a four-digit code—highlights individual distilleries and takes the branding out of the spotlight.

The idea came to Lustig while working for one of the largest distribution companies in the US. During that time, Lustig developed relationships with many distillers and realized that there was essentially no "conversation about the coolest people doing the coolest stuff." Instead, the emphasis was on brands and superficial marketing. And so the idea was born, and one of the first distilleries that caught his eye was NOM 1414, where they use a specific yeast cultivated from their local agave fields to achieve a unique flavor profile.

Only one big problem stood in the way of this brilliant idea: the CRT wouldn't allow labeling of this kind. By the time the CRT blocked the project, Lustig had already invested in it, ordering thousands of custom bottles. He was determined to make the initiative happen. It would take 3 years of lobbying the CRT to get it approved. ArteNOM has bottled from a rotating selection of distilleries, including 1414 (makers of Siembra Azul and Gran Dovejo), 1146 (makers of Fuenteseca and Don Fulano), and 1579 (makers of G4 and Terralta). Whether you like blanco, reposado, or añejo, these Tequilas have something for everyone.

El Tesoro

My short attention span means it's rare for me to give someone my undivided attention for long, but Carlos Camarena makes the time fly when talking about agave and his love for Tequila making. It was through him that I fell in love with El Tesoro, a brand now owned by one of the "big guys" (Suntory).

Founded in 1937, El Tesoro's La Alteña distillery is located in the highlands of Jalisco in the famous Tequila-making town of Arrandas. After earning a degree in agriculture, founder Don Felipe Camarena (Carlos' grandfather) began farming agave and making Tequila. Today, they continue this tradition by employing production methods more closely related to Mezcal and traditional Tequila than most modern brands.

Their agave is estate grown, and rather than harvesting it all at once—a common practice in the Tequila industry, especially when diffusers are involved—their head jimador selects individual agaves for ripeness. The piñas are then cooked in hornos for 10-12 hours, essentially steaming them, which, according to Camarena, causes impurities that he calls "bitter honey" to leak out. Committed to their craft, La Alteña is also one of the few Tequila distilleries still using a tahona to crush the cooked agave. In their case, it's a 2-ton lava rock pulled by a John Deere tractor. Camarena believes it provides a better crush than a roller mill or shredder because the more the fibers are disturbed, the more methanol is released.

Fermentation occurs in wooden vats, a mix of pine and oak similar to those used in Mezcal production. (Remember, for Tequila and most modern spirits, the standard fermentation vessel is stainless steel.) The benefit of wood is that it regulates its own temperature, whereas stainless steel containers require temperature control.

El Tesoro then distills their Tequila in copper pot stills, with the copper removing additional impurities. (Most larger distilleries use stainless-steel column stills.) And though their stills operate at a relatively smaller capacity, this allows for more surface area with the copper. The spirits are also distilled at a lower temperature and to proof, so what comes off the still goes directly into the bottle—no water added.

What I appreciate most about El Tesoro is that they commit to details instead of cutting corners. And thanks to "brand subsidies" and a healthy marketing budget from Suntory, we have access to their beautiful products at a reasonable price.

Don Abraham
Los Valles, Jalisco

NOM: 1480

BLANCO

From the Amatitán region of Jalisco, this certified organic Tequila is cooked in stone ovens and crushed using a roller mill. Fruity and approachable with lots of pineapple notes, the bottle is affordable for mixing but also lovely on its own.

Organic

Tequila Cimarrón
Los Valles, Jalisco

NOM: 1146

BLANCO

Cimarrón's bottling comes at a fair price point and with a pedigree you can trust. The Tequila is light and clean and made with hillside-grown agave that reaches full maturity with an average of 24-26 brix (dissolved sugar). Simply put, this additive-free, column-distilled blanco is the quintessential cocktail bottle.

Margaritas for Days

El Tesoro
Los Altos, Jalisco

NOM: 1139

BLANCO

El Tesoro uses estate grown agaves, removing the core of the piña to reduce bitterness (something they've been doing since 1937), and–similar to Mezcal–fermentation is open tank and includes solids (not just the juices). The result is a complex bottling distilled to proof (no water is added).

Artisanal

Siembra Azul
Los Altos, Jalisco

NOM: 1414

BLANCO

Made from estate grown agave roasted in brick ovens, shredded with hand-powered roller mills, and fermented in stainless steel, this is a clean expression with no shortcuts. The fermenting agave is also serenaded with classical music, a technique thought to optimize the alcohol conversion process.

Traditional Yet Modern

Tequila Ocho
Los Altos, Jalisco

NOM: 1474

REPOSADO

A bartender favorite, this brand was co-founded by 5th-generation agave farmer Carlos Camarena with a focus on respecting the land and traditional processes. Made with single estate grown agave, it's floral with notes of vanilla and citrus–a versatile spirit for cocktails or sipping.

Tried and True

Fortaleza Reposado
Los Valles, Jalisco

NOM: 1493

REPOSADO

For this reposado, tahona-crushed and brick-oven roasted agave is fermented in an open tank and proofed down with natural spring water. It's the perfect beginner's Tequila, complete with roasted sweet potato and caramel notes that don't overwhelm and allow the agave to shine.

Artisanal

Tequila Gran Dovejo
Los Altos, Jalisco

NOM: 1414

REPOSADO

The Vivanco family operates the distillery NOM 1414, a popular destination for brands and distillers who value transparency (it's also where Siembra Azul's blanco is crafted). This estate grown bottling boasts notes of cinnamon and cocoa, setting it on the darker side of the reposado spectrum and making it the ideal sipping dram.

Transparency and Value

La Gritona
Los Altos, Jalisco

NOM: 1533

REPOSADO

Most brands make three expressions, but distiller Melly Barajas specializes in just one. Her woman-run distillery exclusively uses mature agaves that are cooked within 24 hours of trimming the pencas and aged in used, almost neutral barrels. The flavor is full of roasted agave, with subtle notes of caramel.

Women-Owned and Operated

Tequila Tapatío
Los Altos, Jalisco

NOM: 1139

AÑEJO

Don't let this unassuming bottle fool you–this is liquid gold. This copper pot distilled añejo uses open air fermentation in wooden vats (like Mezcal) and is fermented on the fibers, allowing for tons of agave character. The result is a rich flavor profile complete with notes of sweet potato, roasted pepitas, and baking spice.

Traditional Methods

Fuenteseca
Los Altos, Jalisco

NOM: 1146

EXTRA AÑEJO 21 YEAR

A fun fact about Fuenteseca: it has the oldest extra añejo of any distillery, even pre-dating the existence of the category's creation. Copper pot-distilled and aged in Valles in white wine and Canadian rye barrels, their 21-year-old bottling is quite a rare find and worth every penny.

Worth the Splurge

Caballito Cerrero
Los Valles, Jalisco

NOM: Uncertified (formerly 1114)

CHATO BLANCO

This old-school Tequila-producing distillery founded in 1968 prefers to use *angustifolia* agave in combination with classic methods that don't fall under the current legal definition of Tequila. So, they forgo certification and make what they think tastes best. This tasty agave spirit is mineral-driven, verdant, and assertive.

Outside the Box

Siete Leguas
Los Altos, Jalisco

NOM: 1120

AÑEJO

Founded in 1952 and still family run, the distillery was once home to the original Patrón brand before its success outgrew the space. Today they operate 2 facilities sitting side by side, the more modern expansion built in 1984. Aged 24 months, expect woodsy notes, black pepper, and light caramel.

Tried and True

Sugar: whether you pick up a bag of pristine white crystals from your grocer's baking aisle or tear open small packets for your morning coffee, we're all familiar with this pantry staple. In its most familiar form, white table sugar (aka sucrose) is the result of milling, crystallizing, and bleaching sugarcane. And though consumers may take the absence of color to mean purity, it more accurately indicates an absence of flavor; white sugar is designed to be a tabula rasa of sweetness. By contrast, natural or raw sugar appears golden or dark brown due to residual molasses, a natural byproduct of the sugar-making process that offers rich caramel notes and earthy flavors.

For the purpose of distillation, sugar is a water-soluble carbohydrate that can be derived from a variety of natural sources (e.g., honey, agave, sugarcane, corn, sugar beet, fruit) and presented in a variety of forms (e.g., sucrose, fructose, dextrose). And while many types of sugars are used in spirit-making, only one spirit requires cane sugar, and cane sugar only: rum.

Sugar Type	Structure	Primary Source	"Real Talk"
Sucrose	Disaccharides (fructose + glucose)	Cane sugar, sugar beets	Aka table sugar; the body must break this sugar down to absorb it
Fructose	Monosaccharide	Fruit, honey, agave, root vegetables	Common in fruits; direct absorption, but the liver must first convert it to glucose
Glucose	Monosaccharide	Honey, fruits, veggies, grains, nuts	The most common simple sugar in nature; directly absorbed by the body
Dextrose	A form of glucose (usually industrially made)	Refined grains (rice, corn, wheat)	Often used in food manufacturing; essentially identical to glucose

Common sugar types.

Sugar and Sweeteners

Despite not being held in the same esteem it once was (we now know it's responsible for a range of ailments, including dental problems, obesity, and diabetes), we consume more sugar than ever. And thanks in part to abundant corn subsidies in the US and the recent domination of high fructose corn syrup (a sweetener made of corn starch)—cane sugar is now marketed as a more "natural" sweetener by comparison. (Mexican Coke still maintains its status as the more premium version of Coca-Cola for this reason.)

History and Domestication

Sugarcane (*Saccharum officinarum*) isn't shy about what it has to offer. Bite down on a fresh-cut piece of cane and the reward is instantly gratifying. Visually similar to bamboo, this fast-growing grass has undeniably altered our collective palates for millennia.

Archaeological evidence points to the early domestication of sugarcane around 10,000 years ago in what is today Papua New Guinea. Easily propagated and quick to mature (it takes as little as nine months to grow 12–20 feet in height), sugarcane eventually made its way across Southeast Asia and India, where it is known to have been cultivated since at least the 5th century BCE. Several hundred years later, by 100 CE, it was being refined into the crystalline sugar we know today. During refinement, the cane was crushed, and the juices boiled until all the liquid evaporated. The resulting misshapen crystals were called *Khanda* in Sanskrit and later *qandi* in Arabic—the origin of the word "candy."

Fast forward to the present and sugarcane is cultivated across the globe and at scale in over 120 countries including India, Mexico, Japan, Brazil, the US, and nations throughout the Caribbean.

Sugar and Colonialism

Like pulque derived from agave, sugarcane was fermented into "sugar wine" in places like India, China, and parts of South America long before it was distilled. And like pulque, it was banned during colonial rule. In the Philippines, for example, all fermented sugarcane beverages were outlawed in the 18th century, including the popular *basi* (made by cooking the cane juice before fermenting it, allowing the fermented beverage to be aged and bottled.)

Sugarcane farming was never easy, but it was during European imperialism that sugarcane production exacted its most heinous toll. The British Empire, in particular, bears outsized responsibility for taking cane sugar from an occasional upper-class treat to a staple in Western pantries. They did this by commercializing sugarcane agriculture throughout the Caribbean islands (where it was bound to thrive) and relying on the racialized enslavement of Africans to provide the necessary labor. The economic exchange of manufactured goods, enslaved peoples, and sugar (among other Caribbean exports) came to be known as the transatlantic slave trade, and it formed the backbone of the sugarcane industry.

Rhum J.M. cane fields, photo by Nat Harry.

Cane harvester at Rhum J.M., photo by Nat Harry.

Raising Cane

Sugarcane grows quickly and easily given warm temperatures, full sun, and plenty of water, and it's deemed ready for harvest once it reaches the ideal brix level, which takes between nine to sixteen months in warm climates, depending on plant and distillation need. It is also unique among the grasses in that it can be harvested more than once (sometimes as many as four times) before replanting becomes necessary.

The crop can be harvested either by hand (a method prone to egregious labor rights abuses when done on a commercial scale) or with specialized equipment like a sugarcane harvester. Invented in Louisiana in the 1930s, the machine looks like a villainous transformer, with long arms ending in rotating blades that cut sugarcane stalks, strip the leaves, chop the cane into segments, and deposit the waste material back onto the field where it acts as a fertilizer. Their efficiency is unrivaled, but harvesters are *very* expensive (some cost several hundreds of thousands of dollars), making them best suited for big operations on large tracts of land. For smaller, artisanal producers or those in elevated terrain, the cost and logistics are prohibitive, meaning their sugarcane is usually cut by hand at great toil and trouble. (Unfortunately, the true labor cost is seldom factored into the final price tag.) And it's not just sugarcane planting and harvesting that require intense physical labor. Sugar mills—responsible for refining the cane into raw sugar—also rely on hard labor, especially in underdeveloped countries.

The True Impact of Sugarcane's Success

Even today, industrialized sugarcane processing is mired in controversy over accusations of human rights violations and environmental destruction—and the larger the operation, the greater the chance for safety oversights, putting laborers at greater risk of severe chronic illness and even death. Sadly, one of the main problems facing field workers is Chronic Kidney Disease of Unknown Etiology, or CKDu. First documented in the 1970s, it's likely as old as the first colonial sugar plantations. As the name indicates, its causes remain unknown, though the leading theory is that it's a combination of excessive working hours, dehydration, improper sun protection causing heat exhaustion, and overexposure to pesticides and chemical fertilizers. (There is often little oversight of their working conditions, and workers may work fourteen-hour days in the field with temperatures around 100°F.) As marginalized people make up the bulk of the agricultural labor force when it comes to the sugarcane industry, they are at greatest risk. And while some attention has been given to CKDu in the last two decades, and responsible farm owners have begun putting preventative measures in place, it's far from eradicated.

The human toll isn't the only price paid. Since the 1700s, one of the most significant ecological impacts of large-scale sugarcane cultivation has been mass deforestation—and not just in the Caribbean. In the rainforests of Central and South America, native plants and animals have been decimated to make way for the cash crop, leaving ecosystems permanently affected. Even today, Brazilian rainforests are burned to make room for sugarcane plantations that further the booming biofuel business. (Brazil is the largest producer of sugarcane in the world, and as of 2020, was second only to the US in terms of biofuel ethanol production—but that's a rabbit hole for another time.) In short, if you want to ensure your rum is ethically sourced, do a little digging on who brands and distilleries partner with and how they obtain their raw ingredient.

Types of Sugarcane and Their Mysterious Code Names

Sugarcane variants are selected by producers as much for a particular flavor and yield as for resistance to certain pests, diseases, and even weather (like the ability to withstand a hurricane). In Haiti and parts of Mexico and Hawaii, heirloom, or ancestral, varieties are still very much around, and in some parts, they remain dominant, with names changing from village to village (similar to agave).

Heirloom/Ancestral Varieties	Country
Caña Criolla (aka Canne Créole) / Caña Dulce / Caña Nayarit	Mexico
Canne Cristalline / Madame Meuze / Canne Hasco	Haiti
kō Manulele / kō Pilimai / kō Kea/ kō Lahi / Mahai'ula	Hawaii (United States)

Heirloom/ancestral sugarcane varieties.

However, when it comes to spirits, most producers don't get super specific with customers regarding the cane variant they use. Instead, they rely on descriptors like "red," "blue," and "green" (referencing the color or tint of the stalk).

By comparison, most modern cane hybrids are identified by a seemingly random code of letters and numbers. And while many varieties have colloquial names, you're more likely to see them referred to by this code within academia, cane breeding programs, and the sugar and rum industry. Here's how to decipher what this code actually means:

Red cane (left); purple cane (right); photos by Nat Harry.

ID Code	Colloquial Name	Place of Origin	Year of Development	Number of Breeding Attempts
B 51-129	Canne Vanille (Vanilla Cane)	B (Barbados)	1951	129
B 73-419	Red Eyed Cane	B (Barbados)	1973	419
HoCP 96-540	Unknown/None	HoCP (Louisiana)	1996	540
RB 86-7515*	Unknown/None	RB (Brazil)	1986	7,515
Mex 69-290	Unknown/none	Mex (Mexico)	1969	290
CP 96-1252	Unknown/none	CP (Canal Point, Florida)	1996	1252

Rum code names.
*Figuring out some of these codes can be tricky as the letters are not always intuitive. For example, MEX is Mexico, but Brazil is either "SP or "RB," and La Réunion Island is simply "R."

SUGARCANE

That Crazy Little Thing Called Rum

Like the rest of the spirit's history, the origin of the word "rum" is as murky as molasses. Some say it was taken from the suffix of *saccharum* (a type of grass). However, it's more commonly believed to be a shortened version of the word "rumbullion"—a term that first appeared in the 1650s in reference to a sugarcane molasses distillate from Barbados. Back then, "rumbullion" was slang for "a great uproar," perhaps an indication of what could follow a few drams of it while at one of the island's many tippling houses.

At some point, the Anglophone world collectively settled on "rum," though the spirit goes by many names elsewhere, like *ron, rhum, aguardiente,* and *tafia.* As you can imagine, many countries lay claim to rum's origins, but there's no definitive evidence of a first appearance, and that's in large part because rum, as we know it, is the product of a melting pot of influences. Apart from being shaped by the licit and illicit trades in sugar and human beings in the West Indies, sugarcane has been cultivated globally for millennia, drawing influences from Africa, Asia, Europe, and the Americas. As a result, rum, as a category, quickly roots and branches off into older, traditional spirits with different names depending on the home country (think Cachaça in Brazil, Clairin in Haiti, and Charanda in Mexico). The bottom line is that rum lacks a unifying identity, even throughout the Caribbean where it thrives. This means the best way to explore its many iterations is region by region.

One example is Authentic Caribbean Rum (ACR), which represents a dozen countries, including Belize, Haiti, Guyana, and Jamaica, and follows the rum rules set forth by the political and economic union known as the Caribbean Community (CARICOM)—an intergovernmental organization representing fifteen member states and five associated members, all of which share the goal of building stronger economies.

One Definition, Many Styles and Rules

Rum, like whiskey, is a class that contains a range of styles under one (in this case, big and bulky) umbrella. The TTB defines rum as: "Spirits distilled from the fermented juice of sugarcane, sugarcane syrup, sugarcane molasses or other sugarcane byproducts at less than 95% alcohol by volume (190 proof) having the taste, aroma, and characteristics generally attributed to rum and bottled at not less than 40% alcohol by volume (80 proof)." That is an exceptionally broad definition, especially considering sugarcane's global presence.

Because of this complexity, there's little regulation around rum and surprisingly few DOs. So, while the US has Bourbon and Tennessee whiskey, and Scotland has Scotch, rum is still catching up when it comes to regional protections (which could contribute to the general lack of public interest in its finer details). Because of this, consumers commonly shop for rum by subclass, like white, gold/aged, flavored, or blended. Though these are helpful guideposts, knowing about regional styles is just as—if not more—important.

As is the case across the board, having a set of rules or defining characteristics helps establish a spirit as a serious global contender (even though DOs are sometimes not recognized in trade agreements). Many distillers recognize this hard truth and are banding together to compel regional structures and overarching guidelines to help improve rum's reputation—particularly for rum made in Caribbean nations.

Given the diversity of cane spirits, "rum" is much too general a spirit class to offer the average tippler much guidance. And despite the public's tendency to view rum as a category devoid of rules—partly due to the many producing regions and expressions—most regions have actually developed their own unique style, with quite a few being highly regulated.

To understand rum (and other cane spirits), we need to be familiar with the two main types: molasses-based and cane juice-based. Like "whiskey" and "whisky," rum has an alternative spelling ("rhum"), and the spelling clues you into the flavors you can expect. What we commonly refer to as "rum" in the US is a molasses-based distillate that largely stems from European influence. The other rum, which we commonly see spelled with an "h"—rhum—is a distillate made from fresh-pressed sugarcane juice and referred to in the industry as a "cane distillate." So, rum and rhum are two *very* different spirits with unique profiles and qualities.

FRESH CANE JUICE RHUM

If you've only ever tried molasses-based rum, you may be surprised to know that cane juice rhum has an entirely different production process, flavor, and style. Despite being the name of a specific rum (most famously from Martinique) with its own AOC, *Rhum Agricole*—the French term for sugarcane juice rum—has become the generic name for this light and grassy, fresh and bright, sometimes funky, and always potent spirit. These spirits have a more earth-driven character than their molasses siblings owing to a stronger agricultural connection—the raw material is processed directly after harvest and is less refined than molasses—which may be why the word *agricole* stuck. Regardless of its official status, agricole-style cane spirits will often showcase the earthier qualities of freshly pressed sugarcane juice.

Time is of the Essence

One of the critical production factors for cane juice spirits is time. Oxygen is the enemy, and the countdown begins as soon as the cane is harvested. (Sugarcane oxidizes quickly, and letting the cane sit for too long—even just 24 hours—can cause off-flavors to develop during fermentation.) After harvest, the cane is washed and crushed in large mills to release the juice—a process that's now industrialized at most large distilleries.

Stepping into a Martinican rhum distillery for the first time feels like walking onto a giant Mousetrap board, with an added bonus of a distinct heady scent of sweet cane juice and machine oil. Often taking place in a covered, open-air facility, the entire process is frenetic and very loud, and while not all distilleries operate the same way, most follow a similar script. Large trucks unload their cargo from a steep incline above the covered area. Gravity then moves the stalks down onto a conveyor belt to the heart of the crush, where mechanical mills tear them apart and create a muddy, sweet liquid. Once the juice is extracted, the fibrous pulp left over—*bagasse*—is typically dried and burned as a biofuel used to power the distillery or sugar mill.

Clément Rhum Museum, photo by Nat Harry.

Not all agricole-style rhum is crafted on such a grand scale; smaller producers in rural areas tend to crush the stalks using hand-fed mechanical juicers. In places like Haiti or Oaxaca, sugarcane is transported by burro or horse, especially in high elevations or areas without roads.

It's Not Always Pretty

Generally speaking, fermentation is not a visually attractive process, no matter the raw material. Even before the yeast begins its job, the color of the juiced sugarcane resembles dirty honey—murky and unappetizing. But this unassuming sugar slurry is actually quite delicious, exhibiting a raw sweetness reminiscent of fresh coconut water but earthier. Agricole-style rhums are typically made using open fermentation, though a producer might choose to inoculate with a specific yeast to control the flavor profile. Still, traditional styles like Haiti's Clairin often let nature take the wheel, leading to a funkier, less predictable outcome.

Fresh cut sugar cane being unloaded at Rhum J.M., photo by Nat Harry.

Whereas molasses rum is often bottled as a blend of rums from pot and column stills, fresh cane distillates are usually made using one still type, determined by the region's rules and traditions. For example, in Martinique, only column stills are allowed per the AOC, and in the Oaxacan mountain regions, pot stills are common (but by no means preferred) for cane aguardientes. Overall, regardless of the distillation method, the unifying characteristic of agricole-style rhum is its tendency to highlight the fresh and vibrant nature of the sugarcane.

RHUM AGRICOLE (MARTINIQUE)

Did you know you can visit the EU in the Caribbean? Believe it or not, Martinique, an island in the eastern Caribbean Sea (the Lesser Antilles, to be exact), is an overseas department of the French Republic, meaning it has the same status as mainland France's departments and regions. So, when you step foot on Martinique, you technically enter the EU. Perhaps for this reason, Martinique feels slightly different from its neighbors; it's a bit like being transported to the French countryside—if that countryside showcased palm trees and rainforest.

Creole column still at Habitation Clément, photo by Nat Harry.

RHUM AGRICOLE

Plant: Sugarcane (juice)

Place: Martinique (23 municipalities)

Production: Fresh-pressed cane juice; favors open fermentation; column distillation

Protection: AOC

The French established the first European settlement in Martinique in 1635, and the cultivation and distillation of sugarcane began shortly thereafter. But establishing and holding are two very different things. Finding themselves in a contested "frontier," the French struggled to maintain domination of the island, which was often attacked, and even intermittently controlled, by the British. Over time, aspects of the British imprint stuck, including what was then considered the latest sugarcane distillation methods. In 1815, when Martinique was traded back to France for the last time as part of the peace negotiations ending the Napoleonic Wars (and after Haiti had won its independence), French investment in Martinique kicked into high gear. It became the hub of French sugar and rhum production and, by the end of the 19th century, contained no fewer than 215 distilleries. Today, thanks to the tireless efforts of the multi-generational emancipation movement, only around a dozen remain in existence.

Having always been a drink of the people, rhum-making (at least the artisanal kind) was spared the ire of decolonization-minded reformers. The situation has evolved, and today cane spirits are a fully naturalized symbol and product. Martinique and other French rhum-producing islands, like Guadeloupe, have established well-respected AOCs for rhum agricole—though Martinique has the most stringent rules by far and holds the highest reputation outside France. Chartered in 1996, the AOC has very specific requirements for a distillate labeled "rhum agricole," down to the tract of land the cane is grown on. These requirements are:

- Sugarcane variants are limited to those from the species *Saccharum officinarum* and *spontaneum* (wild);

- Crop irrigation is limited by time and frequency, and substances that assist in cane maturation are forbidden;

- Production must occur within one of 23 designated areas on the island. (Though Martinique is only 50 miles long, the trade winds create microclimates, making certain areas more favorable for cane than others);

- No additional sugar or molasses can be added to aid fermentation;

- The minimum brix level is 14. (As we know, sugar is essential to fermentation, and because no additives are allowed in rhum agricole, maximizing the natural sugar content is important);

- Fermentation time is restricted to a maximum of 120 hours; and

- Distillation must take place in column (continuous) stills.

Saccharum Spontaneum

Though *Saccharum officinarum* is the sugarcane species most commonly used for rum, it's not the only one. *Saccharum spontaneum,* as the name suggests, is a wild variety that grows seemingly spontaneously. In India, for example, it's even considered an invasive weed. Compared to *officinarum*, it's shorter and thinner, contains less sucrose, and is much more fibrous. Still, breeding programs use this wild cane to add genetic diversity when creating new hybrids. *Spontaneum* is also officially allowed in the Martinique AOC.

Ti' Punch

- 2 oz. Rhum agricole
- 1 Barspoon (approx. ½ tsp) Sirop de canne*
- Wedge of lime

In a single rocks glass, add cane syrup and a squeeze of lime, then drop the wedge into the glass. Add the rhum and a handful of ice cubes (no more than would fill half the glass), and stir until the syrup is dissolved.

*Sirop de canne is the silky, sweet syrup you get after boiling down fresh cane juice. Commonly bottled by rhum producers like Rhum J.M.. and Clément Rhum, it's a standard cocktail ingredient in Martinique and a must-have for Ti' Punch.

(the national cocktail of Martinique)

Categories of Rhum Agricole

BLANC: These rums are colorless and considered unaged despite resting in vats for at least 6 weeks before bottling. Flavors can span from grassy and hay-like to overripe tropical fruit.

ÉLEVÉ SOUS BOIS: Translating to "raised in wood," these rhums are lightly aged in oak for a minimum of 12 months and up to 2 years. If we were to liken rhum to agave spirits, élevé sous bois would be the reposado of the category, as it mellows the cane's herbaceous notes with age, allowing the barrel to offer a subtle vanilla and spice profile.

VIEUX: Meaning "old" or "aged" in French, this rhum is aged in oak containers for at least 3 years. And if "vintage" is used on the label, that minimum goes up to 6 years. Like the élevé sous bois, the oak cuts the sugarcane's herby flavor, but the longer age time offers more tannins and imparts a stronger flavor from the barrel.

Mechanical cane juicer in Michoacán, Mexico, photo by Nat Harry.

Homère Clément

In 1887, a Creole Martinican politician named Homère Clément purchased a bankrupt sugarcane plantation on the island. Clément, the first person of color to become a licensed medical doctor in France, also served in the French National Assembly and would later become mayor of Martinique's Le François arrondissement. However, Clément's political life was far from the most significant impact he left on the island.

At the time of his investment in the 300-acre plantation, sugarcane, as a commodity, was well in decline. This downturn in demand was partly due to the rise of sugar beet farming back in Europe, which gained popularity in response to the abolishment of slavery across England and its overseas territories in 1848. (For more on sugar beets, see the chapter on root vegetables.) However, newly emancipated farmers in Martinique still had cane crops waiting to be harvested and sold, and though the global sugarcane market was in free fall, demand for rum was on the rise.

Clément saw an opportunity and began distilling the spirit directly from cane juice rather than from molasses or sugar byproducts (thereby removing the need for the cane to be refined). By encouraging the practice across the island, he soon eliminated Martinique's dependence on sugar processing for export, pulling the cash crop out of a depression and earning him the reputation of the "Godfather of Rhum Agricole." Though Clément was not the first to make this style of rhum, he promoted agricole-style rhum and elevated its profile to a much larger scale than ever before. When his sons eventually took over the business, they rebranded with the family name. Today, Clément Rhum produces unaged and aged rhums, as well as a handful of liqueurs.

Martinique Mai Tai

- 1 ¾ oz. aged rhum agricole vieux
- ¾ oz. creole shrubb
- ¾ oz. fresh lime juice
- ½ oz. orgeat

Shake all ingredients with ice, strain into a double rocks glass over fresh ice, and garnish with a lime wheel.

CUVÉE DE L'OCÉAN

Located on the southern tip of the island, Trois Rivières is the largest and oldest plantation on Martinique. The single-estate cane used for this bottling is grown seaside and is sometimes covered by salt water during high tides. The flavor profile offers a blend of freshly cut grass and lightly tropical notes with a touch of a lactic texture.

Funky but Cool

VSOP

You'll note a bit of Cognac-related buzzwords on this bottling, as it's aged for 3 years in American oak and then another year in ex-Bourbon and French oak. Spicy and tropical, this is the ideal bottle to explore aged rhum agricole.

Tried and True

CRÉOLE SHRUBB

This cordial focuses on the medicinal shrubs of the island (the spirit is infused with local herbs and spices). It's not quite a liqueur, though it is lightly sweetened and made using a base of aged and unaged rum. Infused with dried orange peel and spices, this bottling comes in at 40% ABV (higher than most traditional liqueurs).

For the Bartender

LE RHUM AGRICOLE BLANC

One of the first agricole rhums to make its way into back bars in the US, this is a classic unaged rhum filled with overripe tropical flavors, some floral notes, and a hint of hay. It's bottled at 50% ABV, making it perfect for mixing cocktails.

Typification of the Category

CACHAÇA

In 2019, sugarcane was the world's largest crop, with Brazil producing 627 metric tons for human consumption and ethanol production. It should come as no surprise, then, that Brazil has its own national rhum expression. After all, Brazil was distilling cane juice well before the appearance of Caribbean rhum, and its history reaches back nearly 500 years, predating colonial, Barbadian molasses-based rum by almost a century.

Cachaça (*kah-sha-sah*) arose from the synchronization of Portuguese, African, and native South American cultural traditions. The Portuguese took sugarcane to eastern South America, along with the estimated 5.8 million enslaved Africans they forced to tend to it, and it was these Afro-Brazilian communities that invented the spirit.

The word "cachaça" is thought to derive from the name given to the foam that accumulates when boiling sugar, which was skimmed, fermented, and later distilled. And just like any native-born spirit (especially agriculturally focused ones like shochu or Mezcal), it was considered a rustic drink of the lower classes by snooty Europeans (and other pretentious folks).

To the unfamiliar eye, Cachaça could easily be considered an agricole-style rum. However, it's rarely referred to as such, and certainly not by those making it. As the national spirit of Brazil, Cachaça has its own DO, which dictates that the spirit must be made from fresh cane juice (*garapa*), be distilled a single time, be produced in Brazil (though there are no region-specific limitations), and fall within a range of between 38 and 48 percent ABV.

Cachaça is officially divided into two categories: industrial and artisanal, and the difference between the two is distillation method—column stills are used for industrial spirits and copper pot stills for artisanal. Furthermore, industrial producers tend to use extremely fast fermentation processes, having adopted techniques used to make ethanol, like rapid fermentation and extra-large stills. (That said, it's important to remember that fermentation is where flavor is developed, so rushing this step leads to a less complex spirit.) Conversely, artisanal producers usually undergo longer fermentation processes, often using native yeasts, which take longer to break down sugars but provide a unique flavor profile. Distillers of both types are allowed to use up to six grams of sugar per liter, but any more than that and it must be labeled "Cachaça dulce."

CACHAÇA

Plant: Sugarcane (juice)

Place: Brazil

Production: Fresh-pressed juice; any still type

Protection: DO

Cachaça's World Dominance

Brazil is the world's largest grower of sugarcane, which is why it's so surprising that Cachaça rarely finds its way outside the country's borders. In 2015, the country produced 1.8 billion liters of the spirit, though that number has fallen substantially since the pandemic, now hovering at around 800 million. In fact, production is spread across an estimated 40,000 producers—Brazil includes "unofficial," or legally unregistered, distilleries in this figure—but only about 1% of the spirit is exported. Given Brazil's massive population, the spirit is still just the 3rd or 4th most-consumed spirit worldwide, a circumstance not unlike China's national spirit, baijiu.

While most exported Cachaça is unaged, aging is still commonplace in Brazil, with many artisanal producers resting their distillate in casks (which legally can be no larger than 700 liters), sometimes opting for native Brazilian wood to rest the spirit. Hop on a flight to Brazil, and you'll see Cachaça aged in amendoim bravo (*Pterogyne nitens Tul*), Brazil nut (*Bertholletia excelsa*), cabreúva (*Myrocarpus frondosus*), jequitibá-rosa (*Cariniana legalis*), and Amburana (*Amburana cearensis*.) (We'll touch on Amburana and its effect on spirits in the chapter on wood.)

CACHAÇA

Aguaviva has been growing sugarcane biodynamically without chemicals or pesticides since 1902. Their fields in Rio de Janeiro are surrounded by lush rainforest, and their cane is juiced and fermented using native yeast found right on the stalks. The result is an herbaceous bottling with notes of freshly cut grass, olive oil, ginger, and peppercorn.

Biodynamic

SILVER CACHAÇA

A zero-waste distillery (recycling or re-using all byproducts), Novo Fogo's bottling uses estate-harvested sugarcane, is certified organic, and is still easy on the wallet. Produced in 130-liter batches using traditional methods, this unaged bottling offers flavors of banana, fresh ginger, and herbaceous, grassy notes.

Sustainable and Certified Organic

AMBURANA CACHAÇA

Amburana-aged expressions are, as a whole, distinct and transformative, but of all the ones I've tried, this bottling knocks it out of the park. Full of flavors, including banana bread, incense, cinnamon bark, chaga mushroom, and damp earth, this Cachaça is beautiful on its own and exciting in cocktails.

For the Adventurous Palate

CACHAÇA

This distiller uses hand-cut sugarcane from an agricultural region of Minas Gerais. After fermenting the cane within 3 hours of harvest and distilling the juice in copper pot stills, they rest the Cachaça for a month before bottling. The expression offers notes of hay, cucumber spa water, and unripened plantain with a soft, light finish.

For the Bartender

HAITIAN RHUM

By 1790, Haiti—then the French colony of Saint Domingue—was growing 50 percent of the world's sugarcane and 40 percent of the world's coffee supply. But the following year, the enslaved people of the island revolted in what would become the largest and most successful slave rebellion in the history of the Western Hemisphere. In the end, the Haitian Revolution upended the global sugarcane market and ushered in the hard-earned freedom of millions.

By the time Haiti declared its independence in 1804, most, if not all, of the colony's sugar and coffee plantations had been destroyed (queue a tiny French violin). Vengeful and humiliated, France soon demanded reparations from the newly independent country under threat of renewed warfare. Saddled with war debt, Haiti relented and took out enormous loans from—giant eye roll—French banks to repay the French government in exchange for formal recognition of independence. To add insult to injury, Haiti also found itself severely limited in what nations were willing to engage in trade after its precedent-setting rebellion. To make a long story short, the country's sugar industry never recovered on an industrial scale.

HAITIAN RUM

Plant: Sugarcane (juice) and its byproducts

Place: Haiti

Production: Non-specific requirements, but all production must take place in Haiti

Protection: Recent regional certification (HaïRum), not recognized by the TTB

The flip side is that the island's sugarcane has remained relatively unaltered by modern agriculture, not counting some hybridization undertaken by distillers and farmers. This means the sugarcane of Haiti is as close as it gets to what was first introduced by the Spaniards—a truly unique selection of heritage varieties. And despite recent political turmoil, Haitian rhum—notably Clairin (see below)—is having a moment.

Almost all of the rhums coming out of Haiti, including Clairin, are exclusively made from cane juice. In 2021, Haiti created a set of production requirements for producers wishing to certify their rhum as a product of the island. It's branded as HaïRum and is more along the lines of a trademark than a traditional GI. Though not overly detailed, the requirements note that all production, from fermentation through bottling, must occur on the island. Interestingly, they don't specify that the raw ingredients must be sourced on the island.

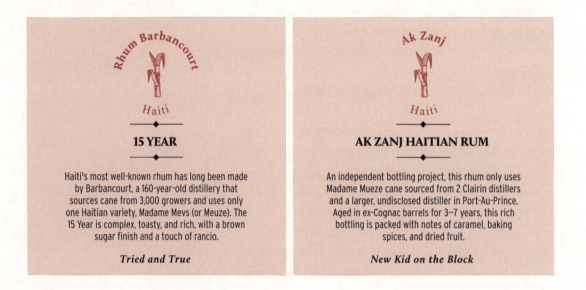

Rhum Barbancourt — Haiti — 15 YEAR

Haiti's most well-known rhum has long been made by Barbancourt, a 160-year-old distillery that sources cane from 3,000 growers and uses only one Haitian variety, Madame Mevs (or Meuze). The 15 Year is complex, toasty, and rich, with a brown sugar finish and a touch of rancio.

Tried and True

Ak Zanj — Haiti — AK ZANJ HAITIAN RUM

An independent bottling project, this rhum only uses Madame Mueze cane sourced from 2 Clairin distillers and a larger, undisclosed distiller in Port-Au-Prince. Aged in ex-Cognac barrels for 3–7 years, this rich bottling is packed with notes of caramel, baking spices, and dried fruit.

New Kid on the Block

CLAIRIN

Clairin is another Haitian cane spirit made from island-grown, sometimes even wild, sugarcane. Like traditionally made Mezcal and destilado de agave, Clairin is typically produced in tiny batches for local consumption using rudimentary equipment. It's often (but not always) made using fresh-pressed cane juice that's then openly fermented in wooden containers using natural yeasts. Some distillers also choose to extend fermentation time in sweltering weather by stabilizing the pH and adding naturally acidic ingredients such as lemongrass or citrus, increasing the complexity of their unique profile. *Vinasse*, the solid remnants left behind from previous distillations (akin to sour mash or dunder [see page 233]), is another common ingredient and can be beneficial to fermentation.

As for the crushing of the cane itself, there is little mechanical assistance, with most producers using an animal-powered *trapiche* (a mill with a wheel or wooden rollers, similar to the tahona used in Mezcal production) or similar contraption. The hyper-local and tedious process means few outside of the Caribbean have heard of this spirit category. However, with recent trends favoring traditionally made spirits, these bottles have begun trickling into the US. Haiti only hosts a few dozen legal Clairin distilleries, but there are probably hundreds of small producers on the island making small batches with homegrown cane.

While fresh cane juice is the standard among small Clairin distillers, it's certainly not a universal practice. For example, *Clairin Le Rocher* (in Pignon) is distilled by producer Romulus Bethel using *sirop de canne*, a sugarcane syrup (rather than molasses or cane juice) that is slowly cooked down to preserve aroma while retaining the character of the cane. To differentiate between this and the main Clairin made throughout the island, its label reads "rhum sirop de canne." The benefit of using sirop de canne is that cane syrup is more shelf stable, allowing distillers to make Clairin year-round and not just immediately after harvest.

Clairin distillation typically occurs over an open flame in rudimentary stills kitted with copper plates (remember that copper is ideal for heat conduction and removing impurities). And as with ancestral Mezcal, each batch of Clairin is small, unique, and carries the mark of the producer. Though it may appear similar to the rhum of Martinique (fresh and vegetal) or other American cane spirits (i.e., higher proof and rustic), Clairin maintains a cultural and agricultural identity, showcasing its terroir. As the "rhum of the people" in Haiti, it's the drink of choice for special occasions and represents an important aspect of native religious ceremonies.

CLAIRIN (KLÉREN)

Place: Haiti

Plant: Heirloom sugarcane (juice) and its byproducts

Production: Traditional, rustic distillation methods; hand-harvested cane

Protection: None

Saint Benevolence

Saint Benevolence was founded in 2017 in Saint Michel de l'Attalaye by longtime Habitat for Humanity volunteer Calvin Babcock and local distiller and community pillar Reverend Gueillant Dorcinvil. Their humanitarian-centric brand combines their two passions: charity and rum. Every bottle purchased directly contributes to the island and the town of Saint Michel by funding surgeries, providing meals, and building schools. They bottle three expressions: a traditional, unaged Clairin; a barrel-aged version; and a 5 year, molasses-based, sourced Caribbean rum that's great for cocktails. Their Clairin is distilled using a field blend of cane types: Cristalline, Madame Meuze (Mezs), Farine France, and 24/14.

Saint Michel de l'Attalaye

RUM CLAIRIN (UNAGED)

Made with a field blend of native cane, this Clairin uses a base of fresh cane juice and syrup—the rhum-style of Saint Michel. It leans on the more vegetal side, with notes of unripe plantain and a touch of lychee–perfect for cocktails like a classic daiquiri.

Giving Back to Community

Various Regions

CLAIRIN COMMUNAL

Blended and bottled from the Clairin of 4 small distilleries by French independent bottler Velier (which also bottles each distillery's expression separately), this release is a wonderful introduction to Clairin. It's fruity, funky, herbal, and still approachable, and at 43% ABV, its alcohol content is lower than some.

A Good Introduction

Pignon

CLAIRIN PIGNON RUM

Made in one of Haiti's top sugarcane-growing areas, distiller Boss Méles uses a combination of vinasse and cane syrup for this twice-distilled Clairin. The result is a complex spirit that's ester heavy, vegetal, and green and complemented with warm caramelized citrus notes.

Funky but Cool

Milot

CLAIRIN MILOT

Made with fresh cane juice and syrup that's slowly fermented for 10-15 days and then double distilled, this Clairin is surprisingly approachable, given its 55% ABV. When enjoying, expect lots of dried stone fruit, minerality, herbaceous notes, and a bit of heat.

Packs a Punch

AGUARDIENTE DE CAÑAS (MEXICO)

Previously inconspicuous Mexican spirits have recently begun making their way into the hearts and back bars of the world, including traditionally made Mexican cane spirits like aguardiente. Since locally made and native spirits were heavily restricted and virtually illicit during the colonial era (partly to encourage consumption of European imports), aguardiente production occurred in domestic kitchens where it was common for women to take over the distilling.

AGUARDIENTE DE CAÑAS

Plant: Sugarcane (juice) and its byproducts; molasses

Place: Mexico

Production: Traditional, rustic distillation methods; hand-harvested cane

Protection: None

Mexican aguardiente is made from various cane-based products, including fresh cane juice and its byproducts piloncillo (i.e., unrefined cane sugar), boiled syrup, and molasses. It also uses traditional tools and methods such as wood-fired stills and open fermentation. Additionally, these spirits aren't always proofed down. Instead, they lean toward higher ABVs—often starting at 100 proof and sometimes much higher—and are generally priced well below their worth.

OAXACA AGUARDIENTE DE CAÑA

In the Sierra Mazateca cloud forests of Oaxaca, the 3rd-generation farmers and distillers of Paranubes grow heirloom sugarcane without pesticides or chemicals. This unaged expression uses fresh-pressed juice and wild (open) fermentation and is bottled at still strength (54% ABV). Flavors include overripe pineapple and fresh coconut.

For the Adventurer

AGUARDIENTE AÑEJADO

This Michoacán-based rum is a blend of pot-distilled cane juice and column-distilled, molasses-based rum—all derived from local cane. The aguardiente is then aged in a combination of ex-Sherry, whiskey, and new oak barrels, and is packed with notes of brown sugar, crème brûlée, and cinnamon toast.

Best of Both Worlds

CHARANDA

CHARANDA

Plant: Sugarcane (juice) and its byproducts; molasses

Place: Michoacán, Mexico (16 municipalities)

Production: Any still type, but copper and Filipino stills common

Protection: DO

Charanda is an *aguardiente de caña* and the only Mexican cane spirit to have a DO—a rare feat in a place where rum is almost an afterthought given the pedigree of agave spirits. Production is limited to 16 municipalities within Michoacán, making this a small production region. Charanda can use sugarcane of any form, as well as cane molasses, but the raw cane must be sourced from the designated regions allowed by the DO. The cane varieties of this area are heritage types, such as Cristalina, Criolla, Mexicana, Nayarit, Mayarí, and Morada.

BLANCO RUM

This dynamic white rum is a 50/50 blend of fresh-pressed sugarcane and molasses that are fermented and distilled separately before blending. The cane is grown at 4,000 ft. above sea level and ground using a water-powered mill. The result is a juicy, tropical bottling filled with overripe mango flavors and funky hogo notes (see the section on Jamaican rum).

Tried and True

SOL TARASCO

Made with only fresh cane juice, this expression is aged for 3 years in ex-Bourbon barrels and infused with local Blue Indigo and Oyster mushrooms. (Mushrooms were historically added to Charanda for medicinal purposes.) It's earthy and offers funky umami notes paired with flavors of vanilla and baking spices.

For the Adventurous Palate

AMERICAN CANE SPIRITS

Historic cane-growing regions in the US—of which there are several—make some very exciting agricole-style rums. Louisiana produces about thirteen million tons of cane annually and has a growing rum industry to show for it, even recently surpassing Florida in terms of output (seventeen Louisiana distilleries make some form of rum). A byproduct of the sugarcane industry, rum production in Louisiana began in the late 17th century (see section on molasses-based rums). Tobacco couldn't grow in the region's humid climate, just as it couldn't in the Caribbean, so the French opted for sugarcane. As the sugar industry expanded, rum, as usual, wasn't far behind.

> **AMERICAN CANE SPIRITS**
>
> **Plant**: Sugarcane (juice)
>
> **Place:** US (notably Hawaii and Louisiana)
>
> **Production:** Any
>
> **Protection:** None

Hawaii, in particular, is having a—notably less commercialized—sugarcane renaissance. Hawaiians have been farming cane long before the first *haole* (non-native/white person) showed up. When they first landed on the Big Island of Hawai'i between the 4th and 7th centuries CE, Polynesians introduced crops like sweet potato, coconut, and sugarcane (*kō*), along with domesticated animals like pigs and chickens. Known as "canoe plants," these staple resources quickly became entrenched on the islands. The two to four varieties of sugarcane stalks brought from Polynesia were soon cultivated into thirty-five unique varieties that early Hawaiians used for food, medicine, shelter, and even fuel.

While native Hawaiians had long been farming sugarcane when Europe first made contact in 1778, it wouldn't be until 1835 that the first (successful) European sugarcane plantation was founded in Kauai. By 1840, the sugar industry was thriving, and by 1880, sixty-three plantations were scattered across the islands. Once the US officially annexed the islands in 1898, the industry would shift but not slow down, as contract workers from nations like China, Japan, and the Philippines were banned and protectionist US labor laws enforced. By 1959, one in twelve Hawaiians worked in the commercial sugar industry.

SUGARCANE

But, as the years passed, Hawaii became less economically dependent on sugarcane, partly due to a burgeoning—and then booming—tourism economy.

In 2016, when the last commercial sugarcane factory in Hawaii closed, it seemed sugarcane as an economic crop was poised to die out completely. However, a resurgence of rum distillers and a movement to reclaim Hawaiian heritage has helped revive this facet of agriculture and the heirloom sugarcane varieties that were once prized.

KEA (UNAGED)

This bottle from kō Hana is made on a small scale with 3 types of estate grown heritage cane: Lahi, Manuele, and Pakaweli. "Eau de vie de cane" would be a more fitting name for this agricole-style rum. It's funky and complex, with notes of oil-cured black olives and hints of overripe mango.

Heirloom Cane

HAWAIIAN RUM AGRICOLE

While they also produce a handful of molasses-based rums, this bottling showcases Hawaiian kō. Forty types of sugarcane are grown on a 44-acre plot on Kohala to make this French-style, copper-pot-distilled agricole rum. The result is a grassy, light, and tropical bottling fit with green plantain and lemongrass.

New Kid on the Block

CALIFORNIA AGRICOLE RUM

Using California-grown sugarcane from the Imperial Valley (near the Southeast border of California), the cane used in this bottling is hand-pressed with a sugarcane press. Distillation occurs in copper pot stills, creating a rich, robust flavor profile of earth and oil-packed olives.

For the Adventurous Palate

RHUM LOUISIANE CANE JUICE AGRICOLE

While the Oxbow Rum Distillery also produces molasses-based rums and operates a sugar mill from estate grown cane, their annual agricole-style rhum release is a beautiful example of terroir in cane spirits. Pot distilled with no additives, the rum is bright, grassy, and vegetal.

Farm to Bottle

MOLASSES-BASED RUM

If rum were a coin, agricole would be one side, and molasses-based rum would be the other. In its most familiar form, rum is a molasses-based concoction "first invented in the early seventeenth century on the British island colony of Barbados. Or not." This opening sentence of Wayne Curtis' immersive book *And a Bottle of Rum: A History of the New World in Ten Cocktails* reminds us that rum's origins are still very much a mystery. Between the scant written records kept in the spirit's early days and sugarcane's vast territorial expansion across the Western Hemisphere, it's not surprising that this category features producers from over eighty countries around the world, each with their own cultural expressions, rules, and allowances for additives and flavors.

Just the same, we'll begin our approach to molasses-based rum in the Caribbean island of Barbados. As explained earlier, the Caribbean once teemed with sugar mills. In Barbados, companion stills eventually began popping up. These stills were not meant to process the cane itself but rather the sweet, syrupy byproduct of the sugar-refining process, otherwise known as molasses. (Apart from rum, you've likely encountered molasses if you've done any baking or lived in the southeastern US.)

Before its reinvention as a distillate, molasses was initially treated as industrial waste—sugar producers couldn't get rid of it fast enough. Of course, there were some uses for it as a livestock feed supplement, cheap sweetener, caloric source for enslaved workers, and medicine (used in a syphilis treatment that was truly cringeworthy). Despite these uses, the ratio of raw sugarcane input to molasses byproduct rendered it more of a nuisance than a boon. Producing four pounds of crystalized sugar from the inefficient cane mills of the colonial era resulted in roughly three pounds of molasses. (Today, the numbers are closer to ten-to-one.) Eventually, though, sugarcane mills found a more lucrative solution for this industrial waste: rum.

So, What Exactly is Molasses?

Molasses is a mixture of sucrose, ash, minerals, other natural sugars, and vitamins created by processing sugarcane. When cane is juiced and then boiled down to form crystals, the gooey liquid left over—typically separated by a centrifuge process—is known as molasses. Though not nearly as sweet as the cane itself, molasses contains considerable amounts of sucrose, making it excellent for distilling.

Molasses Types and the Legend of Blackstrap Rum

As the demand for rum increased, and the secondary market for molasses evolved into a primary one, distillers began developing a taste for specific flavors, sugar contents, and chemical compounds in their molasses. For example, Puerto Rican brand Don Q makes its rums using three different types of molasses from Guatemala, Colombia, and the Dominican Republic—each a mix of varying qualities graded from "A" to "C." As Silvia Santiago, who's been the Maestra Ronera of Don Q for over forty years, points out, "not all molasses is equal . . . remember that, in making rum, we are dealing with a living organism, the yeast. It [the yeast] needs the proper nutrients to be happy."

Molasses is graded based on the amounts of sucrose, ash, and brix (in this case, brix only refers to specific gravity, not sucrose content because of the other sugars present). Though grades reflect clear parameters, batches of molasses differ from one another like any other agricultural byproduct might, and the distiller must analyze each one to make sure they're getting the fermentation just right. It should also come as no surprise that the higher the grade, the more expensive the molasses.

USDA Molasses Grades

- **GRADE A:** This grade is the "fancy" molasses. It has the highest sugar content and must be deemed to have "good" flavor and be mostly free of defects. For these reasons, it's considered the baker's choice.

- **GRADE B:** A step down from A, this grade has less sugar content and a "reasonable" flavor. It is "reasonably" free of defects and typically undergoes a second boiling, making it thicker and darker.

- **GRADE C:** This is the product of a third boiling and is usually referred to as "blackstrap" in reference to its dark color—the word "strap" comes from the Dutch *stroop,* meaning "syrup." It has the least amount of sugar, is somewhat bitter, and has a higher sodium content.

Grade C molasses, or "blackstrap," has become a confusing and often misused term within the world of rum. True blackstrap is a thrice-boiled reduction of molasses, making it much lower in sugar but higher in mineral content than Grades A or B. (This high mineral content is why it's so often used in feedstock.) It's dark, bitter, and even a bit salty, and was once the go-to grade for rum distillers as it's inexpensive, readily available, and has a sugar content sufficient for distillation. Since the early days, industrial methods have increased the efficiency of sugar processing, which is great for sugar producers but less so for distillers. More sucrose extraction means less sugar content left behind in the molasses, making it difficult for most distillers to ferment Grade C on its own.

Here's where it gets confusing. *Blackstrap* is also the name of a type of rum: well, sort of. There is no official definition—it's a self-defined subcategory with enough gray area for a fleet of pirates to sail through— and many rum purists argue there's no such thing. Still, the marketing departments of many brands might beg to differ. Blackstrap rums—or, more accurately, "black rums," as many are not made with blackstrap molasses at all—typically contain added caramel coloring, flavorings, and/or molasses that's been added post-distillation. It's these additives, rather than any unique process, barrel aging, or raw ingredients, that give black rums their severe dark color. And while there are no rules or regulations, many blackstrap rums strive for a coffee, maple, gingersnap, or fresh molasses profile. These aren't fancy sipping rums, but they're loads of fun in cocktails. Classic brand examples include Goslings, made famous by the Dark 'n Stormy cocktail, and Myers's Rum, a long-time denizen of the back bar. More de nouveau examples would be Cruzan or Coruba.

How the Vacuum Pan Changed Sugar

At the height of the sugar boom, colonial sugar plantations, mills, and distilleries were prolific across the Caribbean, and often operated in tandem. Some islands, like Barbados, had hundreds. At the height of production, the small island had 339 plantations, each with their own mill. Then, in 1843, Norbert Rillieux, a scientist from New Orleans, invented the *vacuum pan evaporator*, a machine that would revolutionize the sugar industry. Rillieux, a baptized Roman Catholic from a prominent Creole family, had access to privileges that few people of color—enslaved or free—had in the American South at that time. He attended one of the top engineering schools in Paris and became an expert in steam-powered engines—technology he would implement in his evaporator.

Dark 'n Stormy

- 6 oz. Ginger beer
- 2 oz. Goslings Black Seal Rum
- Lime wedge

Add ice and chilled ginger beer to a Collins glass. Top (float) with rum and garnish with a lime wedge.

(Trademarked since 1991 by Goslings, this mule variation, created in 1920, is Bermuda's national drink.)

SUGARCANE

231

Sugar refining was an expensive, inefficient, and dangerous endeavor in those days, so Rillieux decided to address all three issues at once. He invented a machine that lowered the temperature needed for industrial evaporation. By stacking pans inside a vacuum chamber, he figured out the bottom pans would transfer heat (via steam) to the ones above. This method provided better heat control, improved distillate quality (by preventing the sugar from burning or discoloring), reduced cost (because distillers only had to pay for a single heat source), and eliminated the burn risk for workers who, until then, had to manually transfer boiling cane juice from pot to pot as it thickened.

From a mechanical engineering standpoint, Rillieux's accomplishment was extraordinary. However, the invention of the vacuum pan evaporator had unintended consequences. Because the machine produced higher quality sugar using less fuel, it led to a decline in molasses quality and the centralization of sugar processing plants, moving readily available molasses further from distilleries and eventually off some islands altogether. At the same time, the British Slavery Abolition Act was beginning to take economic effect, leading to a decrease in sugarcane plantings and, by extension, molasses. As a result, many distilleries either shuttered or were consolidated. Soon, molasses was being imported from other islands and even farther afield. Through Rillieux's invention, the rum industry and culture would change forever but would by no means disappear.

Today, most Caribbean islands grow very little (if any) sugarcane, meaning rum distilleries have to import molasses—often from bulk suppliers far away—which raises the price for average consumers. Anyone who's spent time on an island can attest to the cost of groceries and fuel, both of which impact molasses importation. For example, molasses (including freight) represents 70 percent of Don Q's direct cost in making a gallon of rum, especially now that Puerto Rico's commercial cane fields have drastically decreased in number.

Still, while we generalize rum into two styles—fresh cane-based and molasses-based—there's another option. As mentioned in the Clairin section, some rums use sugarcane syrup, or "sugarcane honey"—that is, fresh cane juice that's boiled down but not further processed or separated into components, thereby preserving the shelf life of the cane and its juice. At Saint Nicholas Abbey in Barbados, they've been milling estate grown sugar and making syrup using a steam-powered mill for their rums since 2006. This sugarcane "honey," sometimes referred to as "high test molasses" (though it's not molasses at all), might be the missing link between rum and agriculture for islands with no interest in the sugar industry. (For them, rum is the end goal.)

The Same but Different

If so many rums come from molasses, then why is there such a wide variety of flavors? In short, a combination of factors, including yeast type, molasses grade, distillation process, fermentation length, etc. (Okay, maybe there's no short answer.) Let's use Jamaican rum as an example—it has such a distinct style that it's developed a nearly rabid cult following, of which I count myself a member. Spirits writer Paul Clarke once wrote that Jamaica "makes the fuzz box of rums, a distortion pedal that takes the simple tones of sugarcane and water and gives them a tropical buzz." And I can't think of a better description of the funky, fruity notes found in so many Jamaican rums.

Jamaica secured its DO in 2016 and is one of the few molasses rum-making Caribbean islands that can argue a sense of place. As per the DO, all molasses for Jamaican rum must come from cane grown on the island. But that's not all. Jamaican rum tends to have a little something extra: *hogo.* Borrowed from the French *haut-goût,* meaning "high taste," and later adopted into English in the 18th century to describe the rums of Jamaica, hogo refers to tainted or particularly gamey meat and other similarly strong (yet surprisingly enjoyable) flavors. In scientific terms, it comes down to esters, the natural chemical compounds created during fermentation when yeast feasts on the buffet of sugar. Esters are responsible for several of Jamaican rum's characteristics, including its overripe tropical fruit flavors (think banana and pineapple) and its medicinal and phenolic notes that are detectable by both the nose and palate. The longer the fermentation time, the more esters can be coaxed out, meaning pot still distillation is preferred, as it's ideal for preserving heavy, oilier compounds. Like umami in Japanese cuisine, the funkiness of high-ester rum transcends how most folks evaluate flavor.

Some of the intensity of Jamaican rum esters comes from the somewhat mysterious organic material *dunder.* To put it plainly, dunder is the residue, or waste, that remains after distillation (sometimes also called "stillage"). It's high in acids, making it the perfect environment for hungry yeasts to snack on. In some ways, dunder is not so different from sour mash in whiskey or a sourdough starter. These dunder-influenced esters create the flavor funk—the hogo—offering generous helpings of overripe banana backed by burnt rubber or well-worn leather mixed with pungent tropical notes. Some distilleries have a more significant hogo reputation than others and even go so far as to put their ester count on the bottle. Hampden Estate is one such producer known for its eye-popping ester counts in the thousands. (Though I suspect the human palate can only detect so much.)

Light vs. Heavy: The Art of Blending

While most rum is made using column (aka continuous) stills, it's not uncommon for molasses-based rum producers to blend column and pot still rums. Doing so combines the lighter profile that comes from using column stills with the meatier, oilier body of a pot-distilled distillate. But still type affects more than just the body of the spirit, it also coaxes out different flavors. Pot still rum will be much higher in esters such as fatty acids, allowing the complex flavors developed during fermentation to be preserved and concentrated. However, a pot still rum on its own may prove too overbearing for many drinkers' palates, even in a cocktail. That's not to say single pot still rum doesn't exist; it's just not very common. Blending pot still rums with a more reserved, leaner style helps achieve balance and consistency across bottles and vintages.

Don Q

The Serrallés family of Puerto Rico has been making rum since the late 1800s, long before establishing the Don Q brand in the 1930s (around the same time the Bacardí family launched their venture in Cuba). Don Q doesn't just make tasty rums or give its spirits interesting barrel finishes (e.g., vermouth and Sherry); its distillery also has a sustainable wastewater management program onsite—one of the first in the Caribbean.

Though it's a concern for all distilleries, wastewater is not a super sexy topic. Rum is supposed to be fun, after all. But it's a reality of the spirits industry and is especially important to distilleries near bodies of water.

Initially, Roberto Serrallés, a 6th-generation member of the family distillery, had no intention of carrying on the family rum legacy, opting to leave his island home to earn a PhD in environmental sciences from the University of Oregon. Ironically, his career choice would be the thing to bring him back to the family business. Serrallés instituted a disposal system that takes the distillery's post-distillation water through anaerobic digesters to remove impurities by as much as 70%. Because this process occurs in an airtight chamber, it also creates a biogas. Technically, this gas can be captured, and it was, at one point, used to power parts of the distillery, such as the stills, reducing oil fuel use by half. However, the gas corroded the equipment, so Don Q is now looking at other ways to make their energy use more efficient. Despite that setback, the cleaned water is still used to replenish the local aquifer.

Rum by Type

Despite rum's lack of uniformity, there are a couple of ways to better understand the category's classes and styles. Most rum-related terminology isn't defined by law unless it's specific to a regional regulation or DO. This means it's up to the producer to define terms and the consumer to interpret them. The graph below outlines what you can expect when not seeking out a specific regional flavor profile. And while choosing a rum based on color is not ideal, knowing what these classes mean is useful, as they're the most common way retail shops present rum options.

	Definition	Character	Notable Brands and Bottles
White/Silver	Can be aged or unaged, though many white rums will have been rested for several years in oak and have their color filtered out with charcoal	Clear; relatively dry (if without added sugars); if aged, they may be lightly tinted and have detectable notes of sweetness	Don Q Crystal, Banks 5 Island, Bacardí Superior, Planteray 3 Stars, El Dorado 3 Year, Caña Brava
Gold/Dark	Implies some barrel aging, but will likely be relatively youthful; overall color may simply be darker due to added caramel or caramelized sugar	Ranging from light brown/straw-colored to darker, russet tones; light sweetness from oak aging or added sugars; can expect baking spices and vanilla notes	Mount Gay Eclipse, Flor de Caña 4 Year, Bounty Dark, Denizen, Equiano, Pusser's Rum
Black or "Blackstrap"	Can be aged or unaged; colored with dark caramel; may or may not contain/be made from blackstrap molasses	Dark, so as to appear almost black; typically flavored and/or sweetened; toffee, coffee, and maple syrup flavors	Myers's, Cruzan Blackstrap, Coruba, Goslings
"Navy" Strength and Overproof Rum	Bottled at much higher ABVs, usually around 151 proof	High proof; intense flavor	Lemon Hart & Son 151, Hampden Estate Rum Fire, Planteray O.F.T.D.
Spiced	Often aged, can be infused with botanicals, but typically enhanced with artificial or natural flavorings and additional sugar	Gold/dark or even black in color; prominent notes of baking spices, citrus, vanilla, and ginger	Chairman's Reserve, Kraken, Canerock, Lemon Hart & Son Blackpool

Rum types and examples.

Rum by Region

Country	Style/Typification	Additives Allowed (additional sugar/flavoring)	Notable Distilleries and Brands ----------- Independent Bottlers	Protections
Barbados	Varied; fruit-forward; showcases aged expression; can be light or heavy and ester-forward; mix of pot- and column-distilled	Yes	Foursquare (Doorly's), Mount Gay, Hamilton West Indies ----------- Velier	Applied for GI
Cuba	Dry; light; preference for column distillation; minimum of 2 years aging in oak	No	Havana Club, Ron Santiago de Cuba, Legendario ----------- Samaroli	GI (recognized by the EU)
Guatemala	Varied styles; mix of column and pot distillation; solera aging	Yes, including flavoring extracts and oils	Ron Zacapa, Botran, Magdalena ----------- Bapt & Clem's, Planteray	GI (PDO-protected DO that's recognized by the EU
Guyana (Demerara rum)	Medium-bodied; structured with age; fruit-forward; various still types used, including historic wooden column still	Yes	Diamond Distillery (El Dorado) ----------- Samaroli, Hamilton	GI (recognized by the EU)
Jamaica	Varies; blend of column and pot stills; often leans heavy and toward intense esters	It's complicated**	Appleton Estate, Hampden Estate, Worthy Park, Clarendon, Long Pond ----------- Mezan; Blackadder	GI (recognized by the EU)

Country	Style/Typification	Additives Allowed (additional sugar/ flavoring)	Notable Distilleries and Brands ----------- Independent Bottlers	Protections
Panama	Varied; leans medium-bodied; fruit-forward	Allowed but limited—prohibits the use of artificial essence, artificial sweetener (saccharin, etc.) or color other than caramel	Hacienda San Isidro (Ron Abuelo), Las Cabras (Caña Brava), ----------- Transcontinental Rum Line, Planteray	Regional standards
Puerto Rico	Light; dry; crisp; preference for column distillation; aged a minimum of 1 year in oak	Unknown/not documented	Don Q, Ron del Barrilito, Bacardí	Regional guidelines
United States	Varied; medium-bodied; expressive	Yes	Montanya, Richland Rum, Wright & Brown Distilling Co., Greenbar Distillery	Rum standard of identity (SOI), otherwise none
Venezuela	Varied; tends toward caramelized sugars; dried fruit notes	Yes	Diplomático, Santa Teresa, Pampero	DOC (recognized by the EU)
Virgin Islands (St. Croix)	Light-to-medium-bodied; leans toward Puerto Rican/Cuban style; preference for column distillation	Yes	Cruzan	None

**According to an old legal requirement (not the current GI), only caramel color is allowed in Jamaican rum. However, this can only really be enforced within the country. The loophole is that bottlers can purchase the spirit in bulk, sweeten or further age it, and then label it as Jamaican rum for sale in the EU or US.

Hiding in Plain Sight

If rum is made from sugar, what's the problem with adding a bit more down the line? The answer to this question is especially nuanced if we consider that rums were historically adulterated—usually to improve their taste but also for medicinal purposes. Rum's modest roots include rudimentary equipment, the not-so-finest of raw ingredients, nor the highest level of expertise, meaning most early rums likely tasted as though they could strip the paint off a house. (There's a reason rum went by the moniker "Kill-Devil.") Sweeteners and flavorings were a welcomed addition.

Though a lot has changed in rum's palatability over the last few hundred years, additives are still around, and these approved sweeteners can range from a burnt caramel syrup made from cane sugar to pineapple juice to flavorless glycerin, which adds a "smooth" mouthfeel. The main issue with the contemporary practice of adding sugar or "dosing" is that brands don't disclose that they're doing it. In fact, the US government allows up to 2.5 percent of "harmless coloring and flavoring" to be added to rum without disclosure. This lack of transparency not only misleads consumers but also contributes to reductive expectations of what a rum "should" taste like. The industry's overuse of added sugar and reliance on other additives has led most casual drinkers to assume all rum is a one-dimensional, overly sweet spirit when that's not the case. On the production side, additives mask distillation faults, allowing brands to put out subpar products obscured with sweetness. (It's amazing what a little sugar and cinnamon can do for a poorly made or otherwise lifeless spirit!) This is why quality and transparency are so important to making an informed decision.

Richard Seale

Thankfully, there are always folks working to make the industry more transparent, and one of them is Richard Seale, a 4th-generation distiller. Seale is a staunch opponent of additives in rum, so if you find yourself tasting a product he distills, you can bet it's additive-free. Since founding Foursquare Rum Distillery in 1996, he's sought to change the unruly world of rum categorization. As a purist, his mission is to increase transparency and improve rum's image while showcasing its potential—a long but rewarding road.

For now, there's at least one way to research added sugars in spirits: Sweden's Systembolaget. This government-owned chain of liquor stores allows consumers worldwide to see the added sugar levels for any spirit on the Swedish market (admittedly, the spectrum of products is somewhat limited).

If you've already been using this handy little website, you may have noticed sugar contents have generally dropped in the past five years. That's because the EU updated their rules in 2019 and reduced the amount of sugar permitted in rum to twenty grams per liter, forcing some producers to cut their added sweeteners by half or more!

Taking a hint from consumer market trends, some Caribbean rums already limit or prohibit the use of additives. As mentioned earlier, Jamaican rum is only permitted to have caramel color added, and Cuban rum is also free from additives and sweeteners (unfortunately, Americans can't score bottles without traveling). So, while there is currently no formal certification or organized movement for additive-free rums (like there is with Tequila), it's still possible to find unadulterated options.

Is Rum a Sweet Spirit?

It's a popular misconception that all rum is sweet. This myth is partly due to its raw material but is also the result of the number of sugar-added rums on the market. There's nothing wrong with a sweet drink, but the other edge of the sword is that since disclosing added sweeteners isn't required, consumers think all rum is sweet. Rum without added sugars is as dry as any other spirit off the still. That's not to say it's devoid of *perceived* sweetness (which other spirits can also have). Sometimes, perceived sweetness is a result of barrel aging. For example, American oak provides classic notes of brown sugar, vanilla, and baking spices. While Port, Sherry, and other barrels previously used to age wine can also add sweetness and color variation.

Sugarcane stalks after harvest, Mexico, photo by Nat Harry.

SINGLE BLENDED RUM EXCEPTIONAL CASK SELECTIONS

These aged, high-proof single blended rums (i.e., made by one distillery), combine column and pot still distillates and showcase what the category can really do. The flavor profile varies from bottling to bottling, but expect higher esters and a fruit-forward profile.

Worth the Splurge

WHITE RUM

Made using unaged column-distilled rum sourced from the Dominican Republic and heavy ester, pot-distilled rum from Jamaica, this rum has enough funk to satisfy rum nerds while remaining approachable for those exploring more intense styles. This additive-free bottling bursts with overripe tropical fruit and finishes dry.

Best of Both Worlds

12 YEAR RARE CASKS

I've long been a fan of Appleton rum and blender Joy Spence, and their 12 Year bottling is the sweet spot for me. Affordable enough to mix yet extremely sippable, this complex expression offers notes of rum cake, citrus, and rich caramelized pineapple and finishes dry.

Tried and True

3 STAR RUM

Founded in 1880, this distillery favors Oloroso Sherry barrel maturation and no additives (including sugar). Unfortunately, this blend of 6-10 Year rums is sometimes overlooked due to its comparatively higher price. Still, it's worth it for its rich flavors of dried fruits, brandy, and caramelized citrus.

The Underdog

EL DORADO 3 YEAR (SILVER)

This bottling is a cocktail workhorse. Aged for 3 years in oak, this rum is filtered using charcoal, which strips it of its amber color but leaves much of the oak's flavor. Leaning dry, with a touch of vanilla and citrus, this is a classic and versatile white rum.

Daiquiris for Days

DARK RUM

This funky, Jamaican-inspired rum is made in Oakland using Grade A molasses from Georgia. Distilled in copper pot stills and aged for 2 years, this is one of the first American-made rums to pique my interest. Its flavor profile of crème brûlée and overripe tropical fruit maintains delicious structure and balance.

California Dreamin'

SPICED RUM

Spiced rums can be a tough category to nail. If they don't taste artificial or over-sweetened, they tend to be unduly intense, like tasting a Yankee candle. But this expression is practically a cocktail in a bottle with its perfect blend of spice and fruit, notes of cinnamon, ginger, and citrus peel, and touch of sweetness.

Pirate-Free Spiced Rum

EQUIANO ORIGINAL

Developed by rum expert Ian Burrell, this bottle's name is an homage to Olaudah Equiano, an enslaved man who bought his freedom trading rum. This blend sourced from Mauritius and Barbados is aged in French and American oak, respectively, and offers dried fruit, brandy, and notes of cacao.

Additive Free

RESERVE 10 YEAR

Using molasses from the Dominican Republic and Guyana, this open-fermented and column-distilled rum is an approachable sipper. It's aged in ex-Bourbon American oak casks and boasts notes of brown sugar, baking spice, and dried fig, complete with a nutty and complex finish.

Off the Beaten Path

MAGGIE'S FARM WHITE RUM

This rum uses a blonde-colored sugarcane known as "Louisiana turbinado" and is pot-distilled in Spanish-made copper stills. Native Caribbean yeasts are then introduced, and their longer fermentation times coax out higher-than-average ester values. The result is wonderfully fruit-forward with just a touch of hogo.

Molasses Adjacent

4 YEAR EXTRA SECO

Having worked hard in the last decade to improve sustainability, Flor de Caña is now Fair Trade certified and working to plant 1 million trees by 2025. With no added sugars, their 4 Year oak-aged "white" rum is charcoal filtered, resulting in a light, dry rum, with subtle vanilla notes, making it perfect for classic cocktails.

Fair Trade

8 YEAR SINGLE JAMAICAN RUM

A longtime producer for other brands and blends, Hampden Estate's high ester, higher proof (46% ABV) pot still rum represents some of the finest craftsmanship on the island. Aged 8 years, this funky, wild-fermented rum is for sipping or next-level cocktails.

Worth the Splurge

ROOT VEGETABLES

Having grown up in North Carolina, I'm no stranger to sweet potatoes. Whether roasted, mashed, fried, or served as a classic southern sweet potato pie—I've had them prepared just about any way you can imagine. But in the form of vodka or gin? Well, that's been a relatively new experience for me.

Of all the raw ingredients we've explored so far, root vegetables—true to their underground nature—are the most overlooked in the spirits industry despite their ubiquity in distillation worldwide. The sugar beet, for example, is a neutral spirit workhorse in European distilling, and the Japanese have long embraced the sweet potato in spirits (and cuisine). Even carrots have been known to make an appearance in vodka and eau de vie. The range and history of root vegetables in distillation may surprise you, so let's give them the attention they deserve and dig a bit deeper.

As an ingredient category, "root vegetables" is a bit of a misnomer, used more often in culinary rather than botanical settings. But for the sake of simplicity and in keeping with its use within the spirits industry, we'll use *root vegetable* as an umbrella term for a variety of plants, including:

- "True roots": whose edible part is the plant root (e.g., sugar beets, carrots, and turnips);

- Tubers: whose edible part is not a root but a stem (e.g., potatoes and sweet potatoes);

- Rhizomes: which grow continuously and horizontally underground, putting out lateral shoots (e.g., ginger and turmeric); and

- Bulbs: short underground stems consisting of leaves or fleshy "scales" that hold food reserves for the plant to pull from in dormancy (e.g., onions and garlic).

Overall, root vegetables are hardy, easy to grow, and store well, making them a global staple food, particularly in times of hardship or famine. No matter what you call them, these essential, underdog ingredients are something to root for.

SUGAR BEETS

Fresh off the sugarcane chapter, it's time to explore another sucrose-producing crop—sugar beets (not to be confused with table beets (*Beta vulgaris*), leaf beets (e.g., Swiss chard), or livestock fodder beets.) Although average consumers rarely encounter this vegetable in its natural plant form, it's a big player in industrial food production, including as a neutral spirit base or liqueur sweetener.

Beet Molasses

As mentioned in the sugarcane chapter, molasses is a byproduct of the sugar refining process and can be made from both sugarcane and sugar beets. But unlike the sugarcane variety, sugar beet molasses goes through a secondary extraction to pull out even more sucrose, and any leftover pulp and molasses are mixed into pellets to become feedstock. Notably, you won't see the word "rum" anywhere around beets because although beets produce the same sugar as sugarcane, regulations dictate that rum can only be made from sugarcane and its byproducts.

Sugar beet cultivation, photo by Yevhen Smyk.

But how did we end up using beets for sugar of all things? In the mid-1700s, a German chemist by the name of Andreas Marggraf discovered that beet sugar (aka sucrose) was chemically identical to cane sugar. However, nothing really came of the discovery until a world historical event unfolded decades later. During the Napoleonic Wars (1803–1815), the French couldn't access their colonial sugar supply due to British blockades. As a result, they turned to sugar beets, commercializing the sugar extraction process and unlocking the vegetable's full potential. Forecasting commercial success, Napoléon, then Emperor of France, became an early backer. By 1813, 334 sugar factories had been built, ensuring the French—and the largest army Europe had ever seen—could source the sweetener for themselves without disruption.

Engraving of the French Minister of the Interior presenting beet sugar to Emperor Napoléon.

Then, just twenty years later, in 1833, Britain passed the Slavery Abolition Act, outlawing the owning, buying, and selling of humans as property throughout its colonies around the world. Without forced, racialized labor, true agricultural costs were passed down to consumers, and Britain's sugarcane industry swiftly collapsed, rendering mass sugarcane

ROOT VEGETABLES

production irrelevant. In other words, the jig was up. Sugar beets soon became the new sucrose source for rich and poor Europeans alike, proving Napoléon's investment was sound and leaving a lasting impression on France—the country remains the largest sugar beet producer in Europe.

Breaking Ground

Sugar beets resemble a cross between an unsightly parsnip and a lumpy white potato. They are harvested by machine, and after being pulled from the ground, their leafy tops are lopped off by a rotor. The beets are then washed, sliced thinly (think skinny fries), and treated to a hot water bath, which begins the sugar extraction process (aka diffusion). Each sugar beet contains up to 20 percent sucrose by weight, and after this sugar is steeped out, the remaining fibers are dried and pressed for animal feed. Meanwhile, the sugar juice—which is 10 to 15 percent sugar—is purified, crystalized, evaporated, and turned into crystals visually and chemically identical to crystallized white cane sugar. It's so similar that you may have inadvertently used crystallized beet sugar to bake your last batch of cookies. In fact, if your baking sugar doesn't specify "cane" on the label, it's likely made from sugar beets or a mix of both.

NEUTRAL BEET SPIRIT

NEUTRAL BEET SPIRIT

Plant: Sugar beet

Place: Anywhere

Production: Typically column still

Protection: None

While they never really see the spotlight, sugar beets are a workhorse crop in the spirits industry, acting as a quiet competitor to cane sugar and a widely used base for neutral alcohol (mainly in Europe). Though we typically hear more about *grain* neutral spirits in the industry (especially in the US), sugar beet molasses also makes an inexpensive, neutral spirit. In fact, it's often used as a base in European distilling, serving as a blank slate for a range of spirits, including gins, liqueurs, and amari, and for other distilled products like vinegar and bitters.

Truthfully, we rarely know what kind of sugar sweetens our liqueurs or forms the neutral base of our favorite gin. As imbibers, we're much more interested in the botanicals and other ingredients that create the flavor profile; the sugar (whether cane or beet) is meant to fade into the background. This is neither good nor bad, but as a consumer, it's interesting to consider how and why we might get locked out of this information, which has been largely deemed "need-to-know" by those who turn the gears of the industry.

LIQUEURS AND CRÈMES

We've talked a lot about spirits made from sugar and the use of sugar as a sneaky additive, but now it's time to discuss intentionally sweet spirits. Liqueurs and crèmes aren't just meant to be sweet; they're required to contain a minimum amount of sugar. And while this sugar can be from sugarcane, sugar beet, honey, or agave, in Europe, beet sugar tends to be the industry standard.

Base Spirits

In the US, many small distilleries source neutral grain spirits for their gin or amaro from a large-scale, food-grade ethanol producer. Similarly, it's the industry standard that small, specialized distillers in the EU source neutral beet spirits on an industrial scale, even if they produce other agriculturally focused wines or spirits.

Invisible Hands

You may notice there are no bottle recommendations in this section, but that's not because I don't love artisanal crèmes and liqueurs or neutral beet spirits. Recommendations are supposed to showcase a raw ingredient that stands out or performs a function unique to a spirit's profile, like corn in Bourbon or grapes in Cognac. Beets are meant to do the very opposite—to blend in and explicitly *not* stand out. For this reason, we'll simply appreciate the hard work they do behind the scenes.

Sugar beet harvest, photo by Majo.

Liqueur, sometimes called a cordial in the US, isn't just a fancy way to spell "liquor"—it's a particular class of spirit defined by its sugar content. To make liqueur, sugar is added post-distillation to a (typically) neutral spirit or brandy, which might also contain fruit juice, flavorings, and/or herb infusions. A crème is a specific type of liqueur with an even higher sugar content, making it considerably sweeter—almost like a syrup—and giving it an even silkier mouthfeel. Liqueurs and crèmes are typically considered secondary ingredients in cocktails rather than a base. For example, a triple sec like Cointreau would be the secondary spirit in a Margarita or Sidecar.

In Europe, the rules for liqueurs are more nuanced than almost anywhere else, which is unsurprising as they've been distilled for significantly longer and enjoy a much larger fan base there. In most cases, one hundred grams of sugar per liter is the minimum amount of sugar required; however, in cases of liqueurs that use tart cherry and bitter herbs/flowers (e.g., gentian), the minimum allowable sugar is slightly less to accommodate such sour or bitter ingredients.

	Liqueur	Crème
Sugar Requirements	US - 2.5% volume by weight EU - 100 g/L (70 g if cherry; 80 g if gentian/bitter)	US - None EU - 250 g/L
ABV Range	Typically, 15%-30%	Typically, 15%(minimum)-30%
Common Examples	Amaretto, Ouzo, Triple sec, Curaçao	Crème de menthe, Crème de cacao, Crème de cassis

Liqueurs vs. Crèmes.

POTATOES

Contrary to popular belief, though potatoes are used to make vodka (and technically gin, which is essentially vodka flavored with juniper and other botanicals) they don't get utilized much in distillation today. Still, they hold deep historical and cultural significance and remain a vital and versatile crop.

If you've ever harvested potatoes, you know the strangely gratifying sensation that comes from feeling around in the dirt and pulling out this staple food. The experience is akin to a messy Easter egg hunt. Though commonly lumped together in the "root vegetable" class along with radishes, carrots, and turnips, potatoes are actually tubers, meaning they're a specialized stem composed of starch-storing tissue. This tissue is what's valuable to distillers.

Seed vs. Seed Potato

Unlike most crops, potatoes are usually not grown from seed. Instead, they're grown from bits of sprouted potato planted underground. These tiny, sprouted potatoes are known by their misnomer, "seed potatoes," which refers to tubers not treated with a sprouting inhibitor. This method of planting creates clones, similar to how agave produces pups (see the chapter on agave). By comparison, potatoes grown from true seed (i.e., from the plant's flowers) will produce a new potato variety (similar to apples; see the chapter on apples).

Freshly picked potatoes, photo by LightFieldStudios.

"It'll be Okay"
Vodka Gibson

A savory-leaning, classic cocktail historically made with gin and garnished with a pickled onion, I will blasphemously recommend a hearty potato vodka as the spirit base. It's a great way to showcase a texture-driven spirit. Purists will balk, but I promise the world will keep turning.

- **2 oz. potato vodka**
- **½ oz. dry vermouth (such such as Noilly Prat)**
- **a modest dash of onion brine**

In a mixing glass, stir all ingredients with ice for about 30 seconds, then strain into an extremely cold (ideally from the freezer) Nick and Nora glass and garnish with a pickled onion.

Potatoes (*Solanum tuberosum*) are the world's third most important food crop (in terms of human consumption), the first and second being rice and wheat. This is pretty incredible considering that, unlike rice and wheat, potatoes were independently domesticated in just one place—Peru. Even more impressive is that about 10,000 years ago, ancient Peruvians began ingeniously transforming the too-bitter-to-eat wild potato into at least 4,000 native varieties, augmenting their genetic diversity through cultivation to include different shapes, colors, and sizes that varied by region and even village. With options like these, it's no surprise potatoes are consumed in a myriad of ways.

The Humble Potato

For a crop that's provided food security to millions of people and countless nations over the centuries, spuds weren't always met with open arms. (The Spanish took the gift of potatoes back to Europe in the 16th century, though with considerably less appreciation than for other domesticated crops like maize and tomatoes.) Given their ability to overwinter in harsh climates, they often successfully competed with local staples, like grains, and as such, were met with considerable suspicion and slander throughout Europe. The plant's status as a nightshade didn't help—it's true that a dangerous compound called solanine can be found in green or sprouted potatoes and that the above-ground parts of the plant, including the leaves and "berries" can be poisonous, but it's rare for humans to consume these bits or to be seriously affected by them if they do.

Amid their defamation, potatoes were also rumored to cause maladies like leprosy and lead to immoral behavior as "aphrodisiacs." (In the face of such accusations, it's important to mention that aristocratic landowners were also threatened by the potato's ability to feed poorer populations a little *too* efficiently.) Despite the campaign against it, by the end of the 17th century, the potato had become a significant food source outside South America and had begun spreading across Europe in a slow but steady climb to global popularity.

Market stall displaying varieties of potatoes grown in the Andes mountains of Peru, photo by R Parobe.

ROOT VEGETABLES

VODKA AND GIN

Conjecture has surrounded potatoes for centuries, and misunderstandings continue to abound when it comes to spud-based distillates. Among the more common misconceptions are that most vodka is made from potatoes, all Russian vodka is made from potatoes, and that potato vodka is the best quality vodka. None of these statements are true. In fact, vodka made from 100 percent potatoes accounts for only about 3 percent of the spirit worldwide.

It may also come as a surprise that potatoes made their distillation debut not in Russia but in Sweden. The root vegetable from America made its way to the Nordic country via Spain by the mid-17th century, destined for animal feed (as was the case throughout Europe initially). However, a severe grain shortage in 1746 changed everything. With her country facing famine, Swedish countess and scientist Eva Ecklebad funded research and discovered that both alcohol and flour could be derived from the ubiquitous tuber. Using her privilege to apply the knowledge at scale, Ecklebad's efforts changed the course of history and went a long way toward mitigating the grim reality then faced by Swedes. (She was even honored with admission to the Swedish Royal Academy of Sciences, though, unsure what to do with a woman in their ranks, the Academy would demote her status to "honorary" a few years later.)

Before long, France, Germany, and Poland followed Sweden's lead, making flour and distillate from potatoes. The exported distillate (which hadn't yet been dubbed "vodka" and was simply referred to as a brandy, whiskey, or "spirit") was considered cheap and inferior and was often used to fortify low-quality or "weak" wines. Still, potato "spirit" became such a popular German export that by the early 20th century, it had its own moniker, Berlin Spirit, defined as "a coarse whiskey made chiefly

Distillation

Distillation from potatoes starts with a mash (no pun intended) either from whole potatoes or dehydrated potato flakes, the latter being the more cost-effective route. If using whole potatoes, the spuds are usually peeled, sliced, and then steamed. The cooking stage comes next, which activates saccharification, turning the starch into sugar. Little, if any, water is added; however, due to the starchiness of potatoes, additional enzymes are often needed to help break it down into fermentable sugars. Of course, yeast is added to begin fermentation, and from there, distillation can occur in any kind of still—though many potato vodka and gin producers favor hybrid or pot stills.

from beetroot, potatoes, etc." It was even alleged to be "converted into Fine 'Old Highland Malt whiskey'" in the UK, which, if true, makes one wonder what shenanigans Scottish distillers were up to at the time.

Fast forward to today, and the potato vodka we drink is weightier, meatier, and filled with more character than its grain-based cousin. Some may even have a creamy texture, perhaps a reflection of the producer's appreciation for the vegetable; one doesn't choose to work with such an interesting raw ingredient only to strip it of its unique qualities.

From a bartender's perspective, potato spirits represent a series of missed opportunities spanning decades, largely owing to their undeserved reputation as "cheap" or poorly produced. In fact, in terms of cost, the opposite is the case; it's comparatively more expensive to produce potato spirits, which is one of the main reasons we don't see as much potato distillation. The raw material is mostly water—up to 80 percent—making it a pricey investment by weight if you don't already grow the crop. Grain, corn especially, is a much cheaper option for vodka today. But in places that produce potatoes by the ton, like the US, potato vodka is making something of a comeback with a few invested distillers.

Despite the cost, making potato spirits can be done economically; it just takes a bit of strategy. Will Chase, maker of Chase Potato Vodka, started as a potato farmer in the UK, selling commodity spuds to grocers. He then pivoted to providing specialized varieties used to make crisps (chips to us Americans) before eventually expanding his sights to distillation. Founded in 2008, today the brand makes vodka and gin utilizing "seconds," potatoes deemed imperfect in appearance or otherwise unfit for major grocery stories.

Ahead of Its Time

Potato vodkas received a bit of a profile boost in 2005 when two brands began hustling hard to impact the market: American distiller Boyd and Blair and the now-defunct Karlsson's Gold from Sweden. While they were very different in style and production, both leaned hard into the savory elements and creamy texture potatoes can offer, at a time when vodka was still very much perceived to be a neutral category.

I admit, I was skeptical when I first encountered Karlsson's—their marketing strategy was to serve the spirit over ice with a few turns of freshly ground black pepper for a drink they called Black Gold. At first glance, it seemed like a gimmick, but the vodka was savory, meaty, and a far cry from neutral. Using Swedish-grown "virgin" new potatoes (i.e., younger spuds that have not yet developed their tough, protective skins), they released a special series of vintage potato vodkas to showcase the crop's variance. Sadly, Karlsson's quietly disappeared, perhaps the result of being ahead of its time in its agricultural focus.

VODKA

Chopin Vodka — Krzesk, Poland

While Chopin also makes high-quality single-grain vodkas, their potato vodka is often overlooked. This family-owned distillery has 17 acres of farmland and grows or sources all its raw materials within 20 miles of the estate. Classic, elegant, and still budget friendly.

Tried and True

100% POTATO VODKA

Woody Creek Distillers — Colorado, US

Using Colorado-grown Rio Grande potatoes, a portion of which are estate farmed, Woody Creek uses fresh mash, distills twice, and chooses not to filter to showcase the bottling's chewy yet clean and approachable character.

Farm Distillery

ORIGINAL POTATO VODKA

Chase Distillery — Herefordshire, England

Made with estate grown Lady Claire, Lady Rosetta, and Maris Piper, these potato farmers-turned-distillers use a copper pot still for this bottling. Savory and creamy, with a crisp (but not neutral) finish, it's ideal for spirit-forward cocktails.

Crisps, Chips, and Vodka

VODKA MONOPOLOWA

J.A. Baczewski — Vienna, Austria

Originally a Polish brand, the word "Monopolowa," which means "state monopoly," is a nod to Poland's history of state-run distilleries. For this bottling, the distillers slice, steam, ferment, and distill high-starch, Alpine-grown potatoes onsite. The vodka leans toward a neutral profile, offering a soft, almost creamy texture ideal for cocktails.

For the Back Bar

COLORADO GIN

Woody Creek Distillers — Colorado, US

Using their potato distillate as a base, this gin is re-distilled after infusing with juniper and 12 other botanicals, including citrus peel, lemongrass, cranberry, and rose hips. Bottled at 47% ABV, its creamy mouthfeel and citrus-driven profile make it perfect for a classic martini.

High Proof

MONOPOLOWA DRY GIN

J.A. Baczewski — Vienna, Austria

Easy on the wallet, this hardworking and approachable potato-based gin is versatile in just about any cocktail, from a Negroni to a gin and tonic. Botanicals include juniper, anise, fennel and ginger, resulting in a classic, dry gin, bright with just a hint of pine sap.

For the Bartender

SWEET POTATOES

Unrelated to the "common" potato just discussed or the yam (for which they're often mistaken), sweet potatoes (*Ipomoea batatas*) are a relative of the vining morning glory. The history is a little murky, but it's believed sweet potatoes were cultivated as early as 2500 BCE in the tropics of South America, namely Ecuador and Peru. As the story goes, they expanded well beyond their homeland, making the incredible 5,000-mile journey across the Pacific Ocean to Polynesia. And while it's possible birds or even ocean currents carried the vines, it's more likely that the Polynesians, the greatest seafaring people the world has ever known, made contact with South Americans much earlier than conventionally believed and brought the crop back to Polynesia around 1000 CE. In support of this theory is linguistic evidence—the word for sweet potato in Quechua (the most widely spoken Indigenous language of Northwestern South America) is *cumal*, or *kumara*. In Samoan, it's '*umala*, in Marquesan, it's *kuma'a*, in Hawaiian, it's '*uala*, and in Māori, it's *kūmara*.

Sweet potatoes set sail again during colonial times, traveling to the Caribbean where they would flourish, making a comfortable home in Barbados until a pest devastated the island's farmland, allowing sugarcane to rise as the preferred cash crop in its wake. While Europeans were

A Staple Crop

Due to its ease of growth and high nutritional value, the 5,000-year-old domesticated sweet potato is considered a staple crop, particularly in tropical countries. These tubers are packed with vitamins A, C, and B6, and though they readily adapt to a wide variety of climates and soils, they flourish in tropical regions with notoriously poor soils. And unlike potatoes, these vegetables are perennials with a lifespan of several years, making them an ideal crop in places facing food insecurity.

Sweet potatoes are also an example of how agriculture can shift over time. As perennials, sweet potato varietals naturally "wear out," losing color and flavor after each year of planting. After 30–40 years, these varieties are replaced with new ones, meaning farms and distillers are constantly working alongside universities to test and develop new types.

Sweet potatoes at the Corbin Cash farm in Atwater, California, photo by Nat Harry.

Shochu Outside of Japan

Since the US doesn't recognize the DO for Satsuma shochu (or any shochu for that matter), American distillers are free to make their own versions, just like they do with Grappa, Sotol, and baijiu. One surefire way to know if you're tasting traditional Japanese shochu or a Western version is the proof. Japanese shochu tends to hover around 20%-35% ABV, whereas American-made shochu is typically bottled at 40%, the standard ABV for most US spirits.

generally unimpressed with the starchy root, sweet potatoes were widely planted on the Azores islands of Portugal in the 1800s, after insects and other trade factors all but destroyed the region's orange industry. Most notably, the vegetable found great success in Japan, where it was not only readily accepted into cuisine and distillation but took to the climate without fuss.

Outside of shochu production, sweet potatoes have a spotty history as a spirit base, partly because they're mostly water and, thus, a very costly way to obtain fermentable sugars. Though records show their conversion into alcohol was quite common in the late 1800s, their long-term success as distillation material was likely overtaken by the comparatively less waterlogged sugar beet. However, in the US, sweet potatoes are beginning to find their way into vodka, domestic American shochu, and even liqueurs.

IMO SHOCHU

IMO SHOCHU AND SATSUMA SHOCHU

Plant: Sweet potato

Place: Anywhere (mostly Kagoshima Prefecture, Japan); Satsuma shochu must be made in Japan

Production: Koji fermentation; pot still distillation (vacuum allowed/included)

Protection: DO granted by the WTO for Satsuma shochu (not recognized by the TTB)

As discussed in the rice chapter, early shochu was made from rice and other grains like barley and buckwheat. In fact, the *Satsuma-imo*, as the Japanese dubbed the sweet potato, would not make its debut on the island until long after shochu production was up and running. The crop arrived in modern day Okinawa in 1605 and spread quickly throughout Japan, aided by the welcoming physical and social environment, though rice remained the primary staple crop. Later, in 1732, it saved lives during a period of famine, outperforming rice in certain parts of Japan—a fact not soon forgotten. For a short time early on, it was also an untaxed crop and provided a cost-saving alternative to rice in

256   SPIRITS DISTILLED

shochu production. Today, over 500 sweet potato varieties are cultivated across Japan, and 50 are used in shochu, with Kogane Sengan, Ayamurasaki, and Joy White being among the most common.

To be labeled a "Satsuma," the shochu must be made from local sweet potatoes and koji, and every step of production must occur within the Kagoshima prefecture. Satsuma shochu accounts for 70 percent of total shochu production in the region, and there are two additional shochu DOs within Kagoshima—most notably, the shochu from the Amami islands, made using brown sugar. Because fresh sweet potatoes have a relatively short shelf life in the region's humid climate, distillation takes place during or close to the harvest season (September to December).

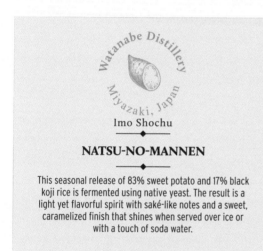

Watanabe Distillery, Miyazaki, Japan

Imo Shochu

NATSU-NO-MANNEN

This seasonal release of 83% sweet potato and 17% black koji rice is fermented using native yeast. The result is a light yet flavorful spirit with saké-like notes and a sweet, caramelized finish that shines when served over ice or with a touch of soda water.

Shochu for Summer

Hawaiian Shochu Company, Hale'iwa, Hawaii

Imo Shochu

NAMI HANA

During production season, the Hawaiian Shochu Company processes 1,000 lbs. of sweet potatoes every 3 days. This particular bottling is made from 82% Hawaiian-grown sweet potatoes and 18% koji rice and is bottled at 30% ABV. The shochu is unfiltered (expect a touch of cloudiness) and vegetal, with earthy undertones.

For the Locavore

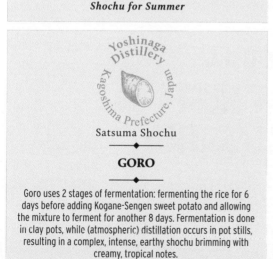

Yoshinaga Distillery, Kagoshima Prefecture, Japan

Satsuma Shochu

GORO

Goro uses 2 stages of fermentation: fermenting the rice for 6 days before adding Kogane-Sengen sweet potato and allowing the mixture to ferment for another 8 days. Fermentation is done in clay pots, while (atmospheric) distillation occurs in pot stills, resulting in a complex, intense, earthy shochu brimming with creamy, tropical notes.

For the Adventurous Palate

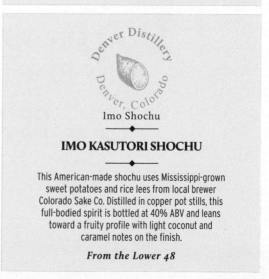

Denver Distillery, Denver, Colorado

Imo Shochu

IMO KASUTORI SHOCHU

This American-made shochu uses Mississippi-grown sweet potatoes and rice lees from local brewer Colorado Sake Co. Distilled in copper pot stills, this full-bodied spirit is bottled at 40% ABV and leans toward a fruity profile with light coconut and caramel notes on the finish.

From the Lower 48

ODDS AND ENDS: VODKA, GIN, AND . . . BLENDED WHISKEY?

But Nat, you said whiskey comes from grains! Arrgh! Well, there's always an exception, so let's dig in. In 1909, after years of squabbling with rectifiers (those tinkering with pre-made alcohol by re-distilling or adding coloring, flavoring, etc.) disgruntled by the Bottled in Bond Act of 1897, President Taft came up with a compromise and approved the first legal definition of whiskey in the US as part of the Food and Drug Act. The law defined *straight* whiskey as being made from 100 percent aged grain spirit and allowed for "cutting" it with a neutral spirit (like vodka, perhaps made from sweet potatoes) to make a blended whiskey.

Today, the TTB requires 20 percent straight whiskey in the mixture, with another type of whiskey or neutral spirit allowed for the remainder. As you might imagine, that leaves a pretty big margin of neutral spirit to whiskey, so generally speaking, these bottles are not usually considered the cream of the crop. Still, some producers are bringing their own quality take on blended whiskey and using sweet potatoes in the process (see producer spotlight on Corbin Cash).

Article from the *Los Angeles Herald*, December 27, 1909

As for the use of sweet potatoes in the industry as a whole, they occasionally pop up as a base for gin, vodka, and even as a liqueur. However, though they're becoming more visible, sweet potatoes are still a far cry from being a mainstream spirit ingredient.

Corbin Cash

We first met Corbin Cash and its founder, farmer-turned-distiller David Souza, in the chapter on Rye and Wheat. In addition to producing Merced rye whiskey, they also make a unique field blend whiskey from an 80/20 mix of sweet potato and Merced rye. Done right, this is where we can make good use of that blended whiskey rule. In this example, the "neutral" spirit is the sweet potato distillate that's aged separately for up to 4 years before being blended at 45% ABV. When enjoying this blend, whiskey purists should be prepared for a pleasant surprise—a warm, rich spirit appeals to Bourbon drinkers and those looking for something a bit off the beaten path.

SWEET POTATO LIQUEUR

Sweet potato pie in a glass, this bottling's estate grown sweet potatoes are distilled to a lower proof than their other spirits and aged in barrels for 4 years. The result is a blend of sweet potato and baking spices, offering a sweet but incredibly balanced flavor profile—perfect for fall cocktails!

For the Sweet Tooth

SWEET BLEND VODKA

Currently the only Black-owned, farm-to-bottle distillery in the US, Delta Dirt's vodka is distilled with sweet potatoes and corn grown on their family farm. Rich, bold, and fruity with a soft texture, their balanced vodka is perfect for your next vodka martini.

Farm Distillery

ROOT VEGETABLES

Without trees, most of our favorite spirits simply wouldn't exist as we know them. Often overlooked by consumers, wood is actually one of the most important ingredients in spirit-making, as the defining profiles of many aged spirits are imparted from their containers. Wooden barrels—particularly those made of oak—have long been prized not just for their durability as watertight vessels, but also for their economical weight when transporting alcohol in bulk, particularly before the industrialization of glass and aluminum. Overall, the barrel-making process, done by skilled artisans and coopers, deserves greater recognition.

While the wooden barrel has been vital to storage, fermentation, and trade for millennia, that wasn't always the case. The practice of using clay pots to store fermented liquids is much older. Notably, the Romans (and before them, the Etruscans, Phoenicians, and countless others in and outside Europe) used clay vessels to store most things: water, wine, olive oil, grain, and other goods. Though airtight and able to withstand subterranean storage without decomposing, clay pots were prone to breakage during transportation (even the sturdy Roman amphorae). As trade increased and networks extended across the globe, deliveries got bigger (and heavier), which in the case of liquids, meant a more practical solution was needed.

A multitude of people across time and space have turned to wood for storage. For example, First Nations people of the Pacific Northwest have been bending wood with steam to make oceangoing boats and watertight containers since time immemorial. However, for the purpose of fermentation, distillation, storage, and trade, it's the Celts who are credited with the version closest to what we use today. As early as 350 BCE, they were bending and shaping large pieces of lumber to make watertight barrels (a natural extension of the same technique they used to make boats). Roughly 450 years later, their cultural barrel-making knowledge had become widespread, aided in large part by contact with the Roman Empire and its advance across the continent. Soon, wood—particularly oak due to its tight grain—was a premier choice for storage and trade. Wooden barrels could be repaired, had a much longer lifespan, and held a significantly higher volume than clay pots safely could. Plus, they were more versatile and could be used to store and safely transport a greater variety of goods, including flour, meat, salt, and potable water.

However, when it came to volatile products like wine, beer, and spirits, the transition from clay pots to wooden barrels led to some unintended outcomes. Early on, merchants and consumers noticed that the *wooden staves* (the slats that make up the barrel) introduced new flavors and mellowed some of the spirits' harsher qualities, particularly over longer journeys. But the observation didn't impact the spirit-making process right away. In fact, the use of barrels to *purposefully* modify or age alcoholic beverages is a relatively modern development of the last two centuries. (You may recall from the grapes chapter that the first VSOP Cognac, released in 1818 by a little company called Hennessy, was a novelty at the time.)

Fast forward to the present, and today barrel aging has become so ingrained in spirits production that there are often rules regulating it, and not just in terms of how long a spirit can rest in barrel but also in the type of vessel (i.e., wood species) permitted and its treatment (e.g., char vs. toast). The practice has also been shaped by a few political influences

Egyptian Buckets

In Egypt, open, multi-piece wooden buckets made of softer woods, such as palm, were used as storage containers as far back as 3000 BCE. In a tomb dating back to 2690 BCE, researchers recovered a wooden bucket believed to have been used to measure grain. Another tomb, dating to around 1,000 years later, contained a small vat beside the deceased and a mural depicting the same vessel holding grapes after harvest.

along the way. For example, Bourbon regulations were updated by Franklin Roosevelt's New Deal, which required aging in *new* charred oak barrels rather than used, refurbished ones.

	Common Uses	Size
Quarter Cask	Typically used for aging whiskey and historically valued for portability	13 gal. (50 L)
Barrel (American Standard)	Typically, the first use is for American whiskey, and the secondary use is for rum, Tequila, and/or whiskey	53 gal. (200 L)
Hogshead	Almost exclusively recoopered from ex-Bourbon barrel staves with new heads added; most often used for aging Scotch	59-66 gal. (225-250 L)
Port Pipe	Used for holding and maturing Port	350-600 L (no standard size)
Butt	Often called a Sherry butt as it's commonly used for Sherry	500 L
Puncheon	Used for a range of wine and spirits	500-700 L (no standard size)

Commonly used barrel sizes.

Boisé Is Not in Idaho: An Open Secret in the World of Cognac

Depending on who you ask, boisé (pronounced *bwah-zay*) is a dirty word. To some producers, it's just another tool in their distiller's toolbox. For others, especially purists, it's considered cheating. So, what exactly is this contentious ingredient?

Boisé is a tannic solution made from soaking oak chips in hot (or even boiling) water—think of a strong tea with an hours-long steep time. It's often added to Cognac and occasionally other spirits to provide style consistency or to achieve a unique profile that softens the spirit and offers notes of nuts, spice, and vanilla. Though there is no one method to making boisé, the process always begins the same way: soaking the wood to extract its tannins. After about seven hours, the oak chips will

Wood Beyond Aging Spirits

Trees serve other vital purposes beyond spirit maturation. For example, Mezcal and agave spirits are often fermented in large wooden vessels called *tinas,* usually made of pine or other local wood. Furthermore, wood serves as fuel to roast the agave used in agave-based distillates. Just as peat imparts flavor in whisky, the wood smoke penetrates the agave as it cooks. Therefore, the type of wood used matters quite a bit. For example, depending on the region and its native vegetation, you may encounter mesquite, which lends a robust evocation of barbecue, or pine, which gives the spirit a light, tangy profile.

Essentially, trees are a vital component of traditional Mezcal and agave spirit production, and as these spirits become more universally popular, the risk of tree shortages and irresponsible forest management present real concerns for locals and producers alike. Deforestation has only recently made it into mainstream discourse, but a conscientious approach to distilling (and drinking) should lead the industry toward a more sustainable future.

have exhausted their contribution, and depending on the producer's approach and desired flavor, multiple batches of fresh chips may be needed. Interestingly, water—not alcohol—is used during this maceration process to slow down evaporation and avoid drawing out unfavorable flavors. The alcohol is then added afterward to stabilize and fortify the solution, often along with sugar, resulting in a woodsy syrup of sorts.

To achieve a consistent, unified flavor and add another layer of complexity, most producers will age their boisé in barrels. Similar to barrel aging spirits, each type of oak provides a different aromatic experience and flavor profile, so there is a lot of room to experiment. However, flavor isn't all that's extracted from the wood—color is also imbued, resulting in eye-catching hues of walnut and cacao. These, in turn, affect the coloring of the final spirit (another reason why judging a spirit based on color can be misleading).

As previously mentioned, small amounts of boisé can legally be added to Cognac. Its use is standard for larger houses—especially the "big four"—though it's up to the producer to disclose its presence. (Such disclosure is rare and usually done with great reluctance.) And while this traditional ingredient is often added with honorable intentions, it can just as easily be used to mask a spirit's shortcomings, which is why some view it as an unfair advantage. Nonetheless, I maintain that a well-made boisé can be a work of art.

I first understood how complex these additives can be during a presentation by Maison Ferrand, a long-established Cognac house and the company responsible for the Planteray brand of rums sourced from all over the world. During the seminar, they served a small paper cup filled with a mysterious substance the consistency and color of hot fudge. It wasn't pretty, but it was more delicious than it had a right to be. With intense vanilla, bitter walnut, and toasted coconut rounded out by a healthy dose of sugar, it seemed more like an ice cream topping than a spirit ingredient.

One can see how such a well-made concoction might be considered gaming the system, even when heavily regulated (as it is for French brandy); however, in my opinion, one should think of boisé as a spice cabinet seasoning rather than a substitute for maturation time and flavor development. And while I reserve no judgment for those producers that employ it—not unlike the post-distillation addition of sugar in rum—I do believe consumers have a right to know when it's used so we can evaluate the spirit properly. Transparency, as always, is the key to building a loyal customer base.

Maker's Mark Private Select barrels aging in a limestone cellar, photo by Nat Harry.

Maker's Mark

On its face, Maker's Mark is a straightforward brand: a distillery with a single mash bill and a recipe for success, it's unchanged by fickle trends of the industry. Its front-palate Bourbon with its iconic red wax seals is easily recognizable, beginner-friendly, and fairly priced (so much so that it might be easy to overlook).

So how does one innovate in an institution so deeply rooted in tradition? Jane Bowie, the former Master of Maturation and Director of Innovation at Maker's Mark and the wizard behind the brand's barrel program until her departure in 2022, had an answer: wood. Since Maker's Mark doesn't tinker with their whiskey (aside from proof), the experimentation occurs during maturation. "If you were to put a nutrition label on a bottle of Bourbon, it would be: water, yeast, grains, and wood," said Bowie, who I first met in 2018 on a behind the scenes tour of the facility.

Over the course of my visit, it became clear to me just how important barrels were in the process of spirit-making, and the depth of flavor they could impart. While most single barrel programs are centered around choosing a standout barrel from the rickhouse, Maker's Mark's Private Select program is about creating a unique profile rather than finding it by chance. As a spirits buyer, I was fortunate enough to take part in the experience, which I could best describe as an exercise in blending by tasting whiskeys aged with different staves, noting their properties, and then combining a ratio of wood types and profiles to achieve balance.

The last step to finessing these flavors? Controlling the environment. The Private Select barrels, along with Maker's 46 (aged in French Oak), aren't stored in traditional rickhouses but in a temperature-controlled limestone cellar (its creation involved a few sticks of dynamite) to prevent drastic changes to final outcome.

OAK

Distillers and coopers utilize a wide variety of wood, but the industry most heavily relies on oak. Centuries of trial and error have left oak (particularly white oak) as the MVP when it comes to making wooden barrels, as they're durable yet flexible (allowing the staves to be easily manipulated). Oak also acts as a great natural insulator, helping to regulate the temperature of the liquid inside—an essential detail in areas lacking temperature control, as is often the case with whiskey and rum storage.

Oak's backstory begins fifty-six million years ago, when, the flora and fauna of our planet were vastly different—better suited to the warmer, wetter climate of that time. (For example, lush tropical rainforest covered what is now the Southwestern US.) Though it's impossible to know exactly where oak trees (genus *Quercus*) originated (some of the oldest pollen samples have been discovered in present-day Austria near Salzburg), it's believed vast swaths of oak forests spanned the Northern Hemisphere. But not all oaks would go on to evolve the same way. If we were to fast forward on our time-traveling journey, we'd find that 8 million years later (i.e., 48 million years ago), the oak trees of Europe, Asia, and North Africa were already genetically distinct from their cousins in America. From that point to the present, oak trees have divided into over 435 species spanning five continents.

These acorn-bearing, monoecious trees (i.e., they have both male and female flowers) have proved to be an ecological and economic boon. The trees create a robust habitat from the forest floor—where they support mushrooms and diverse microorganisms—to the canopy— where insects, birds, and other organisms large and small thrive. Often spreading as wide (or wider) than their height, these massive trees also clean the air around them by absorbing comparatively large amounts of carbon dioxide. And as far as humans are concerned, the oak has provided a staple food source for millennia, and its wood has provided the raw material for constructing ships, houses, and, of course, barrels.

Keeping Healthy

In recent decades, the white oaks of the Missouri Ozarks and parts of the Midwest have been increasingly susceptible to premature death, also known as oak decline, as climate change brings stark seasonal shifts including frequent and extreme droughts. Since 2012, there's been a rise in Rapid White Oak Mortality, or RWOM, a severe type of oak decline that stems from environmental stressors and vulnerability to pathogens. A quick-onset syndrome, RWOM can kill a mature, otherwise healthy tree in a matter of weeks. Though changes to forest management, like more aggressive sustainability tactics, have shown progress in slowing oak decline, they're not expected to eradicate the issue. Without a more significant change of course, oak decline will continue to devastate not only spirit producers who rely on American oak barrels but entire ecosystems that depend on these vital trees.

Many people are unaware that our close human relationship with oak trees is due, in part, to their unique granular structure. As hardwood trees, they're slow-growing and, consequently, offer up very dense, durable wood. However, at a microscopic level, they have larger cell structures than most hardwoods. This means their wood is more porous, which has particular advantages when it comes to storing and maturing spirits, including decreased leakage. Though all trees in the genus *Quercus* share this commonality, not all oak species are created equal when it comes to spirit-making.

The Building Blocks of Wood

Each oak type imparts its own unique flavor profile, further altered by how it's charred and/or toasted by the cooperage. Each cooper must consider four vital compounds when working with oak: cellulose, hemicellulose, lignin, and tannin. These four components are intricately bound and form the building blocks of wood. Just as barley must be malted to access the grain's sugar stores, a cooper must break down these bonds to unlock the wood's true potential.

Before becoming a barrel, the raw oak staves must be *seasoned*, typically by leaving them outside for at least two years and up to four (though some French oak may be seasoned for up to six years). Seasoning the wood exposes it to natural light, temperature fluctuations, and microorganisms that "prepare" the wood and significantly reduce its moisture content. This gradually softens the tannins and removes other undesirable traits like excessive amounts of aldehydes and other organic compounds.

- **CELLULOSE:** As a structural component of the primary cell walls of trees, cellulose gives wood much of its strength. Though wood is roughly 45 percent cellulose, this organic compound is odorless, has no taste, and is insoluble in water, and thus has little effect on the flavor the wood imparts.

- **HEMICELLULOSE:** Forming 22–25 percent of wood's cellular structure, hemicellulose is a vital supporting actor. It helps form the fiber that fills out the overall structure of wood and affects its overall quality. These complex carbohydrates contain sugars that are only accessible when the staves are heated (i.e., when the barrels are "cooked"). The "wood sugars" can then be caramelized for flavor or coloring.

- **LIGNIN:** Lignin is small but mighty and makes up anywhere from 15 to 35 percent of wood's composition. Structurally, this little polymer fills in the space between cellulose and hemicellulose. From a spirit-making perspective, lignin bestows a tremendous amount of flavor and aroma, including notes of vanilla, clove, smoke, and leather. (Bourbon drinkers might want to take note because these flavor compounds are the secret sauce in American whiskey.)

🍾 **TANNINS:** These are the compounds you've most likely heard of, as they are essential to many spirits including wines and Bourbons. Tannins are a group of organic compounds called polyphenols that naturally occur in plants and can be found in fruit skins, seeds, leaves, bark, and wood. And while they alter the structure, texture, and flavor of a wine or spirit, too many tannins can lead to unwanted side effects, like extreme bitterness or a very dry, almost chalky, mouthfeel. This is one of the reasons why seasoning wood is so essential—it softens the tannins.

Maker's Mark Private Select barrel with selected staves, before filling, photo by Nat Harry.

WOOD

From the Forest to the Cooperage

Like any other agricultural product used in distillation, trees aren't harvested willy-nilly. Intentional practices and specialists are vital to the spirit-making process, and for their part, cooperages work closely with loggers to source their timber. Just as a jimador deems when an agave is ready, a forester or logger will decide which trees to harvest. Foresters typically survey a stand of trees, searching for mature or otherwise "merchantable" ones, in a process called "timber cruising." Cruising can also include thinning or removing unhealthy trees, a forest management practice referred to as timber stand improvement (TSI).

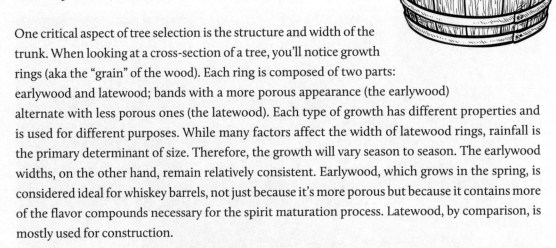

One critical aspect of tree selection is the structure and width of the trunk. When looking at a cross-section of a tree, you'll notice growth rings (aka the "grain" of the wood). Each ring is composed of two parts: earlywood and latewood; bands with a more porous appearance (the earlywood) alternate with less porous ones (the latewood). Each type of growth has different properties and is used for different purposes. While many factors affect the width of latewood rings, rainfall is the primary determinant of size. Therefore, the growth will vary season to season. The earlywood widths, on the other hand, remain relatively consistent. Earlywood, which grows in the spring, is considered ideal for whiskey barrels, not just because it's more porous but because it contains more of the flavor compounds necessary for the spirit maturation process. Latewood, by comparison, is mostly used for construction.

As for harvesting, logging is a year-round industry, though fall and winter are ideal seasons because the sap has retreated. Dry spells also make it easier to harvest for the same reason. And while different countries and regions have specific harvesting rules and guidelines, Europe demonstrates the greatest oversight, partly because European oaks grow more slowly than their American counterpart. Another major consideration in forestry is how land is owned and managed (i.e., private land vs. government ownership with stricter regulations). In the US, private landowners are encouraged, but not required, to make sustainable choices. Conversely, state-managed forests in central Europe are tightly regulated—particularly in France—though 70 percent remain privately owned. Still, many private owners of forests in France work closely with the government and specialized buyers to protect their investments. For example, in 2020, forest industry stakeholders submitted a plan to the French Ministry of Agriculture and Food to help lower carbon emissions and promote sustainable practices.

How Would You Like Your (Oak) Barrel Cooked?

Wood is no different than other spirit ingredients in that it needs to be exposed to heat before all the flavors it offers can be accessed. Cooking the staves is, therefore, a critical step in barrel-making, as it's where a distiller works with the cooperage to choose the overall profile of their spirit. The decision usually comes down to one of two methods: charring or toasting.

Charring is the quick but tricky technique of burning the inside of the barrel without setting the whole thing on fire. The process caramelizes the wood's sugars (think the crispy top of crème brûlée or a nice sear on a steak) and is used for spirits (not wine), most notably Bourbon. There are four commonly used char levels, with char one being the lightest and taking around 15 seconds, and char four being the heaviest and most widely used in Bourbon. (Char four is also called "alligator char" due to the texture left behind on the barrel.) Despite the heavy burning, even char four can be reached in under a minute of flame exposure. And though there are technically higher char levels, these four are the industry standard.

Re-charring barrels at Kavalan Distillery, Taiwan, photo by Nat Harry.

Alligator char, photo by Nat Harry.

Char Level	Time	Uses	Flavor Profile
1	15 seconds	First level beyond toasting; meant for quick aging (less time in barrel); least commonly used in commercial distilling	Least complex; perceived sweetness; smokey or campfire notes
2	30 seconds	Still comparatively rare in commercial distilling and American whiskey	Increased complexity; notes of roasted coffee, baking spice, and cacao
3	35 seconds	Often used in American whiskey, particular Bourbon and rye	Complex flavors, including baking spice, caramel, and vanilla; sugars begin caramelizing at this char level
4 (aka alligator char)	55 seconds	Often used in American whiskey, particularly Bourbon	Most complex, with the addition of partial charcoal formation that aids filtration; the barrel begins to crack at this char level, taking on an "alligator skin" appearance

Common barrel char levels.

While playing with fire is fun, a lot of chemistry occurs during barrel cooking that determines how a spirit will taste. Specifically, heat changes the chemical composition of wood, breaking down the cellulose and hemicellulose and, as mentioned earlier, caramelizing the sugars. It also releases lactones—esters that significantly affect the spirit and offer notes of coconut and fresh wood. As the char level increases, the lactones actually decrease; so while American oak contains significantly more lactones, higher char levels counter some of their intensity.

In some cases, such as winemaking, charring isn't preferred because the char's robust flavors risk overwhelming the profile. This is where toasting comes in, as it uses lower heat and is a slower process than charring. As with charring, there are also toasting levels. A toast can be categorized as light, medium, medium plus, or heavy, with a bonus category called toasted heads, where the head of the barrel receives the same treatment as the staves. And while some coopers use an open flame, others prefer ovens or even infrared heat to toast the staves. This gentler cooking method results in a more delicate flavor profile as the sugars never truly caramelize, and different esters can be showcased, allowing the distillate to shine. For this reason, you'll see toasting used in the production of elegant spirits like Cognac and wines—where the fruit is often meant to be the star—as well as in brandy distillation, ensuring the eau de vie remains front and center.

The preferred wood types and cooking methods reflect the distinct products and regional tastes found throughout the industry. For example, French and other European oak are toasted more often than American oak, which is more commonly charred for spirits like Bourbon. Whatever the method, both toasting and charring share the same fundamental goal: soften the tannins, remove the raw notes from the wood, and release the complex flavors and aromatics trapped inside.

Humidity, Heat, and the Angel's Share

Depending on the char level and the external elements, changes will begin soon after the spirit has entered the barrel. The invisible hand of maturation is guided by two factors: temperature and humidity. In hotter climates where barrels aren't stored in a temperature-controlled environment, the angel's share, or evaporation loss, can be high. This is one reason you don't see many age statements on Caribbean rum or on spirits made in warm climates like those of Australia or India. Kentucky *rickhouses* (tall storage warehouses that stack barrels four or five stories high and have about as much insulation as your average shed) can see temps as high as 100°F and as low as 0°F. Barrels near the top of the rickhouse receive the most extreme treatment, leaving their contents with higher ABVs, as water evaporates quickly in these conditions.

Rickhouse at Jim Beam, photo by Nat Harry.

In Cognac, France, brandy is stored and aged in buildings called "chais," which get their name from *cahier de chai*, meaning "cellar register"—a feature that all producers must keep per the DO. Chais are typically made of limestone and are either subterranean or built at ground level (not stacked high like a rickhouse). Each chais' cellar master takes great care to maintain the internal environment, as temperature and humidity significantly affect the flavor and maturation process. Storage is typically classified as either humid or dry, and a humid chai will have 90–100 percent humidity, while a dry one will have about half that. Higher humidity facilitates less water evaporation, as the air is already saturated. But it also means a higher rate of alcohol loss, which can quickly tame the spirit but drop the ABV. To account for this, large producers will often have a range of wet and dry storage, rotating the barrels to achieve a specific profile.

AMERICAN WHITE OAK

The white oak—also known as the American white oak as there are species of it in Europe—is native to Nortth America and comprises one of the most ubiquitous trees across the central and eastern US, particularly in and around the Ozark Mountains. These giants oaks take roughly ninety years to reach maturity (plus or minus a decade), a tall order (no pun intended) considering one of the defining rules for Bourbon is the use of a *new* charred oak container. It's wild to think of a tree growing for nearly a century just to be cut down and used for a single purpose, just once. Of course, beyond the world of Bourbon, the barrel will go on to live a long, boozy life (possibly another hundred years or more), aging other spirits without the "new oak" requirement.

Plant: American White Oak (*Quercus alba*)

Place: North America (especially the Ozark Mountains)

Barrel Qualities: Vanilla; baking spice; toasted coconut; banana; dill (appears more in wine and rye whiskey)

American Oak and The Life Cycle of a Bourbon Barrel

There's a common misconception that Bourbon barrels must be made from American oak (this isn't technically a requirement). So, why is the belief so prevalent even among bartenders and industry pros? Because American oak is the most efficient and practical choice. It's far cheaper and less laborious than importing European oak, and it's easily accessible, with most Kentucky Bourbon barrels made from trees grown in the Ozarks. And while using American oak may not be the rule, it does tend to be the standard by which Bourbon is judged because it heavily influences some of the spirit's most classic attributes: vanilla, caramel, and baking spice. Still, it's not unheard of to find a Bourbon aged in French oak—Buffalo Trace released a limited bottling under the label "Old Charter"—but that's a rare and expensive undertaking.

Obviously, distilleries aren't just chucking these costly barrels afterward—not only would that be wasteful, it would also be financially

Recycle, Recooper, Refire

Barrels get around! A worn-out barrel is one that has either fallen into disrepair or exhausted its tannins. But even in these cases, there are ways to extend its life. Coopers will dismantle the worn vessel, discard any wood that's too thin or beyond repair, re-toast/re-char the remaining staves, and use them to build a new barrel.

unsustainable. Barrels are expensive, and Bourbon distillers use a lot of them (you may have heard the aphorism that there are more barrels of Bourbon aging in Kentucky than people living in the state). Some distilleries choose to sell the barrels to breweries or other distillers, and in fact, many of them travel to Scotland where they can be used multiple times to age Scotch whisky. Others will sail to the Caribbean, where they can be used to age rum until they literally fall apart. And we can't forget about Tequila! Your favorite reposado or añejo is likely aging in an ex-Bourbon or Tennessee whiskey barrel right now.

Those distillers who choose not to sell them will often use ex-Bourbon barrels to age other types of whiskey, such as corn whiskey. They may even have their own workspace on site where they break down the barrels and refurbish the staves, which involves taking the barrel apart, scraping and sanding down the wood, and then toasting or charring the staves as desired. Both Rhum J.M. and Kavalan have onsite coopers to breathe new life into their barrels.

With a lifespan that can last more than a century, it's not unusual for a barrel to have more than a few stamps on its passport. As the only spirit category with a single-use requirement, ex-Bourbon barrels are numerous and found around the world. For example, one barrel may travel to Mexico to age Tequila for a few years and then head back to Kentucky to finish off a specialty whiskey. Other times, a rum barrel will hitch a ride to Scotland to either finish a single malt for a few years or spend the rest of its days aging Scotch whisky

Barrels and Boats

Along with Limousin oak, Tronçais oak was used extensively in shipbuilding during French war efforts in the late 1700s. Anticipating the need for building materials nearly a century earlier, Louis XIV had both species heavily planted throughout the French countryside beginning in 1669 as part of a large-scale forestry program. Today, these forests remain nationally managed and are planted, thinned, and harvested like any other crop.

LIMOUSIN OAK

Quercus robur (aka English oak) is one of the most abundant trees found throughout the European continent, especially within the Limousin region in Southwest France (from where it gets its common name in the spirits industry). The Limousin forests sit about ninety miles east of Cognac, making this oak the obvious barrel choice for the region's famous wine and brandy.

Slower to mature than other species, Limousin oak is typically harvested between 140 and 180 years old. Compared to other European oaks (see Tronçais below), it has a relatively loose grain, allowing changes in the spirit to occur more quickly thanks to more surface contact with the barrel staves. As a result, Limousin oak is particularly favored for wine, brandy, and Scotch maturation. The species also has higher concentrations of tannins and phenols than American white oak. So, while its American cousin may be more aromatic, Limousin oak offers more spice to the palate. (Interestingly, only 20 percent of the wood yielded from Limousin oaks is suitable for barrel production compared to 50 percent yielded by American white oak.)

Plant: Limousin Oak
(*Quercus robur*)

Place: Limousin forests of Southwest France

Barrel Qualities: Heavy tannins; nutty; baking spice; coffee; cacao

TRONÇAIS OAK

Known as Tronçais oak within the spirits industry due to its abundance within the forests of Tronçais in Allier, France (around eighty miles northwest of Limousin), *Quercus petraea* acts almost inversely to Limousin oak when it comes to Cognac. Tronçais oak's grain is finer than Limousin's, and its tannins are more subtle, contributing an elegant profile and an even longer maturation time than its already slow-maturing neighbor. Sometimes, brandy producers leverage this yin-yang relationship, using barrels made from both oak species for a more balanced profile.

Plant: Tronçais oak
(*Quercus petraea*)

Place: Allier, France

Barrel Qualities: Fewer tannins; clove; nutmeg; nutty; creamy mouthfeel

MIZUNARA OAK

Native to East Asia and Japan in particular, Mizunara oak might be the trendiest wood in whisky today—it's also notoriously difficult for coopers to work with. This popularity, combined with the tree's scarcity, means barrels made from this finicky Japanese oak have become prohibitively expensive for many distilleries.

Plant: Mizunara oak
(Quercus crispula)

Place: Hokkaido, Japan

Barrel Qualities: Honey; incense; baking spices; sandalwood; toasted coconut

Mizunara oak has deep historical and cultural connections to the northernmost Japanese island of Hokkaido. And though it's been used by Japanese whisky makers since the 1930s, it's jumped into the global limelight within the last decade, catching a ride on the spirits' rising popularity. The relatively late adoption of the oak in the spirits industry came about as a result of necessity rather than choice. During WWII, trade barriers prevented Japanese importers from acquiring barrels and other goods from the US and Europe. So, to keep up with demand (which increased during the war), they made do with the native species on hand.

The structure of Mizunara oak is vastly different from that of American white oak—the branches are slim in comparison, and both the trunk and branches are prone to twists and turns, showcasing the tree's complex cellular structure. Making cooperage more complicated still, these majestic trees have a high moisture content, and the wood is incredibly porous and much softer than other oak species. This leaves the barrels prone to leakage, which amounts to a higher product loss. Lastly, these trees are scarce, as they must mature for at least 200 years to be suitable for staves—more than twice the wait compared to American white oak! Some distillers have worked around these issues by using the Mizunara oak barrels for shorter aging stints, chiefly for finishing. This means the spirit is primarily aged in a different type of barrel—preferably one less porous and expensive—before moving to the more premium cask for its final years of aging, a process called cask finishing. Some

Japanese whisky makers disagree with this practice, arguing that it takes twenty or more years for Mizunara oak to truly bestow its gifts. However, this opinion clearly hasn't hindered the popularity of Mizunara oak in Japanese whisky and beyond, as the oak is now being used by distilleries and barrel programs globally.

When it comes to flavor, Mizunara oak wood offers a unique profile that extends beyond the usual spectrum of vanilla, baking spice, and brown sugar. Extremely high in lactones (the compound responsible for the coconut influence in American oak), Mizunara oak barrels imbue subtler flavors like honey and flower blossoms, along with more unusual notes of sandalwood and nutmeg. As Bourbon, Scotch, and even Cognac makers continue experimenting with the oak and its flavors, it will be interesting to see how the Mizunara oak impacts the industry as a whole.

Amburana

Plant: Amburana (*Amburana cearensis*)
Place: Brazil; Argentina; Paraguay; Peru
Barrel Qualities: Cinnamon; Overripe banana; Butterscotch; Nutmeg; Gingerbread

Clearly, oak dominates the spirits industry. However, there is one specialty wood breaking through the competition: Amburana. Over thirty types of wood can be used to age Cachaça (see chapter on sugarcane), and though Amburana is relatively unknown outside of Cachaça-producing regions (until recently, that is), it is one of the most popular woods among producers. It's also easily identified by its flavor. Once you taste an Amburana-aged spirit, you won't confuse it with anything else. It has a unique profile of intense vanilla, caramelized plantain, and banana, providing a subtle sweetness that rounds out the spirit. Unfortunately, due to overharvesting for barrels and for its medicinal qualities—essential oils can be extracted from the bark—this tall and slow-growing tree is now endangered. Responsible distillers, such as Avuá Cachaça (see the chapter on sugarcane), work to ensure sustainable harvesting and replanting, which will go a long way to preserving the specimen, especially as American whiskey producers begin to adopt the wood as a finishing cask.

STOCKING YOUR HOME BAR . . . WITH BOOKS

TO LEARN MORE ABOUT THE PROCESS AND HISTORY OF DISTILLATION:

Proof: The Science of Booze by Adam Rogers
The Maturation of Distilled Spirits: Vision and Patience by Hubert Germain-Robin

TO LEARN MORE ABOUT MEZCAL, TEQUILA, AND THE COMPLICATED WORLD OF AGAVE SPIRITS:

Agave Spirits: The Past, Present, and Future of Mezcals by Gary Paul Nabhan and David Suro Piñera
Divided Spirits: Tequila, Mezcal, and the Politics of Production by Sarah Bowen
Finding Mezcal: A Journey into the Liquid Soul of Mexico, with 40 cocktails by Ron Cooper, with
    Chantal Martineau
How the Gringos Stole Tequila: The Modern Age of Mexico's Most Traditional Spirit by
    Chantal Martineau
Mezcal: The History, Craft & Cocktails of the World's Ultimate Artisanal Spirit by Emma Janzen
Mezcalaría: The Cult of Mezcal by Ulises Torrentera
¡Tequila!: Distilling the Spirit of Mexico by Marie Sarita Gaytán

TO LEARN MORE ABOUT WHISKEY IN ITS MANY ITERATIONS:

*Japanese Whisky: The Ultimate Guide to the World's Most Desirable Spirit with Tasting Notes from
    Japan's Leading Whisky Blogger* by Brian Ashcraft, with Idzuhiko Ueda and Yuji Kawasaki
Malt Whiskey: The Complete Guide by Charles MacLean
The Spirit of Rye: Over 300 Expressions to Celebrate the Rye Revival by Carlo DeVito
The Terroir of Whiskey: A Distiller's Journey into the Flavor of Place by Rob Arnold
Whisk(e)y Distilled: A Populist Guide to the Water of Life by Heather Greene

TO GEEK OUT ON THE RAW INGREDIENTS:

Domestication of Plants in the Old World: The Origin and Spread of Domesticated Plants in Southwest Asia, Europe, and the Mediterranean Basin by Daniel Zohary, Maria Hopf, and Ehud Weiss
Sugar: The World Corrupted: From Slavery to Obesity by James Walvin
The Drunken Botanist: The Plants that Create the World's Greatest Drinks by Amy Stewart
The Story of Corn by Betty Fussell
Wood, Whiskey and Wine: A History of Barrels by Henry H. Work

TO ADD TO YOUR REFERENCE LIBRARY:

A Good Drink: In Pursuit of Sustainable Spirits by Shanna Farrell
Doctors and Distillers: The Remarkable Medicinal History of Beer, Wine, Spirits, and Cocktails by Camper English
The Oxford Companion to Spirits and Cocktails by David Wondrich, with Noah Rothbaum
The Ultimate Guide to Spirits and Cocktails by André Dominé
A History of Vodka by William Pokhlebkin

FOR MORE ON THE HISTORY OF RUM (AND PIRATES!):

And a Bottle of Rum: A History of the New World in Ten Cocktails by Wayne Curtis
Modern Caribbean Rum: A Contemporary Reference to the Region's Essential Spirit by Matt Petrek and Carrie Smith
Rum: A Social and Sociable History of the Real Spirit of 1776 by Ian Williams
Rum: The Manual by Dave Broom

STOCKING YOUR HOME BAR . . . WITH BOOKS

TO LEARN ABOUT THE MANY EXPRESSIONS OF BRANDY:

Armagnac: The Definitive Guide to France's Premier Brandy by Charles Neal
Armagnac: The Spirit of Gascony by C.E. Page
Brandy: A Global History by Becky Sue Epstein
Calvados: The Spirit of Normandy by Charles Neal
Calvados: The World's Premier Apple Brandy by Henrik Mattsson
Cognac: The Seductive Saga of the World's Most Coveted Spirit by Kyle Jarrad

FOR MORE ON OVERLOOKED SPIRITS:

Baijiu: The Essential Guide to Chinese Spirits by Derek Sandhaus
The Pisco Book by Gregory Dicum
The Shochu Handbook: An Introduction to Japan's Indigenous Distilled Drink by Christopher Pellegrini

TO EXPLORE BEYOND THE WORLD OF SPIRITS:

The Wine Bible by Karen MacNeil
Sherry: A Modern Guide to the Wine World's Best-Kept Secret, with Cocktails and Recipes by
    Talia Baiocchi
Wine Folly: The Essential Guide to Wine by Madeline Puckette and Justine Hammack
The Beer Bible by Jeff Alworth
Amaro: The Spirited World of Bittersweet, Herbal Liqueurs, with Cocktails, Recipes, and Formulas by
    Brad Thomas Parsons

FOR THOSE WHO WANT A GOOD COCKTAIL:

The Bar Book: Elements of Cocktail Technique by Jeffrey Morgenthaler, with Martha Holmberg
Spirits of Latin America: A Celebration of Culture & Cocktails, with 100 Recipes from Leyenda & Beyond
    by Ivy Mix
Mindful Mixology: A Comprehensive Guide to No- and Low-Alcohol Cocktails with 60 Recipes by
    Derek Brown

ACKNOWLEDGMENTS

This book was made possible through a shared passion and enthusiasm for spirits and all the people who work behind the scenes to make them. Every person mentioned in this book has been a source of inspiration.

Big thanks to my long-time Bay Area industry colleagues Eli Spector, Jake Lustig, Sam Filmus, Rob Easter, and Romina Scheufele for answering so many questions and putting me in touch with the right folks.

To Camper English and Emma Janzen, for answering my many publishing-world questions.

For every person who took the time to write a kind blurb or review, I'm beyond grateful.

For the above and beyond hospitality of Todd Leopold, Earl Brown, Tyler Burke, David Souza, Christian Huber, Jason Cox, David Harrison, and the always welcoming team at Maker's Mark.

A huge thank you to all those who worked behind the scenes, including copyeditor Chelsea Jackson, interior designer Morgane Leoni, and cover designers Zoe Norvell and Paul DuVernet. And, of course, to Edward Zegarra and Jessica Kaplan at Westwood Press for taking a leap on this project.

Thank you also to photographers Sara Reeves and Liz Devine, and for all those who contributed images and helped make this book beautiful.

Julie Feinstein, for her patience and support, and Andrea Burnett, who was kind enough to offer up a bit of guidance.

William Scanlan, outstanding human being and importer of amazing spirits, for introducing me to some of my favorite parts of Oaxaca.

Rachel and David of Left Margin Lit in Berkeley, for providing a wonderful space for community and creativity.

Leah and Amelia, who got me started on this wild journey at a little place called Felicia's Atomic Lounge.

Most of all, thank you to Kelly—my spouse, my biggest supporter, and my most patient proofreader—to whom I owe a lifetime supply of cocktails.

Photo by Liz Devine

NAT HARRY is a spirits and cocktail professional with more than 20 years' experience in the industry that includes running the farm to table bar program at Berkeley's Revival Bar & Kitchen and curating the spirits portfolio for fine spirits distributor Cask. Harry has been a judge for the prestigious San Francisco World Spirits Competition since 2020 and currently serves as Director of Education for the San Francisco chapter of the US Bartenders' Guild.